A. J. Hunter

15⁰⁰

Meaning, Quantification, Necessity

International Library of Philosophy

Editor: Ted Honderich

A Catalogue of books already published in the
International Library of Philosophy
will be found at the end of this volume

Meaning, Quantification, Necessity

Themes in philosophical logic

Martin Davies

ROUTLEDGE & KEGAN PAUL

London, Boston and Henley

First published in 1981
by Routledge & Kegan Paul Ltd
39 Store Street, London WC1E 7DD,
9 Park Street, Boston, Mass. 02108, USA and
Broadway House, Newtown Road,
Henley-on-Thames, Oxon RG9 1EN
Set in Press Roman by
Hope Services
Abingdon, Oxon
and printed in Great Britain by
St Edmundsbury Press
Bury St Edmunds, Suffolk

British Library Cataloguing in Publication Data

Davies, Martin

Meaning, quantification, necessity.
(International library of philosophy)
1. Logic
I. Title
160   BC6
ISBN 0-7100-0759-0

To the memory of Gareth Evans

To the memory of Gerald

CONTENTS

Contents

Part Two: Quantification and Reference

Part Three: Necessity and Actuality

PREFACE

In a certain sense of the word 'introductory', this is an introductory book on philosophical logic. It is not introductory in the (positive) sense that it would be readily intelligible to someone who had no prior acquaintance with philosophical logic. On the contrary, I have assumed some familiarity with philosophical logic and with elementary formal logic (including, for example, the notions of theory, rule of inference, rule of proof, function, interpretation, and isomorphism). It is, rather, introductory in the (negative) sense that nobody who has engaged upon serious research in philosophical logic will find much, or perhaps anything, that is new here. For this is not a work of originality, but of synthesis. I have aimed to bring together ideas in such a way as to provide a final year undergraduate, or a first year graduate student, with the sort of background which will enable him or her to proceed with serious research.

The philosophical logician, or philosopher of language, raises, and attempts to answer, questions at two different levels. At the lower level the questions concern the linguistic or semantic function of particular words, or kinds of words, in natural or formal languages. The philosophical logician seeks to articulate the contributions made to the meanings of whole sentences by, for example, names, predicates, quantifier expressions, definite descriptions, pronouns, demonstratives, and adverbs. To this extent he shares a project with other theorists, principally with linguists. At the higher level the questions concern the theoretical concepts which are crucially employed at the lower level; for example, the concepts of meaning, truth, and semantic structure.

These questions are characteristically philosophical, and by raising them the philosophical logician parts company with some other theorists and, in particular, with the linguist. His answers to questions at the higher level guide and inform, and are in turn informed by, his answers to questions at the lower level.

It has seemed to me natural to begin with questions at the higher level and, amongst such questions, to begin with the concept of meaning and to proceed thence to the concept of truth. It may seem that in this last matter I am simply reversing an order of priorities which has been constitutive of what might be called 'Davidson's programme', and preferring an order of priorities constitutive of what might be called 'Grice's programme'. But in fact I do not believe that there is, or needs to be, any such opposition between these two programmes. In any case, we cannot hope to elucidate the concept of linguistic meaning without having recourse to some fundamental facts about language use, facts about the propositional attitudes of language users. And once the concept of meaning is thus elucidated (whatever the details), the concept of truth can be elucidated in one more step. For if a sentence *s* means that *p*, then *s* is true if and only if *p*.

At the lower level the philosophical logician shares a project with the linguist. But even here the philosopher may take steps where the linguist has no desire to follow. For example, names, being unstructured expressions, are formally rather simple. A name only has to be assigned a bearer. Yet names give rise to deep philosophical questions clustering around so-called description theories of names, questions which serve as a reminder of the connection between linguistic meaning and propositional attitudes. For example, again, certain features of quantifier expressions in natural languages may suggest philosophical questions about, say, the essential features of quantification. In order to answer those questions, the philosophical logician might consider quantifier expressions of a kind which do not occur in natural languages and which, to that extent, have no call upon the attentions of the linguist.

There is another way in which the interests of the philosophical logician and the linguist may fail to coincide. A formal system which is set up to reproduce certain features of natural languages may invite a generalization which does not itself answer to any feature of natural languages. Such a generalization need be of no concern to the linguist, and on many occasions it will be of no proper concern to the philosopher either. But sometimes such a generalization may arm the philosopher with the resources to dissolve a philosophical puzzle. Such, indeed, seems to be the case with two dimensional modal logic and the puzzle of truths which are contingent yet knowable *a priori*.

The differences between the philosophical logician's project and the linguist's project should not be underestimated. But they leave a considerable area of common interest. This common interest has not, perhaps, been quite as fruitful as might have been hoped ten or fifteen years ago. (Work on Montague grammar constitutes a single, but sizeable, exception.) One might conjecture that this lack of fruit is not unrelated to attacks made by many philosophers upon what they regard as the psychological pretensions of linguistics. Such attacks seem to me mistaken, and I should have liked to have written a book about philosophical logic for linguists as well as philosophers. Unfortunately, my lack of the requisite expertise in linguistics has prevented this. But I hope that this book will, at least, not be counter-productive.

When I arrived in Oxford in 1973, interest in philosophical logic was approaching its peak. The doctoral thesis which is a rather distant ancestor of this book was written over the next three years, and owed a very great deal to the prior and continuing work of Gareth Evans, John McDowell, and Christopher Peacocke. This book has accumulated further debts to those three, and to others. I am grateful to Mark Platts for the suggestion that the thesis might be turned into a book, and to Anita Avramides, Jennifer Hornsby, John McDowell, Christopher Peacocke, Mark Sainsbury, David Wiggins, and Stephen Williams for reading greater or smaller portions of the manuscript and suggesting many improvements. Geoffrey Pullum and Deirdre Wilson gave me helpful advice on linguistics. Lloyd Humberstone kindly allowed me to use the main ideas of a paper which we wrote jointly.

I have made more detailed acknowledgments in the notes at the end of each chapter, but it is not always easy to trace the ancestry of one's thoughts. So it is virtually certain that at some points I have used other people's ideas in a way that is not acknowledged here, or in the text or the notes. I apologize in advance for any such oversights.

I gladly acknowledge a great debt to the Fellows of Magdalen College for electing me to a Fellowship by Examination and thus providing me with the opportunity to write the book, and to the members of the Department of Philosophy at Monash University for inviting me to visit there for the first half of 1979.

During the time that I have been at Magdalen my approach to

philosophical logic has been influenced by many conversations with Peter Strawson. He has taught me much, and has been an unfailing source of encouragement and good advice.

Some months after this book was delivered to the publisher, Gareth Evans died (at the age of 34). In writing this book I have been greatly indebted to him, so perhaps it may be allowed to stand as a partial testimony to his interest in, and influence upon, graduate students and others over the past decade.

PART ONE

MEANING AND TRUTH

I

MEANING

---

1   THEORIES OF MEANING

The phrase 'theory of meaning' occupies a central place in philosophical logic. Yet that phrase is ambiguous. We need to distinguish:

(1) a (perhaps formalized) theory which, for some particular language L, yields a meaning specification for each well-formed sentence of L; that is, a theory which yields a theorem of the form

$$s \text{ means (in } L) \text{ that } p$$

for each sentence s of L;

(2) a (discursive) theory which illuminates the concept of meaning; that is, a philosophical account which analyses meaning in terms of other concepts, or at least reveals the location of the concept of meaning with respect to other concepts.

Concerning theories of meaning in the first sense (theories$_1$ of meaning), there are five brief preliminary points to be made. Someone might be concerned that, if a theory$_1$ of meaning for English is a theory which yields such theorems as

'Everest is a mountain' means (in English) that Everest is a mountain

then a theory$_1$ of meaning is something with an air of triviality about it. The first three points are intended to ease that worry, although the third also has a stipulative component.

3

(1) A theory$_1$ of meaning is a theory about a particular language, the object language (*OL*), and it is itself cast in a particular language, the metalanguage (*ML*). But what the theorems of the theory state in the *ML* about particular *OL* sentences could as readily be stated in any of a host of languages. What a Frenchman knows when he knows what the English sentence 'Everest is a mountain' means is just what an Englishman knows when he knows what that sentence means, although what a Frenchman would write down as part of a theory$_1$ of meaning for English would be a French sentence mentioning that English sentence and so would be different from what an Englishman would write down as part of a theory$_1$ of meaning for English.

(2) A theory$_1$ of meaning for one language cast in a second language is very different from a theory of translation for the first language into the second, even if the language in which the theory of translation is cast is itself the second language. We must contrast:

  (i) 'Kungen vet att Stockholm är en stor stad' means (in Swedish) that the King knows that Stockholm is a large city;

  (ii) 'Kungen vet att Stockholm är en stor stad' means (in Swedish) what 'The King knows that Stockholm is a large city' means (in English).

In (i) a certain English sentence is used in specifying the meaning of a Swedish sentence. In (ii) that same English sentence is mentioned as a sentence which means the same as the Swedish sentence. What obscures the difference is that, since the translation theory is cast in English as well as being a theory of translation into English, anyone who can read the theory probably knows what the mentioned English sentence means, and so can come to know what the Swedish sentence means. But the difference remains. What is stated by (i) is something knowledge of which itself suffices (e.g. in a Frenchman) for knowing what the Swedish sentence means. What is stated by (ii) is something knowledge of which does not itself so suffice (e.g. in a Frenchman). (On this point, see Lewis, 1972, pp. 169-70, and Evans and McDowell, 1976, pp. vii–xi.)

(3) The meaning specifications provided by a theory$_1$ of meaning for a language might or might not provide conceptual analyses of the meanings of sentences of that language. A theory$_1$ of

4

meaning for Swedish in English might specify the meanings of Swedish sentences containing the present tensed verb 'vet' either by using the simple verb 'knows' or by using the phrase 'has a justified true belief'. Using the phrase to provide a conceptual analysis provides greater philosophical illumination, but that illumination is a contribution to epistemology rather than to philosophical logic. A meaning specification may be conceptually unilluminating, in this sense, without being trivial or empty. What is stated by a meaning specification which does not provide conceptual analysis, for a Swedish sentence containing 'vet', is something that most people do not know. It is not built into the notion of a theory$_1$ of meaning, as that notion is used here, that the theorems of such a theory should provide conceptual analyses. (We allow, in the terminology of Dummett, 1975, that a theory$_1$ of meaning may be *modest* rather than *full-blooded*.)

The fourth and fifth points are of an almost wholly stipulative character. The fourth is related to the topic of Chapter III. The full significance of the fifth will be seen in Chapter VIII.

(4) A theory$_1$ of meaning for a particular language L might have for each sentence of L an axiom specifying that sentence's meaning. If L had infinitely many sentences then the theory would have infinitely many *proper axioms* (that is, infinitely many axioms other than those of the background logic of the theory). This would prevent a theorist from listing all the proper axioms, but it need not prevent him from specifying them. There might be an effectively recognizable feature such that the proper axioms are all and only the sentences of the *ML* which have that feature. In that case the proper axioms could be specified by a proper axiom schema. As we shall see (in Section III.1) there is a project which a theory$_1$ of meaning will not serve well if it simply has an axiom for each sentence of the *OL*. But it is not built into the notion of a theory$_1$ of meaning, as such, that it should have only finitely many proper axioms.

(5) A theory$_1$ of meaning for a particular language seems to state contingent facts about that language. It seems to be a merely contingent truth that 'Det regnar' means (in Swedish) that it is raining. Here we face a choice. We could regard a language as

a changeable and indeed changing thing. In that case Swedish is a language which has the contingent property that in it, at present, 'Det regnar' means that it is raining. But let us instead regard a language as an unchanging and, indeed, unchangeable thing. It is a consequence of this stipulation that the language which is in fact at present spoken in Sweden has the non-contingent property that in it 'Det regnar' means that it is raining. A language in which those words did not mean that it is raining would be a different language. But we still have room for a contingent fact. It is a contingent fact that the people of Sweden speak a language in which 'Det regnar' means that it is raining. A quite different language could, if things had gone differently, have been spoken in that country. Ignoring for the moment both context dependence and ambiguity we could regard a language as an order pair $< \mathscr{S}, \mathscr{M} >$ where $\mathscr{S}$ is a set of sentences and $\mathscr{M}$ is a set of meaning specifications, one for each sentence in $\mathscr{S}$. If $< \mathscr{S}, \mathscr{M} > = L$ and s is a sentence of $\mathscr{S}$ for which $\mathscr{M}$ specifies.

$$s \text{ means that } p$$

then s is a sentence of L and s means (in L) that p (*cf.* Lewis, 1975, p. 3).

With the notion of a theory₁ of meaning thus clarified we must face a very natural question. How could any contribution be made to philosophical logic by attending to theories₁ of meaning for particular languages? For if one seeks to construct theories which provide conceptual analyses then one may contribute to philosophy but not specifically to philosophical logic, while if one seeks to construct theories which do not provide conceptual analyses then one may contribute, at best, to international relations or tourism.

One answer to this question is that a contribution can be made to philosophical logic by stating, quite generally, under what conditions a correct theory₁ of meaning for a language L is an adequate theory for the language of a given population G; that is, by stating under what conditions the language L is the *actual language* of G. (Let us ignore populations with bilingual members.) To state these conditions would be to provide a theory₂ of meaning, that is, a philosophical elucidation of the concept of meaning.

2 PROPOSITIONAL ATTITUDES AND ACTUAL LANGUAGES

The thought that elucidation of the concept of linguistic meaning (meaning in a language) must proceed via an account of what it is for members of a population to speak that language is a compelling one. It does not require us to deny that there are languages which no one speaks. It just requires us to deny that the significance of the claim that a certain sentence *s* means that *p* in a language *L* can be appreciated independently of any consideration of what it would be to speak *L*.

If members of a population *G* share a language *L* in which *s* means that *p* then those members can use utterances of *s* to express their belief that *p*. This claim is very rough, but refining it promises to yield us an account, employing the concepts of the propositional attitudes (belief, desire, intention, and so on), of what it is for *L* to be the actual language of *G*. That account will constitute a condition of adequacy upon any theory which purports to be a theory₁ of meaning for the language of *G*. Let us call any such condition of adequacy a *propositional attitude constraint* (*PAC*).

To see more clearly why there will be some such *PAC* which a theory must meet with respect to a population, if that theory is to be an adequate theory₁ of meaning for the language of that population (equivalently: if the language for which that theory is a correct theory₁ of meaning is to be the actual language of that population) imagine that a language $L = <\mathscr{S}, \mathscr{M}>$ is spoken in a population *G*. Then the meaning specifications in $\mathscr{M}$ can contribute towards our interpretation of the utterances, by members of *G*, of (indicative) sentences in $\mathscr{S}$ and of sentences (in other moods) closely related to sentences in $\mathscr{S}$; that is, towards our redescription of those utterances as linguistic acts of certain *kinds* (assertions, commands, questions, and so on) and with certain *contents* (an assertion *that Everest is a mountain,* a command *that the criminal be found*, a question *whether it is raining*). But the meaning specifications in $\mathscr{M}$ can make only a partial contribution towards our interpretation of the utterances of members of *G*, because the meaning specifications do not by themselves license the redescription of utterances as linguistic acts of certain kinds. Rather, given an utterance (of an indicative sentence *s* or a closely related sentence in another mood) which is already redescribed (at least provisionally) as a linguistic act of a certain kind, a meaning specification (*s* means that *p*) licenses the further redescription of the utterance as a linguistic act with a certain content (an assertion that *p*, a command that *p*, a question

7

whether p). What is needed, in addition to the meaning specifications, is what John McDowell (1976, p. 44) has called a *theory of force*. (A rather different use of that phrase is made in Dummett, 1973, p. 416.)

A theory of force does two things. First, it licenses redescription of utterances, performed by members of G, as linguistic acts of various kinds. Second, it specifies for each utterance type a sentence in $\mathcal{S}$. The meaning specification for this sentence provides the content of linguistic acts performed in utterances of that type. We can suppose that the theory of force does this second thing by having as a component an ordered pair $<U, f>$ where U is a collection of utterance types and f is a function on U such that for each utterance type u, $f(u) = <s, m>$, where s is a sentence in $\mathcal{S}$ and m is a mood. We can suppose that the theory of force does the first thing, at least in part, by taking the mood of an utterance type as a *prima facie* indicator of the kind of linguistic act performed, that is, of force. But we must have it clearly in mind that mood and force may come apart in two ways. On the one hand, an utterance in, say, the imperative mood may be advanced without imperatival (or any other) force so that the utterance is not a command (or any kind of linguistic act at all). On the other hand, an utterance in, say, the indicative mood may be advanced with imperatival force so that the utterance is a command. Let us, for the moment, leave it vague just how (in view of the potential gap between mood and force) the assignment of force is completed. (What seems to be needed, in a full account, is a substantive principle of classification of linguistic acts into kinds; we shall return to this point shortly.)

A theory$_1$ of meaning and a theory of force jointly license the redescription of utterances as linguistic acts of certain kinds and with certain contents. If an utterance of type u is certified as being advanced with assertoric force and if $f(u) = <$'The door is shut', *indicative*$>$, then via the meaning specification

'The door is shut' means that the door is shut

the utterance is redescribed as an assertion that the door is shut. To spell this out generally, but in detail, would be to contribute to a philosophical account of meaning (a theory$_2$ of meaning), for it would be to locate the concept of meaning (in a language) with respect to the concepts of assertion, command, question, and so on. A further contribution would be made by stating (again, generally but in detail) under what conditions licensed redescriptions are correct. The inevitability of some *PAC* follows from the fact that any redescription of behaviour as intentional action must render that behaviour intelligible in the light of the agent's propositional attitudes.

This brief sketch of an argument to show that there will be some *PAC* itself suggests a constraint; a constraint which has been stated very clearly by John McDowell (1976, pp. 44–5):

> *PAC 1*   Acceptability, in a bipartite theory of the sort constituted by combining a [theory₁ of meaning] with a theory of force, would require that the descriptions of [linguistic] acts which it yields should fit coherently into a wider context, in which the speakers' behaviour in general, including their linguistic behaviour, under those descriptions, and their non-linguistic behaviour, under suitable descriptions, can be made sufficiently intelligible in the light of propositional attitudes (centrally, beliefs and desires) whose ascription to them is sufficiently intelligible in the light of their behaviour, again, and of the facts which impinge on them.

No one could object to what this constraint says, but one might doubt whether it says quite enough. For there are two apparent gaps in the account which would be provided by *PAC 1* of what it is for a theory to be an adequate theory₁ of meaning for the language of a population.

The first apparent gap is this. The constraint *PAC 1* does not itself tell us what propositional attitudes can be attributed to a member of a population on the basis of an utterance described as a linguistic act of a certain kind and with a certain content. One might, for example, think intuitively that assertion is an expression of belief. But *PAC 1* does not itself tell us whether, and if so under what conditions, an utterance described as an assertion that p can be made intelligible in the light of the absence, in the speaker, of a belief that p. Nor does *PAC 1* itself tell us whether an utterance described as an assertion that p can invariably be made intelligible in the light of the presence, in the speaker, of a belief that p; whether, for example, it can be made intelligible in the light of the presence, in the speaker, of an intention that no one should know whether he, the speaker, believes that p. What is needed in this case is a fuller specification of the propositional attitudes (beliefs, desires, intentions, and so on) which need to be present if a speaker is to assert that p. What is needed more generally is a fuller specification of the (conceptual) connections between propositional attitudes and kinds of linguistic acts.

The need for such a fuller specification is increased by the fact that mood is, at best, a *prima facie* indicator of force. We left it vague (four paragraphs back) just how the assignment of force is completed. One appealing picture is this. The theory of force assigns to each utterance type an indicative sentence and a mood, and mood is taken as a *prima facie* indicator of force. So the theory of force licenses provisional redescription of utterances as linguistic acts of certain kinds. The redescriptions licensed by the bipartite theory (the theory$_1$ of meaning and the theory of force together) are then checked against *PAC 1*, and the assignment of force is completed by such revisions of the provisional redescriptions as may be required as a consequence of infringement of *PAC 1*. This picture is appealing, but without a fuller specification of the connections between propositional attitudes and kinds of linguistic acts we cannot tell whether a provisional redescription does infringe *PAC 1*, and we cannot tell what revision would be required. On the other hand, if we had such a fuller specification (which would not be specific to any particular language or population) then we could allow that, for any given language and population, a theory of force need have just two components: an ordered pair $<U, f>$, where f assigns to each utterance type in U an indicative sentence and a mood, and a (*prima facie* indication) function from moods to forces (that is, from moods to kinds of linguistic act).

The second apparent gap is this. There is nothing in *PAC 1* about the conventional nature of language use. So suppose that $L = <\mathscr{S}, \mathscr{M}>$ where $\mathscr{S}$ contains just one sentence 'Grrr' and $\mathscr{M}$ specifies that

'Grrr' means that the speaker is angry.

Suppose that members of a population G occasionally come out with utterances of 'Grrr' to 'get across' the message that they are angry, but that on each occasion of use they rely upon the audience's recognition that 'Grrr' is like the sound made by an angry dog. Then it would be odd to say that L is the actual language of G since, intuitively, members of G are not using a language at all; the expression 'Grrr' has no linguistic (roughly: conventional) meaning in that population. But it is difficult to see why *PAC 1* would not be met, with respect to the population G, by a theory$_1$ of meaning for L with just one axiom

'Grrr' means (in L) that the speaker is angry

together with some theory of force. (This example is borrowed from Schiffer, 1972, pp. 119–20.)

A proponent of *PAC 1* might reply that this second gap shows, at most, that *PAC 1* provides a necessary but not a sufficient condition of adequacy upon theories$_1$ of meaning. But for two reasons we should not rest with that reply. One reason is that unless we at least indicate how to advance from *PAC 1* towards a necessary and sufficient condition of adequacy we can hardly claim to have elucidated the concept of linguistic meaning. The other reason is that there is no filling the first gap without filling this second gap too because, for at least some kinds of linguistic act (including assertion), performing an act of that kind by an utterance of a certain type involves trading upon the fact that that utterance type has a certain linguistic (roughly: conventional) meaning in the population.

What all this suggests is that *PAC 1* needs, ideally, to be augmented by a *PAC* which provides a necessary and sufficient condition of adequacy; that is, a necessary and sufficient condition for a language to be the actual language of a population. This would fill the second gap, and could be appealed to in the substantive principle of classification of linguistic acts into kinds which would fill the first gap.

The natural place to look for richer accounts of the actual language relation, and of kinds of linguistic acts, in terms of propositional attitudes, is in Grice's programme. For two concepts employed there promise the kind of elucidation which we seek, namely the concepts of utterer's occasion-meaning (*s-meaning*) and of *convention*. (For a list of books and papers in Grice's programme, see the notes to this chapter.)

Very roughly, a speaker S *s-means* that p by his utterance (token) x directed at audience A, just in case

(1) S intends that x will produce in A an (activated) belief that p;

(2) for some feature F of x, S intends that A should recognize S's primary intention (the intention in (1)) in part by recognizing x to have feature F;

(3) S intends that A's recognition of S's primary intention should be part of A's reason for believing that p;

(4) S does not intend that A should be deceived about S's intentions.

Condition (4) includes:

(4a) S does not intend that A should think that S lacks the intention in (2);

11

(4b) S does not intend that A should think that S lacks the intention in (3);

(4c) S does not intend that A should think that S does intend that A should think that S lacks the intention in (2);

(4d)

    .

    .

    .

S-meaning something need not rely upon any linguistic (roughly: conventional) significance of the utterance type. In the example above, members of G s-mean by their utterances of 'Grrr' that they are angry. The feature F (in condition (2)) in this case would be: resembling the sound of an angry dog.

Similarly, we could define *s-commanding* that p by an utterance x directed at A. We replace (1) by

(1$'$) S intends that x will produce in A the response that A brings it about that p;

and make a corresponding change in (3). And we can define *s-asking* whether p.

Equally roughly, a *convention* in a population G is a regularity R such that it is common knowledge in G that

(1) everyone in G conforms to R;
(2) everyone in G believes that everyone else in G conforms to R;
(3) everyone in G has a reason to conform to R, furnished by the belief in (2);
(4) there is a general preference in G for general conformity to R, rather than slightly less than general conformity;
(5) there is an alternative regularity R' which would have served G reasonably well.

(This definition is taken directly from Lewis, 1975, pp. 5-6.) The notion of common knowledge used in this definition is itself defined as follows. It is common knowledge between x and y that p just in case

(1) x knows that p;
(2) y knows that p;
(3) x knows that y knows that p;
(4) y knows that x knows that p;

12

(5) x does not disbelieve (4);
(6) y does not disbelieve (3);
(7) x does not disbelieve (6);
(8) y does not disbelieve (5);

.

.

.

And perhaps an even weaker notion defined by replacing (3) and (4) by

(3′) x does not disbelieve (2);
(4′) y does not disbelieve (1);

might suffice (ibid. p. 6). We do not have to concern ourselves with the details of these definitions to see how they might be used to provide a further *PAC*. Thus consider the following.

> *PAC 2* A correct theory₁ of meaning for $L = <\mathscr{S}, \mathscr{M}>$ is adequate as a theory₁ of meaning for the language of population G [equivalently: L is the actual language of G] just in case there is an ordered pair $<U, f>$ such that for every sentence s in $\mathscr{S}$, if s means (in L) that p then (i) there is an utterance type u in U such that $f(u) = <s, indicative>$ and there is a convention in G to s-mean that p by audience-directed utterances of type u; [and (ii) if there are utterance types $u!$ and $u?$ such that $f(u!) = <s, imperative>$ and $f(u?) = <s, interrogative>$ then there are conventions in G to s-command that p by audience-directed utterances of type $u!$ and to s-ask whether p by audience-directed utterances of type $u?$].

Implicit in *PAC 2* is an assumption that, in any theory of force, the (*prima facie* indication) function from moods to kinds of linguistic act will associate s-meaning with the indicative mood, s-commanding with the imperative mood, and s-asking with the interrogative mood. According to *PAC 2* (and upon that assumption) what it is for a language L to be the actual language of a population G is for there to be, for each sentence s of that language, conventions in G to use utterances of s, and of closely related sentences in other moods, to perform linguistic acts of kinds determined by the moods of the utterance types and with contents .determined by the meaning (in L) of s.

Although we have a definition of s-meaning, and (in *PAC 2*) a

13

provisional account of the actual language relation between languages and populations, we do not yet have an account of assertion. An assertion that p is, roughly, an act of s-meaning that p, in which the speaker trades upon the fact that the sentence which he uses means that p in the language of the population. If s means that p in the language of the population then there is a regularity of use of utterances of s to s-mean that p (clause (1) of the definition of convention), members of the population believe that there is such a regularity (clause (2)), and this belief provides members with a reason to continue to use s to s-mean that p (clause (3)). That suggests the following definition of assertion. A speaker S asserts that p in his utterance (token) x of type u directed at audience A just in case S s-means that p by x and the feature F in clause (2) of the definition of s-meaning is:

> being an utterance of a type such that there is, in the population,
> a regularity of use of utterances of that type to s-mean that p

(cf. Schiffer, 1972, pp. 122–8). Such a definition would play a part in filling the first gap left by *PAC 1*, for it yields a fuller specification of the propositional attitudes which need to be present if a speaker is to assert that p. And, just as we could define assertion in terms of s-meaning, so we could define command in terms of s-commanding and question in terms of s-asking.

All this suggests a picture of the way in which one might set out to answer the question whether a certain language L is the actual language of a population G. If L is to be the actual language of G then there must be a theory of force which *inter alia* relates the utterance types used in G to the (indicative) sentences in L (that is, to the members of $\mathscr{S}$ if $L = < \mathscr{S}, \mathscr{M}>$). So one might try out a provisional hypothesis about an ordered pair $<U,f>$ and a provisional hypothesis that the indicative mood is a *prima facie* indication of s-meaning, the imperative mood is a *prima facie* indication of s-commanding, and the interrogative mood is a *prima facie* indication of s-asking. The theory of force with these two components, and the meaning specifications for L (that is, the members of $\mathscr{M}$), jointly license the redescription of utterances made by members of G as linguistic acts of certain kinds (at this stage, s-meanings, s-commandings, s-askings) and with certain contents. One would assess these redescriptions in two ways. If L is the actual language of G then, according to *PAC 2*, there are regularities of use of utterances of certain types to perform linguistic acts of certain kinds and with certain contents, and these regularities are conventions. If the regularities are conventions then the s-meanings are acts of assertion, the s-commandings are commands, and the s-askings are questions. The redescriptions might fail on this first assessment; there might be no appropriate regularities, or there might be regularities which are not conventions. Whether they pass or fail on this first assessment, the redescriptions must also be assessed according to *PAC 1*. For the redescriptions yield, via the definitions of kinds of linguistic acts, attributions of propositional attitudes to speakers, and one must judge whether these attributions make sense of the total pattern of behaviour (linguistic and non-linguistic) of the speakers. If the redescriptions fail on either assessment then one might try out other theories of force. If that does not help then one must conclude that *L* is not the actual language of *G*. Perhaps some language other than *L* is the actual language of *G*. Or perhaps no language is the actual language of *G*. (As the example of 'Grrr' indicates, this may be the case even though there are in *G* regularities of use of utterances of various types to s-mean, s-command and s-ask various things.)

Our intuitive grasp upon what it is for a population to use a language will furnish plenty of counterexamples to *PAC 2* as it stands. But there would be little point in considering even modest refinements if there were good arguments against the whole project of augmenting *PAC 1* by a *PAC* of a broadly Gricean kind. Some writers do indeed take themselves to have such arguments quite apart from any detailed counterexamples.

One objection begins from the indisputable point that if *L* is a language with infinitely many sentences then for any population *G* there will be infinitely many sentences of *L* which are never used in *G*. Mark Platts (1979, pp. 89–90) put the objection this way:

> The majority of . . . sentences . . . will never be uttered. They will not therefore be uttered with any intentions. . . . The obvious move . . . is to hold the meanings of such sentences to be definable in terms of hypothetical intentions. . . . But now Grice faces a dilemma: either there is some constraint upon these hypothetical intentions . . . or there is not. If there is none, the meanings of unuttered sentences will be left completely indeterminate. . . . There must therefore be some constraint. Generally *the constraint upon the hypothetical intentions with which a sentence can be uttered . . . is precisely the meaning of the sentence.* . . . the

attempt to define the meanings of unuttered sentences in terms
of hypothetical intentions . . . is hopeless: for it presupposes a
prior notion of sentence-meaning. (My italics)

This objection will be revealed as groundless by the considerations of
Section IV.1, but we can already see in outline how a reply would go.
The problem (briefly) is that we may want to say that *s* means that *p*
in the language of *G* even though no utterances of a type suitably
related to *s* are ever performed in *G*; we may want to say that *L* is
the actual language of *G* even though some sentences of *L* are never
used in *G*. The solution (briefly) is that we shall only want to say the
first thing if *s* is constructed out of building blocks which occur in
sentences which are used in *G*, and, what is more, whose occurrence
there plays a role (to be specified in Section IV.1) in the use of those
sentences in *G*; and we shall only want to say the second thing if *L* is
the smallest language which contains all the sentences which can be
constructed out of the building blocks which occur in, and whose
occurrence plays a role in the use of, the sentences which members
of *G* do use. What constrains the intentions with which members of
G would utter an indicative sentence *s* (or a closely related sentence
in another mood) is not the meaning, in some prior sense, of *s* but
rather the intentions with which members of *G* do utter sentences
from whose building blocks *s* is constructed. (On this problem and
solution, see Loar, 1976, pp. 158-60.)

Acceptance of a solution along these (briefly indicated) lines may
be encouraged once we notice that the same problem would arise if
one settled for *PAC 1* alone, as Platts thinks we should. Suppose that
we have a correct theory₁ of meaning for *L*, and a theory of force. Are
these theories jointly acceptable for a population *G* even if *L* contains
sentences never used in *G*? The answer furnished by *PAC 1* alone is,
presumably, that the theories are jointly acceptable if the redescriptions
which they would license would fit into a wider context in which
speakers' behaviour could be made intelligible in the light of propositional attitudes. But whether such redescriptions would so fit depends
upon what linguistic acts members of *G* would perform using those
sentences, and that, according to the original objection, is constrained
by the meaning of those sentences in a prior sense. But what could the
prior sense be? The only candidate is the meaning of the sentences in
L. But that can constrain linguistic acts performed by members of *G*
only if *L* is their actual language. And whether *L* is their actual language
is precisely the original problem.

A second objection to the project of augmenting *PAC 1* by a Gricean *PAC* is that *PAC 2*, and the accompanying definitions of s-meaning and assertion in terms of propositional attitudes, encourage the implausible view that one can first determine what a man's propositional attitudes are (merely by attending to his non-linguistic behaviour) and then, via the Gricean definitions of s-meaning, assertion, and so on, proceed to describe the man as performing linguistic acts of specific kinds and with specific contents. An extreme version of this view is that one can observe a single utterance x and, on the basis of the non-linguistic behaviour surrounding x and independently of anything one may know about other utterances, attribute to the utterer sufficiently fine-grained propositional attitudes to permit the redescription of x as a linguistic act of a determinate kind and with a determinate and fine-grained content.

The implausibility of this view attaches primarily to the idea that a man's non-linguistic behaviour may put us into a position to assign specific contents to his utterances. For we narrow down the content of the linguistic act performed in a certain utterance, by looking at the circumstances in which the speaker produces other utterances of the same type and of syntactically related types. (In practice, we assume that the contents of linguistic acts are systematically related to the syntactic form of the sentence used.) The extreme version of the view is more implausible still, because attribution of propositional attitudes on the basis of a limited range of behaviour is answerable to other behaviour of the same agent.

But although the view is implausible, and although its implausibility may constitute an objection to certain projects within Grice's programme, we are not committed to the view by accepting *PAC 2* and the definitions of assertion and s-meaning. Consider first the extreme version of the view. To state in psychological vocabulary a necessary and sufficient condition for an utterance to be an act of s-meaning that p is not at all to suggest that it can be determined just by looking at that utterance and the immediately surrounding behaviour whether that condition obtains. What has been argued by Jonathan Bennett (1976, pp. 147-8) is that a short stretch of behaviour may provide overwhelming evidence that a certain man's utterance is an act of s-meaning something, and may provide a reason to ascribe a determinate content to the act. His very plausible example is of a languageless creature s-meaning that his audience risks being hit on the head by a coconut. But it is doubtful whether, if we really restrict ourselves to the immediately surrounding behaviour, we can be justified in ascribing precisely that content as against, for example, that the audience risks being hit on the top by a heavy, edible object, or even just a pain producing object. We need other behaviour to convince us that the speaker has (and here employs) the concepts of a head and of a coconut. And this further need should not be obscured by the fact that it may be very likely indeed that such further behaviour would be forthcoming.

As for the view in its less extreme version, it is no part of *PAC 2* to deny that, in practice, the way to proceed with interpretation of a man's utterances is to try out a scheme of redescription of those utterances as linguistic acts, and see how the resulting propositional attitude attributions contribute to the project of rendering the man intelligible, and then to revise those redescriptions in respect of the kind of linguistic act and of the content. Nor is it part of *PAC 2* to hold that this is merely the best policy in practice. It is consistent with *PAC 2* to hold that this practical policy is sustained by a deep conceptual truth about propositional attitude attribution. (See e.g. Davidson, 1974, especially pp. 311–12.)

3 MEANING, CONVENTION, AND MOOD

Our intuitive grasp of what it is for a language to be the actual language of a population reveals that the condition imposed by *PAC 2* is too severe to be a necessary condition for the obtaining of the actual language relation. For, according to *PAC 2*, if a language in which a sentence *s* means that *p* is to be the actual language of *G*, then there must be, in *G*, a regularity of use of utterances of *s* to s-mean that *p*. But in familiar cases of language use there are too many linguistic acts which are not acts of s-meaning, too many examination answers, confessions, reminders, and utterances directed at counter-suggestible audiences (Grice, 1969, pp. 166–8), too many stories, rote repetitions, illustrations, suppositions, parodies, charades, chants, and conspicuously unmeant compliments (Davidson, 1979, p. 11). It is simply not plausible to maintain that there is a regularity of use of indicative sentences to perform acts of s-meaning.

We can leave the definitions of s-meaning and of convention intact, and we can leave the general form of the definition of the actual language relation intact. The definition will begin

L is the actual language of G just in case there is an ordered pair $<U, f>$ [and there is a (*prima facie* indication) function from moods (assigned to members of U by f) to kinds of linguistic act] such that, for every sentence s in L (that is, in $\mathscr{S}$ if $L = < \mathscr{S}, \mathscr{M} >$), if s means (in L) that p then. . . .

But we cannot complete the definition simply by putting together, in the most obvious way, the concepts of s-meaning and of convention (as in *PAC 2*). We need a new completion of the definition of the actual language relation, and with it a new definition of assertion as a special kind of s-meaning.

To the extent that the condition imposed by *PAC 2* is too severe, we need to make use, in a new definition, of a concept weaker than that of s-meaning (and concepts weaker than those of s-commanding and s-asking), or a concept weaker than that of convention, or both. Grice's programme provides at least two examples of concepts weaker than that of s-meaning. Let us consider those first.

A speaker S s-means* that p by his utterance (token) x directed at audience A, just in case

(1*) S intends that x will produce in A an (activated) belief that S believes that p;

(2*) for some feature F of x, S intends that A should recognize S's primary intention in part by recognizing x to have feature F;

(3*) S intends that A's recognition of S's primary intention should be part of A's reason for believing that S believes that p;

(4*) S does not intend that A should be deceived about S's intentions.

(We are not strictly justified in saying that s-meaning* is a weaker concept than s-meaning, since we have not shown that all cases of s-meaning are also cases of s-meaning*. Nor is it obvious that it can be shown.)

The concept of s-meaning* is usually brought in to meet the fact that examination answers, confessions, reminders, and utterances directed at counter-suggestible audiences are not cases of s-meaning (see e.g. Grice, 1969, p.171). It is not altogether clear that all of these (that all confessions, for example) are cases of s-meaning*. And it is not altogether clear that it would not be preferable to notice the element of ritual in at least some of these cases and to describe them as (derivative) cases in which there is a pretence of s-meaning. But, in

19

any case, there are still too many linguistic acts which are not acts of s-meaning and not acts of s-meaning* either. Even if we alter *PAC 2* by replacing 's-mean' with 's-mean*', the condition which is imposed upon the use of indicative sentences is still too severe to be a necessary condition for the obtaining of the actual language relation.

S-meaning and s-meaning* are both instances of a more general notion. In each case there is a propositional attitude ψ such that a speaker's primary intention is that the audience should ψ that p. So let us define the quite general notion of *weak-s-meaning (ws-meaning)*. A speaker S ws-means that p by his utterance (token) x directed at audience A, just in case there is some propositional attitude ψ such that

(w1) S intends that x will produce in A a ψ that p;
(w2)   as (2*);
(w3) S intends that A's recognition of S's primary intention should be part of A's reason for ψ-ing that p;
(w4)   as (4*).

(For some values of 'ψ' the word 'reason' in (w3) may be inappropriate, and may have to be replaced. In general, one might read 'basis'.)

We need to define appropriate generalizations of the concepts of s-commanding and s-asking, too. A definition of ws-commanding might begin as follows. A speaker S ws-commands that p by his utterance (token) x directed at audience A, just in case there is some propositional attitude ψ such that

(w1') S intends that x will produce in A a ψ to bring it about that p;

Given that beginning, we could easily fill in the other clauses (w2')–(w4'). But s-commanding, as it was defined earlier, is not obviously an instance of this general notion. In order to make it so, we need to replace the clause

(1') S intends that x will produce in A the response that A brings it about that p;

with

(1'') S intends that x will produce in A an intention to bring it about that p;

So let us suppose that this alteration is made, and that the concept of ws-asking is defined analogously to the concepts of ws-meaning and ws-commanding. Then, armed with those three concepts, and with the original concept of convention, we can give a new definition of the actual language relation.

> *PAC 3 L* is the actual language of *G* just in case there is an ordered pair $<U, f>$ such that for every sentence *s* in *L*, if *s* means (in *L*) that *p* then (i) there is an utterance type *u* in *U* such that $f(u) = <s, indicative>$ and there is a convention in *G* to ws-mean that *p* by audience-directed utterances of *u*; [and (ii) if there are utterance types *u!* and *u?* such that $f(u!) = <s, imperative>$ and $f(u?) = <s, interrogative>$ then there are conventions in *G* to ws-command that *p* by audience-directed utterances of type *u!* and to ws-ask whether *p* by audience-directed utterances of type *u?*].

Along with this new definition of the actual language relation we have a new definition of assertion. A speaker *S* asserts that *p* in his utterance (token) *x* of type *u* directed at audience *A* just in case *S* s-means that *p* by *x* and the feature *F* in clause (2) of the definition of s-meaning is:

> being an utterance of a type such that there is, in the population, a regularity of use of utterances of that type to ws-mean that *p*.

And just as we define assertion as a kind of s-meaning, so we can define *saying* that *p* as ws-meaning that *p* in which *F* is that same feature. The concept of saying is very much more general than the concept of assertion, and it is a concept which, intuitively, we need. For many linguistic acts which are performed using indicative utterance types, and which involve trading upon the fact that an utterance type has a certain linguistic meaning in the population, are nevertheless not assertions. Thus, for example, an utterance of the sentence 'The door is shut', performed with the overt intention of getting *A* to believe that *S* desires that *A* bring it about that the door is shut, would count as a saying that the door is shut but not as an assertion that the door is shut. And the same can be said of ironic statements, and of many jokes (Peacocke, 1976, p. 184):

> If in response to a remark that one's tape recorder is malfunctioning, another replies 'Nixon will be pleased to help you with any difficulties you have with the "Erase" button' as a joke, he does strictly and literally say that Nixon will be pleased to . . . etc. But he does not assert that Nixon will be pleased . . . etc.

To the extent that it avoids the problem that there are too many linguistic acts which are not acts of s-meaning (or of s-meaning*), *PAC 3* is an improvement over *PAC 2*. Indeed, *PAC 3* avoids that problem to such an extent that it allows, at least as a theoretical possibility, that a population could have a language L as their actual language even though members of the population never used sentences of L in acts of s-meaning (or of s-meaning*) at all. This theoretical possibility might be important if we were to cease ignoring populations with bilingual members. For a population might use two languages, one of which was reserved for use in stories, rote repetitions, illustrations, suppositions, parodies, charades, chants, and conspicuously unmeant compliments. And we should want to allow (in a fully general account) that each of the two languages was an actual language of that population.

There is, however, a problem with *PAC 3*, for it allows that an utterance type may be classified as indicative even though there is no use of utterances of that type to perform acts of s-meaning (or of s-meaning*), and that is not obviously consistent with the intuition that the use of utterances of indicative types to perform acts of s-meaning (or perhaps, of s-meaning*) is, in a certain sense, the norm. (Similarly, the use of utterances of imperative and interrogative types to perform acts of s-commanding and s-asking, respectively, is the norm. To be the normal use, in this sense, is not to be the usual or statistically most frequent use (cf. Davidson, 1979, p. 11).)

We have already seen how an utterance of 'The door is shut' might be an act of ws-meaning (a saying that the door is shut) which is also classifiable as an act of ws-commanding. It is a theoretical possibility that, in a certain population, all acts of ws-meaning should be acts of ws-commanding. So suppose, for a moment, that in a certain population this is so, and that for each sentence s of L there are two utterance types u_1 and u_2 which can be used interchangeably. For all that *PAC 3* says, one of u_1 and u_2 is indicative and the other is imperative. For all that *PAC 3* says, different moods are used quite indifferently. And this goes against our intuition.

We can approach the same point from a slightly different direction. It is implicit in *PAC 3* that, in any theory of force, the (*prima facie* indication) function from moods to kinds of linguistic act will associate ws-meaning with the indicative mood, ws-commanding with the imperative mood, and ws-asking with the interrogative mood. It seems to be a matter of practical necessity that, in any population, the syntactic form of a man's utterance should constitute, for an audience,

22

prima facie evidence as to what more specific kind of linguistic act is being performed. What is implicit in *PAC 3* is that if, in a certain population, the indicative mood constitutes, for an audience, *prima facie* evidence that an act of s-meaning is being performed, then that is a quite superficial feature of the linguistic behaviour of that population. And this is counter-intuitive, since it is some such facts as that the indicative mood constitutes, for an audience, *prima facie* evidence that an act of s-meaning is being performed that provide the conceptual anchoring of the various moods.

If a mood is to be the indicative mood then it should be the case either (i) that, in the population, that mood constitutes, for an audience, *prima facie* evidence that an act of s-meaning is being performed, or else (ii) that, for some relatively specific kind of linguistic act which is more naturally regarded as derivative from s-meaning than from s-commanding or s-asking (such as s-meaning*), that mood constitutes, for an audience, *prima facie* evidence that an act of that kind is being performed. In a similar way we could spell out what it is for a mood to be the imperative mood, or the interrogative mood.

Let us say that g is a *good* mood function just in case g is a function from moods to pairs $\langle K_1, K_2 \rangle$ of kinds of linguistic act, such that if $g(indicative) = \langle K_1, K_2 \rangle$ then K_1 is ws-meaning and K_2 is either s-meaning or some relatively specific kind which is naturally regarded as derivative from s-meaning; and if $g(imperative) = \langle K_1, K_2 \rangle$ then K_1 is ws-commanding and K_2 is either s-commanding or some relatively specific kind which is naturally regarded as derivative from s-commanding; and similarly for $g(interrogative)$. Then we can provide a definition of the actual language relation which allows, as a theoretical possibility, that there could be use of a language without there being a practice of s-meaning or s-commanding or s-asking, or of any kind of linguistic act which is naturally regarded as derivative from some one of these, but which requires, as a theoretical necessity, that if the indicative, imperative, or interrogative moods are used then they are used in appropriate practices.

> *PAC 4* L is the actual language of G just in case there is an ordered pair $\langle U, f \rangle$ and a good mood function g (such that for each u in U, if $f(u) = \langle s, m \rangle$ then $g(m)$ is defined) such that for every sentence s in L, if s means (in L) that p then
> > (i)   for some mood m there is an utterance type u in U such that $f(u) = \langle s, m \rangle$;

(ii) for any mood m and any utterance type u if
$f(u) = <s, m>$ and $g(m) = <K_1, K_2>$ then
(a) there is a convention in G to K_1 that p by audience-directed utterances of u;
and
(b) an audience-directed utterance of u constitutes, for the audience, *prima facie* evidence that an act of K_2-ing is being performed.

In most cases there will be some mood m such that for every sentence s in L there is an utterance type u for which $f(u) = <s, m>$; namely, the indicative mood. Such a mood might be said to be *comprehensive*. It is not required by *PAC 4* that any mood be comprehensive.

The definitions of assertion and of saying can remain as they were after *PAC 3* save that we shall now require that the utterance be in the indicative mood. This has the (intuitively pleasing) consequence that assertion is the norm for saying (see again Peacocke, 1976, p. 184).

Doubtless there are objections which could be raised against *PAC 4*. Doubtless further refinements are needed. (For example, something needs to be said about the way in which audience-directed utterances in certain moods constitute *prima facie* evidence that linguistic acts of certain kinds are being performed.) But let us conclude this section by doing two things. Let us, first, recall the two apparent gaps in the account provided by *PAC 1* and, second, note briefly some other ways in which one might provide a definition of the actual language relation.

The two apparent gaps were these. The constraint *PAC 1* does not itself tell us what propositional attitudes can be attributed to a member of a population on the basis of an utterance described as a linguistic act of a certain kind and with a certain content. And there is nothing in *PAC 1* about the conventional nature of language use. The definitions of s-meaning, assertion, saying, and the rest go some way towards filling the first gap (see also Schiffer, 1972, Chapter IV). The definition of the actual language relation fills the second gap. And in filling those gaps we have introduced just one complication into the picture. Because linguistic acts of a certain kind may constitute the normal use of an utterance type without constituting a regular use, we have had to allow that a mood is associated with two kinds of linguistic act, one less specific and one more specific.

Here, finally, are three other ways in which one might provide a definition of the actual language relation.

24

(1) The definitions *PAC 2*, *PAC 3* and *PAC 4* all involve the idea of conventions to perform linguistic acts of various kinds, where the kinds of linguistic act are defined in terms of intentions about intentions. According to the definition of convention, language users have knowledge about intentions about intentions, of a quite complicated sort. So one might try to provide a definition of the actual language relation which does not involve the attribution of quite such complicated knowledge to ordinary language users. One might, in particular, require only that there be a convention to use utterances of a certain type with the intention, for some propositional attitude ψ, to produce in the audience a ψ with a certain content (and to do this without any intention to deceive the audience about one's intentions). It is plausible that one could argue that if a speaker were to make an utterance with such an intention, and if the presence of the convention constituted part of his reason for using an utterance of that type, then the speaker would perform an act of ws-meaning (cf. Lewis, 1969, pp. 152-9).

(2) Although there is no regularity of use of utterances of 'The door is shut' to s-mean that the door is shut, an utterance of that sentence does count, for an audience, as *prima facie* evidence (i) that the speaker s-means that the door is shut, and (ii) that the speaker believes that the door is shut. One might provide a definition of the actual language relation which requires not common knowledge about intentions about intentions, but instead, common knowledge that audiences take utterances as *prima facie* evidence about speakers' beliefs. (For this kind of definition, see Peacocke, 1976.)

(3) The condition imposed by *PAC 2* was too severe. We need to make use, in any new definition, of a concept weaker than that of s-meaning, or a concept weaker than that of convention (or both). In *PAC 4* we used the concept of convention and a concept weaker than that of s-meaning (namely, ws-meaning). One might provide a definition of the actual language relation by using a concept weaker than that of convention. In particular, one might borrow from Grice the concept of having a certain procedure in one's repertoire, and require only that members of a population have the use of certain utterances to s-mean certain things in their repertoire (see Grice, 1968 and Schiffer, 1972, pp. 132-6).

25

NOTES

In this chapter I am indebted to conversations with Anita Avramides, Simon Blackburn (particularly in the final paragraph at (1)), Christopher Peacocke (particularly concerning the theory of force), and Peter Strawson. At many points I have followed Peacocke, (1976); my definition of weak-s-meaning, for example, is based upon Peacocke's definition of saying (p. 186).

Some fundamental books and papers in Grice's programme are these: Grice (1957), (1968), and (1969); Strawson (1964a) and (1970a); Schiffer (1972); Lewis (1969) and (1975). Bennett's paper (1973) and subsequent book (1976), and Searle (1969), have also been influential. For a discussion of Strawson (1970a) see McDowell (1980) and Strawson (1980). For a discussion of Lewis (1969) and (1975) and, in particular, an objection to clause (5) in the definition of convention, see Burge (1975).

For the purposes of exposition I have ignored the fact that in many linguistic acts the expression used is, strictly speaking, not grammatical. Thus, when I say, for example, that the actual language of a population contains the sentences which members of the population use, I do not wish to be taken to be denying that specification of the class of (grammatical) sentences which members of the population use already requires syntactic theorizing.

II

TRUTH

1 TRUTH CONDITIONS

If the philosophical account of meaning which was barely outlined in Chapter I were made fully general and fully detailed then it would constitute a map of a certain region of conceptual space, namely a central tract within the broader area which is the territory of philosophical logic. It is certain that the concept of truth lies in that region, and yet its location would not be revealed by the map, for the account in Chapter I did not appeal to that concept. This omission holds the promise of elucidation. If we can say where truth is related with respect to meaning then the account of meaning will furnish an account of truth. And it is not difficult to state the location of truth.

For any language $L = <\mathscr{S}, \mathscr{M}>$ the extension of the predicate 'is true (in L)' is a subset of $\mathscr{S}$ determined by the rule

> (T) From: s means (in L) that p
> infer: s is true (in L) iff p

(where 'iff' abbreviates 'if and only if ').

The converse of (T) is not an acceptable rule. This is particularly clear (a) if 'iff' is read as the material biconditional. From

> s means (in L) that snow is white

we infer by (T)

> s is true (in L) iff snow is white.

Using the undoubted truth

Snow is white iff the earth moves

we can proceed thence to

s is true (in L) iff the earth moves.

And from that the converse of (T) would yield a falsehood. The converse of (T) is no more acceptable (b) if 'iff' is read as a strict or modal biconditional, expressing *broadly logical* equivalence (see Plantinga, 1979, p. 2). For by (T) and the truth

Snow is white iff (snow is white and $12^2 = 144$)

we obtain

s is true (in L) iff (snow is white and $12^2 = 144$)

from which the converse of (T) would yield a falsehood. (It might be thought that on this second reading of 'iff'

s is true (in L) iff snow is white

is itself false, since s could have meant that snow is black, for example. But recall that a language in which s means that snow is black is a different language from L in which s means that snow is white (cf. Wallace, 1972, p. 242 and 1975a, p. 57; Baldwin, 1975, p. 84; Peacocke, 1978, p. 477).)

Corresponding to these two readings of 'iff' there are two notions of a truth condition: (i) a *material* truth condition, and (ii) a *strict* truth condition. The unacceptability of the converse of (T) on either reading of 'iff' shows that for the corresponding notions of truth condition it is not a sufficient condition for s to mean (in L) that p, that a truth (in L) condition for s is that p. For these two notions of truth condition it is false that 'to give truth conditions is a way of giving the meaning of the sentence' (Davidson, 1967, p. 7; for a retraction see Davidson, 1973a, p. 325; see also Section II.3).

Adding rule (T) to a theory$_1$ of meaning for a particular language is one way of providing a theory$_1$ of truth for that language. In general a theory$_1$ of truth is a (perhaps formalized) theory which, for some particular language L, yields a truth condition specification (material or strict) for each well-formed sentence of L; that is, a theory which yields at least one theorem of the form

s is true (in L) iff p

for each sentence s of L.

Concerning theories$_1$ of truth, we can make five preliminary points corresponding to those we made concerning theories$_1$ of meaning at the beginning of Chapter I.

(1) A theory$_1$ of truth is a theory about a particular object language (*OL*), cast in a particular metalanguage (*ML*). But what the theorems of the theory state in that *ML* could be stated in other languages.

(2) There is a world of difference between

  (i) 'Snön är vit' is true (in Swedish) iff snow is white

and

  (ii) 'Snön är vit' is true (in Swedish) iff 'Snow is white' is true (in English).

It would not be correct to mark the contrast by saying that what is stated by (i) is something knowledge of which itself suffices (e.g. in a Frenchman) for knowing what the Swedish sentence means. For it clearly does not so suffice. But what is stated by (i) is something knowledge of which does itself suffice (e.g. in a Frenchman) for knowing that the Swedish sentence does not mean, for example, that snow is black. What is stated by (ii) is something knowledge of which does not itself suffice for even that. (See again, Evans and McDowell, 1976, pp. vii–xi.)

(3) It is not built into the notion of a theory$_1$ of truth, as that notion is used here, that the truth condition specifications which it yields as theorems should provide conceptual analyses.

(4) It is not built into the notion of a theory$_1$ of truth, as such, that it should have only finitely many proper axioms.

(5) Because what a certain sentence means in a language L is a non-contingent property of L, we can assign to sentences strict truth (in L) conditions. But not just any material truth condition specification can be elevated to a strict truth condition specification. If, for example, a sentence s means (in L) that snow is white then (reading 'iff' as the material biconditional) we have both

  s is true (in L) iff snow is white

and

  s is true (in L) iff the earth moves

as correct (material) truth condition specifications. But, if 'iff' is instead read as a strict or modal biconditional, only the first of these is a correct (strict) truth condition specification.

A theory$_1$ of truth for a particular language is no more a theory$_2$ of truth (a discursive theory which illuminates the concept of truth) than a theory$_1$ of meaning is a theory$_2$ of meaning. But just as we can provide a theory$_2$ of meaning by stating, in general, under what conditions the meaning specifications yielded by a theory$_1$ of meaning are correct for the language of a given population, so we can provide a theory$_2$ of truth by stating, in general, under what conditions the (material) truth condition specifications yielded by a theory$_1$ of truth correctly fix the extension of the truth predicate for the language of a given population. And we have the two raw materials with which to state this. For it is obviously a necessary and sufficient condition for a theory$_1$ of truth θ to be correct for the language of a given population G that there be a language L such that L is the actual language of G and θ is a correct theory$_1$ of truth for L. We have (in Chapter I) a (provisional) account of what it is for L to be the actual language of G. And we know what is a sufficient condition for θ to be correct for $L (= <\mathscr{S}, \mathscr{M}>)$, namely that θ should have for each sentence s in $\mathscr{S}$ just one theorem of the form

$$s \text{ is true (in } L) \text{ iff } p$$

and that this should be the result of applying rule (T) to the meaning specification in $\mathscr{M}$ for s. So it is a necessary and sufficient condition for the correctness of θ that θ should determine the same extension for the truth (in L) predicate as a theory meeting the sufficient condition; that is, that for each s in $\mathscr{S}$ the theorems of θ which are of the form

$$s \text{ is true (in } L) \text{ iff } p$$

should be materially equivalent to the sentence of that form which would be a theorem of a theory meeting the sufficient condition. (Similarly, we can state a necessary and sufficient condition for the correctness of a theory which delivers strict truth condition specifications.)

Adding rule (T) to a theory$_1$ of meaning for a language is by no means the only way, or even the most familiar way, of providing a theory$_1$ of truth. Let us fix upon a very simple propositional calculus language L_1 with just three atomic sentences s_1, s_2 and s_3, where

s_1 means (in L_1) that snow is white
s_2 means (in L_1) that the earth moves
s_3 means (in L_1) that grass is blue

and with the connectives '&', 'v' and '∼' with their usual meanings. (To avoid any questions about temporal relativity, read 'snow is white' as 'snow is always white', and so on.)

Here is the familiar way to provide a theory₁ of truth for a language like L_1. First, to list, for the atomic sentences, the truth (in L_1) condition specifications which would be obtained via rule (*T*):

(*T1a*) s_1 is true (in L_1) ↔ snow is white
(*T1b*) s_2 is true (in L_1) ↔ the earth moves
(*T1c*) s_3 is true (in L_1) ↔ grass is blue.

Here '↔' is the material biconditional (in the *ML*). Then second, to provide for each truth functional connective an axiom which states how it contributes to the (material) truth conditions of sentences in which it occurs. To state this quite generally we shall need to quantify (in the *ML*) over all sentences of the *OL*; let us use 'σ' and 'τ' as variables for this purpose.

(*T2*)   ($\forall\sigma$)($\forall\tau$) ['('∩σ∩ '&'∩τ∩ ')' is true (in L_1) ↔
         (σ is true (in L_1) & τ is true (in L_1))]

(Read: for any sentences σ and τ of L_1 the sentence made up of a left bracket followed by σ followed by the symbol '&' followed by τ followed by a right bracket is true (in L_1) iff . . .) The symbol '&' which is used on the right hand side of this biconditional is the conjunction sign in the *ML*.

(*T3*)   ($\forall\sigma$)($\forall\tau$) ['(' ∩σ∩ 'v'∩τ∩ ')' is true (in L_1) ↔
         (σ is true (in L_1) v τ is true (in L_1))]
(*T4*)   ($\forall\sigma$) ['(' ∩ '∼'∩ σ∩ ')' is true (in L_1) ↔
         ∼(σ is true (in L_1))]

(Call this theory '*Tθ*'.) These six proper axioms are adequate to yield, for each sentence of L_1, a truth (in L_1) condition specification in which the right hand side is free of the semantic predicate 'is true (in L_1)'. One example is more than enough to show the general strategy. Consider the sentence '('∩s_1 ∩ '&'∩s_2 ∩ ')'. By universal instantiation from (*T2*) we have

'('∩s_1 ∩ '&'∩s_2 ∩ ')' is true (in L_1) ↔
(s_1 is true (in L_1) & s_2 is true (in L_1))

31

The logic used in the *ML* (standard first-order logic) yields (without any help from the proper axioms of *Tθ*) all instances of the schema

$$(A \leftrightarrow B) \rightarrow (\Sigma (A) \leftrightarrow \Sigma (B)) \qquad \text{(Subst)}$$

where $\Sigma(A)$ is a sentence containing A, and $\Sigma(B)$ results by replacing at least one occurrence of A in $\Sigma(A)$ by B. Equivalently, in the presence of *Modus Ponens* and Conditional Proof, the *ML* logic yields as a derived rule of inference

$$\frac{A \leftrightarrow B}{\Sigma(A) \leftrightarrow \Sigma(B)} \qquad \text{(Subst Inf)}.$$

So, in particular, by (*T1a*) and *Subst* we have

'('$^{\cap}s_1 \cap$ '&'$^{\cap}s_2 \cap$ ')' is true (in L_1) $\leftrightarrow$
(snow is white & s_2 is true (in L_1)),

and thence, by (*T1b*) and *Subst*

'('$^{\cap}s_1 \cap$ '&'$^{\cap}s_2 \cap$ ')' is true (in L_1) $\leftrightarrow$
(snow is white & the earth moves).

Not only is the right hand side of this biconditional free of semantic vocabulary (that is, in this case, free of the predicate 'is true (in L_1)') but also the biconditional has the feature that replacement of 'is true (in L_1) $\leftrightarrow$' by 'means (in L_1) that' results in a correct meaning (in L_1) specification for the mentioned *OL* sentence. Indeed, using the general strategy which this one example is more than enough to show, we can prove for each sentence of L_1 a biconditional with this feature. Using other strategies we can prove biconditionals such as

'('$^{\cap}s_1 \cap$ '&'$^{\cap}s_2 \cap$ ')' is true (in L_1) $\leftrightarrow$
((snow is white v (grass is blue & $\sim$ grass is blue))
& the earth moves)

which lack this feature.

It is instructive to observe just what proof theoretic resources are required in the background logic of the *ML* if at least the biconditionals with the just mentioned feature are to be provable. In the proof sketched the crucial resource is *Subst* (or *Subst Inf*). To demonstrate that all instances of that schema are provable we would proceed by induction on the complexity of Σ and would naturally appeal to the introduction and elimination rules for the various connectives in the background logic of the *ML*. (In the case of negation we might appeal to *Modus*

Tollens.) We would not need to appeal to the rule of double negation elimination. So certainly intuitionistic logic in the *ML* would be sufficient to yield the biconditionals (see Evans, 1976, p. 204). But not even that is required. The schema *Subst* does not distinguish between '&' and 'v' so we do not need the full strength of the introduction and elimination rules for those connectives. What is more, reflection on the difference between a rule of inference and a rule of proof reveals that we do not even need *Subst*. For *Subst* and *Subst Inf* are strictly stronger than either of the rules of proof which result from reading '⊢' in

$$\frac{\vdash (A) \leftrightarrow (B)}{\vdash (\Sigma (A) \leftrightarrow \Sigma (B))}$$

as 'there is a proof from the logic alone of . . .' or as 'there is a proof from the proper axioms of . . .'. The rule of proof which results on the first reading will not help in the proofs of the biconditionals, but the rule of proof which results on the second reading will help. Use of that rule can replace use of *Subst* (or *Subst Inf*) without any loss of formal adequacy. (For a little more on the use of rules of proof, see the last five paragraphs of Section II.5.)

2   THE MARKS OF TRUTH

With a view to drawing out some of the consequences of rule (*T*)'s statement of the location of the concept of truth relative to the concept of meaning let us introduce some terminology. For any theory₁ of truth a *canonical proof procedure* is an effective strategy for producing, for each sentence of the *OL* in question, a truth condition specifying biconditional whose right hand side is free of semantic vocabulary. The theorems thus produced are *canonical theorems*. Here is a canonical proof procedure for *Tθ*:

At any stage at which the truth predicate is applied to a complex *OL* sentence use the proper axiom (from (*T2*)-(*T4*)) for the last connective employed in the construction of the sentence, to yield a result in which the truth predicate is applied to less complex *OL* sentences. At any stage at which the truth predicate is applied only to a simple *OL* sentence use the appropriate proper axiom (from (*T1a*)-(*T1c*)) to eliminate that use of the truth predicate. At any stage at which the truth predicate does not appear, stop.

33

A theory$_1$ of truth (in L), together with a canonical proof procedure, is *interpretational* for L just in case replacing 'is true (in L) $\leftrightarrow$' by 'means (in L) that' in the canonical theorems yields precisely the set of correct meaning (in L) specifications for the sentences of L. (Given a very obvious canonical proof procedure, a theory$_1$ of truth (in L) obtained by adding rule (T) to a correct theory$_1$ of meaning (in L) will be interpretational for L.) If rule (T) succeeds in locating the concept of truth relative to the concept of meaning, then what is stated by the canonical theorems of an interpretational theory$_1$ of truth for L goes to the heart of the concept of truth in L.

If we consider a formal theory$_1$ of truth θ in which the uninterpreted predicate symbol 'Tr' occurs rather than 'is true (in L)', together with a canonical proof procedure for θ, then we can say that θ is interpretational for the language $<\mathscr{S},\mathscr{M}>$, where $\mathscr{S}$ is the set of sentences for which canonical theorems are delivered by θ and $\mathscr{M}$ is the set of meaning specifications which result by putting 'means that' for '$Tr \leftrightarrow$' in those canonical theorems. If $<\mathscr{S},\mathscr{M}> = L$ then 'Tr' can be read as 'is true (in L)'.

If θ is an interpretational theory$_1$ of truth for L and L is the actual language of G, then what θ states, together with the extra fact that θ is interpretational, can be used in the redescription of utterances, performed by members of G, as linguistic acts with certain contents. For, by the definition of an interpretational theory, if a canonical theorem of a theory$_1$ of truth which is interpretational for L states that s is true (in L) iff p, then s means (in L) that p. And if L is the actual language of G and s means (in L) that p, then utterances by members of G, of types related to s by a component $<U,f>$ of a theory of force, may be redescribed variously as assertions or sayings that p, as commands that p, and as questions whether p. There is nothing mysterious about this; certainly nothing as mysterious as might be suggested by saying (more briefly) that a theory$_1$ of truth itself is (or can serve as) a theory$_1$ of meaning (see below, Section II.3). For a theory$_1$ of truth does not itself state enough about sentences to determine their meanings (cf. Davidson, 1976, p.41: 'A theory of truth, no matter how well selected, is not a theory of meaning'). It is the extra fact that the theory is interpretational that licenses conversion of its canonical theorems into meaning specifications. Thereby, the fact that a theory is interpretational guarantees that the theory correctly fixes the extension of the truth predicate for the language in question. But it is not the fact thereby guaranteed which enables the theory to play a role in the interpretation of the speech of members of G (see McDowell, 1977, p. 160).

All of this is by way of an indication how a theory$_2$ of truth can be provided by reflecting quite generally upon theories$_1$ of truth. There remains the question whether any interesting characteristics of truth beyond the familiar rubric

> a sentence s is true just in case the world is as a person who used s to make an assertion would thereby assert it to be

can be wrung from a theory$_2$ of truth thus provided. David Wiggins (1980a) has argued that several interesting characteristics, what he calls 'marks of truth', can be identified once one has a theory$_2$ of truth along the lines suggested here (although he does not explicitly adopt the Gricean developments which led us from *PAC 1* to *PAC 4*). This is not the place to evaluate, or even to rehearse, all of his arguments. It will suffice to do just two things: first, to remark that it is very difficult to see how there could be anything interesting to say about truth unless something interesting can be made to flow from a theory$_2$ of truth which employs the notions of a theory of force and the actual language relation to relate the truth of sentences to human speech (cf. Strawson, 1970a, p. 189), and second, to consider briefly what Wiggins (1980a, p. 205) regards as the first mark of truth, namely that truth is 'the primary dimension of assessment for sentences'.

Let us focus upon the use of indicative utterance types. It is not an immediate consequence of our definition of the indicative mood that utterances constitute, for an audience, *prima facie* evidence that the speaker is expressing a belief. For we allowed that the indicative mood might constitute, for an audience, *prima facie* evidence that the linguistic act being performed is of a certain kind other than s-meaning or s-meaning*, provided that the kind is naturally regarded as derivative from s-meaning. But suppose that the members of a population use just one language (so that there is not a language reserved for use in stories, for example). Then it is very plausible that the members of the population sometimes use indicative utterance types in acts of s-meaning (or s-meaning*), that members themselves regard uses of indicative utterance types in linguistic acts of other kinds as derivative or parasitic, and that the indicative mood constitutes, for an audience, *prima facie* evidence that an act of s-meaning (or perhaps of s-meaning*) is being performed. (These plausible claims may be susceptible of proof, but Wiggins provides no proof, and no proof will be provided here.)

An act of s-meaning or of s-meaning* is typically an expression of belief. This is particularly clear in the case of s-meaning*, for in that case the speaker intends the audience to take his utterance as an expression of belief. Repeated unsignalled deviation from the norm of belief expression in acts of s-meaning* would undermine the readiness of other members of the population to take the utterances of the speaker as expressions of belief. Since the speaker will recognize that this would be the consequence of repeated unsignalled deviation, he has a reason to conform to the norm of belief expression in acts of s-meaning*. Most acts of s-meaning are also acts of s-meaning*. In the most plausible exceptions, the speaker does not intend to produce in the audience an activated belief about the speaker's beliefs, because he knows that the audience is already fully aware of his (the speaker's) beliefs (cf. Schiffer, 1972, p.47). But such acts of s-meaning, although not acts of s-meaning*, are still expressions of belief. And in general, in an act of s-meaning the speaker relies (in his primary intention) upon the audience's trust that he (the speaker) is sincerely expressing his beliefs. Since the speaker will recognize what would be the consequence of repeated unsignalled deviation, he has a reason to conform to the norm of belief expression in acts of s-meaning. Suppose now that in the (unique) language of a certain population a sentence s means that p. Then, if a speaker who is trying to conform to the norm of belief expression doubts that p, he will not utter s (except to perform a linguistic act of a kind which members of the population regard as derivative or parasitic). And that doubt would, in the presence of the minimal mastery of the concept of truth provided by rule (T), go in step with a doubt that s is true. So, finally, it is plausible that in cases where speakers have just one language, and use indicative utterance types, there is a norm according to which the speakers aim at truth in their utterances of sentences. And to agree over this would, it seems, be to agree over the first mark of truth. (For a discussion of conventions of truthfulness and trust in serious communication situations, see Lewis, 1975, pp. 7–10, 28–9.)

This agreement involves acceptance, also, of a primary dimension of assessment for utterances, which we may call 'TRUTH' (to distinguish it from truth of sentences). In some cases (in which context dependence is absent) the connection between truth and TRUTH is very simple (so simple that we can ignore the distinction). In these cases we can say that an utterance token of a sentence type s is TRUE just in case s is true. But the connection is not always so straightforward. The evaluation of an utterance for TRUTH is a once-for-all matter because, as Frege (1918, e.g. p. 37) put it, an utterance expresses a *complete thought*. A TRUE utterance of 'John is hot' does not become FALSE merely because John later cools off. Our grasp of what it is to belong to the category of indicative sentences depends upon the idea that an indicative sentence in use expresses a complete thought, so that utterances of it are TRUTH evaluable. But, as the example of 'John is hot' shows, various utterances of the same sentence may express different complete thoughts, so that some utterances are TRUE and some FALSE. The sentence 'John is hot' itself expresses a complete thought only relative to a context of utterance. (For a little more on TRUTH and context dependence, see Section VIII.3. See also Appendix 1.)

3   MEANING AND TRUTH CONDITIONS

It is obvious that to provide a theory$_2$ of truth one must discuss theories$_1$ of truth, not just theories$_1$ of meaning. But there is another familiar thought, namely that in pursuing other central concerns of philosophical logic we should do well to consider theories$_1$ of truth rather than theories$_1$ of meaning. It is a thought with which Davidson (1967, p. 6) expressed sympathy when he wrote:

> As a final bold step, let us try treating the position occupied by '*p*' extensionally: to implement this, sweep away the obscure 'means that' . . . The plausible result is
>
> (*T*)   *s* is *T* if and only if *p*.
>
> What we require of a theory of meaning for a language *L* is that
> . . . it place enough restrictions on the predicate 'is *T*' to entail all sentences got from schema *T* when '*s*' is replaced by a structural description of a sentence of *L* and '*p*' by that sentence.

And it is a thought which might be developed in either of two ways. In one development it would become the doctrine that a theory$_2$ of meaning should not speak of theories$_1$ of meaning, but rather of theories$_1$ of truth. In the other it would become the worry that there are technical obstacles to incorporating certain desirable features into a theory$_1$ of meaning, but no technical obstacles to incorporating those features into a theory$_1$ of truth. In this section we shall consider the doctrine and the worry in turn.

The doctrine that in providing a theory$_2$ of meaning one should not speak of theories$_1$ of meaning receives a fairly explicit statement from John Foster (1976, p. 6):

> [Even if technical problems are surmounted] our philosophical aims would be better served without [the intensionality of 'means that']. The point of showing how to construct theories of interpretation is to gain insight into the notion of meaning; this insight will be diminished if, to gain it, we have to take intensional idiom for granted.

It is surely correct that if one is to gain insight into the notion of meaning one must not simply make uncritical use of that notion. But it does not follow that one should retreat from theories$_1$ of meaning to theories$_1$ of truth. For it is not a theory$_1$ of meaning which provides insight into the notion of meaning; what provides that insight is an account, in quite general terms, of when a theory$_1$ of meaning is correct for the language of a population. Such an account would, of course, be empty if it were simply to help itself to the concept of meaning. But no one has ever seriously offered such an empty account, and no one offering an account along the lines of the *PAC*s of Chapter I could be accused of offering such an empty account.

McDowell (1976, p. 42) was closer to the mark when he wrote:

> [A] clear and convincing description of the shape which a theory of meaning for any language would take, not itself uncritically employing the notion of meaning, ought to remove all perplexity about the nature of meaning in general.

What will 'remove all perplexity about the nature of meaning' is a theory which speaks quite generally of theories$_1$ of meaning for particular languages, and which does not itself make uncritical use of the concept to be illuminated. This general theory will not be a mere description of the formal character of theories$_1$ of meaning, but rather an account of when such a theory is correct (for the language of a population). Such an account renders the concept of meaning, and the notion of stating the meaning of a sentence, unmysterious. For such mystery as may be supposed to attach to a sentence's having a certain meaning in a language is removed when we reveal the consequences, for the use of that language, of that sentence's having that meaning. Similarly, the supposed mystery of a sentence's being true in a certain language under certain conditions is removed when we relate that fact about a language to facts about the use of that language.

The doctrine that a theory$_2$ of meaning should not speak of theories$_1$ of meaning but rather of theories$_1$ of truth is mistaken. What makes the doctrine sound plausible, no doubt, is the ambiguity of the phrase 'theory of meaning'. What seems to go naturally with the doctrine is the (complementary) view that a theory$_1$ of truth does everything that we want a theory$_1$ of meaning to do. We have already noted Davidson's (1967, p. 7) claim that 'to give truth conditions is a way of giving the meaning of the sentence'. In 'Semantics for natural languages' (1970, p. 18) he wrote, 'I suggest that a theory of truth for a language ... give[s] the meanings of all independently meaningful expressions on the basis of an analysis of their structure'. And in the opening paragraph of Davidson (1979, p. 9) we find the following: 'Elsewhere I have argued that a theory of truth patterned after a Tarski-type truth definition tells us all we need to know about sense.' In a similar spirit, Platts (1979, p. 2) notes that 'A recurrent thought in the comparatively recent history of semantics is that the meaning of a sentence can be given by stating the conditions under which it is true', and goes on to cite passages from Frege, Wittgenstein, Carnap, and Quine, as well as Davidson.

We shall consider, in a moment, whether the familiar passage from Frege (*Grundgesetze*, I.32) really commits him to the view under discussion. But the most important point about that view is just that it is false. What seem to be expressions of the view are, at best, misleading expressions of some other view. The view is false because it is not the case that it is a sufficient condition for a sentence *s* to mean (in *L*) that *p* that *s* should be true (in *L*) iff *p*. It is not sufficient even if 'iff' is read as a strict or modal biconditional. (See again the beginning of Section II.1; and note that all true sentences of mathematics are true under all conditions.) If what seem to be expressions of the false view are simply slogans, summarizing the connection between an interpretational theory$_1$ of truth and a theory$_1$ of meaning, then they are misleading slogans. What is a sufficient condition for *s* to mean (in *L*) that *p* is that a canonical theorem of an interpretational theory$_1$ of truth for *L* should state that *s* is true (in *L*) iff *p*. And that claim is not happily abbreviated to the claim that stating truth conditions is a way of giving, or specifying, meanings.

Davidson's claims (quoted two paragraphs back) are best seen as unhappy abbreviations. We have already noted his clear statement that 'A theory of truth, no matter how well selected, is not a theory of meaning' (1976, p. 41). In that paper and elsewhere (e.g. Davidson, 1973a) he sets out carefully and accurately the connection between (as we would put it) an interpretational theory₁ of truth and a theory₁ of meaning. Similarly, when McDowell (1977, p.161) allows that a theory₁ of truth can 'serve as' a theory₁ of meaning, he sharply distinguishes that claim from the claim that a theory₁ of truth *is* a theory₁ of meaning:

> [Serving] as a theory of sense [meaning] is not the same as being one, on a certain strict view of what it is to be one. It was clear anyway that a truth-theory of the sort Davidson envisages does not, in saying what it does, *state* the senses [meanings] of expressions.

(One might still judge the 'serving as' terminology to be potentially misleading. See again the third paragraph of Section II.2.)

Let us now consider the familiar passage from Frege (*Grundgesetze*, I.32: 1893, pp. 89-90). In Furth's translation it is:

> Every such name of a truth value [i.e. every sentence] *expresses* a sense, a thought. Namely, by our stipulations it is determined under what conditions the name denotes the True. The sense of this name — the *thought* — is the thought that these conditions are fulfilled.

It is very far from clear that on the basis of this passage we should attribute to Frege the false view that it is a sufficient condition for a sentence s to express the thought that p, that s should be true iff p. It is at least as plausible (on the basis of just this passage) to attribute to Frege the very different view that for the sentences of the language under consideration, and given the stipulations which Frege had provided, it is a sufficient condition for s to express the thought that p that it should be determined by those stipulations (alone) that s is true iff p. And this is suggestively analogous to the claim which one would make for an interpretational theory₁ of truth (given a canonical proof procedure which involves following out, in the most natural way, the consequences determined by the stipulations, that is, the axioms). So if this reading of Frege were to be sustained (after scholarly investigation of other passages) then the view which would receive support from Frege would be the view set out, for example, in Davidson's careful and accurate statements, and not the view suggested by the unhappy abbreviations.

We come now to the worry that there are technical obstacles to incorporating certain desirable features into a theory$_1$ of meaning. It was explicit in Chapter I (at (4)) that it is not built into the notion of a theory$_1$ of meaning, as such, that it should do anything other than have an axiom for each sentence of the *OL* under consideration. But a further requirement might be motivated by the familiar (if vague) thought that the meaning of a sentence depends upon the meanings of its constituents; the requirement, namely that the theorems of a theory$_1$ of meaning should follow from axioms which assign semantic properties to expressions in some restricted class. The detailed development of a constraint along these lines must wait until Chapter III, but we can already see how theories$_1$ of truth might seem to have an advantage over theories$_1$ of meaning once some such requirement is in force.

In Section II.1 we saw how to derive a truth condition specification for each of the infinitely many sentences of a propositional calculus language L_1 from a very small finite set of proper axioms — one for each atomic sentence and one for each connective. The derivations in the theory $T\theta$ proceed by substitution inferences. For example, we substitute 'the earth moves' for 's_2 is true (in L_1)' in the right hand side of the biconditional

$$\ulcorner s_1 \ \& \ s_2 \urcorner \text{ is true (in } L_1) \leftrightarrow$$
$$(\text{snow is white} \ \& \ s_2 \text{ is true (in } L_1))$$

on the basis of the axiom

(*T1b*) s_2 is true (in L_1) $\leftrightarrow$ the earth moves.

(Here, and henceforth, we use corner quotes to help abbreviate the descriptions of *OL* sentences previously written out using the concatenation functor '$\cap$'; and we omit brackets where there is no loss of clarity.) But there is a plausible argument which seems to show that similar derivations cannot be provided in a theory$_1$ of meaning for L_1. For to warrant substitution of 'the earth moves' for an expression mentioning the *OL* sentence s_2 (cf. for 's_2 is true (in L_1)') within the scope of 'means that' (cf. in the right hand side of a biconditional) we should need a very strong equivalence (cf. the biconditional (*T1b*)), strong enough, in fact, to ensure that 'the earth moves' and the expression mentioning s_2 mean the same (for what warrants substitution within the scope of 'means that' is just synonymy). But 'the earth moves' is clearly not synonymous with any expression which mentions a sentence of L_1. (In particular, it is not synonymous with 's_2 is true (in L_1)'.)

This argument is plausible, but perhaps we have been too much impressed by the substitution inferences of $T\theta$. Those inferences combine with the axiom $(T2)$ for '&' to allow us to proceed from the axioms $(T1a)$ and $(T1b)$ to the biconditional

$\ulcorner s_1$ & $s_2 \urcorner$ is true (in L_1) $\leftrightarrow$
snow is white & the earth moves.

But we can provide an axiom for '&' which itself warrants just that step, namely

$(T2')$ $(\forall\sigma)(\forall\tau)(\forall p)(\forall q)$ $[((\sigma$ is true (in L_1) $\leftrightarrow p)$ &
$(\tau$ is true (in L_1) $\leftrightarrow q)) \rightarrow$
$(\ulcorner\sigma$ & $\tau\urcorner$ is true (in L_1) $\leftrightarrow p$ & $q)]$.

Doubtless there are reasons for preferring the original axiom $(T2)$ over the new $(T2')$ in a theory$_1$ of truth; reasons having to do with the unfamiliarity of the quantifiers '$(\forall p)$' and '$(\forall q)$'. But in the face of the plausible argument to show that we cannot mimic $(T2)$ in a theory$_1$ of meaning, we might at least try to mimic $(T2')$. And this task is not difficult.

$(M2)$ $(\forall\sigma)(\forall\tau)(\forall p)(\forall q)$ $[((\sigma$ means (in L_1) that $p)$ &
$(\tau$ means (in L_1) that $q)) \rightarrow$
$(\ulcorner\sigma$ & $\tau\urcorner$ means (in L_1) that p & $q)]$

It is undeniable that this axiom can contribute to derivations of correct meaning specifications for complex *OL* sentences, provided that we can proceed from $(M2)$ (universally quantified in the 'p' and 'q' places) to its instantiations in which particular *ML* sentences (themselves not containing quantifiers of the new kind) occupy the 'p' and 'q' places. For if we can so proceed then in particular we shall have

$((s_1$ means (in L_1) that snow is white) &
$(s_2$ means (in L_1) that the earth moves)) $\rightarrow$
$(\ulcorner s_1$ & $s_2 \urcorner$ means (in L_1) that snow is white
and the earth moves).

And then using

$(M1a)$ s_1 means (in L_1) that snow is white

and

(*M1b*) s_2 means (in L_1) that the earth moves

we can proceed (by '&' introduction and *Modus Ponens*) to the desired meaning specification for $\ulcorner s_1 \ \& \ s_2 \urcorner$. It is also undeniable that the instantiations of (*M2*) are true (and, indeed, necessarily true). So what objections might be mounted against a theory₁ of meaning (call it '*Mθ*') incorporating (*M1a*), (*M1b*) and (*M2*)?

It would obviously be wrong to complain that the validity of inferences in *Mθ* will have to be explained by appeal to the concept of meaning which is precisely the concept which we are trying to elucidate. That would just be the mistake of confusing a theory₁ of meaning and a theory₂ of meaning.

Davidson (1967, p.6) says that 'it is reasonable to expect that in wrestling with the logic of the apparently non-extensional "means that" we will encounter problems as hard as, or perhaps identical with, the problems our theory is out to solve', and Foster (1976, p.6) says, 'it is hard to see how, without doing violence to our syntax or our logic, we can condense the infinite set of consequences into a finite set of axioms'. Perhaps the wrestling and violence envisaged only occur when we try to give a theory₁ of meaning for a more complicated language than the very simple L_1. But it is surely more likely that if intractable problems are to arise at all then they will arise as soon as one attempts to incorporate recursive structure into a 'means that' theory. So let us suppose that Davidson and Foster would regard the use of the '($\forall p$)' and '($\forall q$)' quantifiers and the associated rule of universal instantiation in *Mθ* as illegitimate.

Certainly there are philosophical questions to be raised over quantification into other than name position. Equally certainly this is not the place to answer those questions. But the following considerations may help to reduce the suspicion with which '($\forall p$)' and '($\forall q$)' are regarded.

(1) It would be a mistake to regard quantification into a certain position as involving the claim that occupants of that position are names (cf. Section VI.3). An argument would be needed to show that there is something illegitimate about quantification into sentence position *per se*.

(2) It would be a mistake to confuse the quantification in, for example, (*M2*) with the quantification 'in and out of quotes' in

   ($\forall p$) ('p' means that p).

There is no reason to believe that the acceptability, in a

theory$_1$ of meaning, of the former turns upon that of the latter.

(3) Interpretation of '($\forall p$)' in $M\theta$ does not require a domain of propositions, conceived as independent of all languages. It is sufficient that '($\forall p$)' can be instantiated by any ML sentence from a restricted class (restricted, in particular, to exclude ML sentences which already include such quantifiers). Thus '($\forall p$)' can be given a substitution interpretation (for which, in general, see Section VI.4 and Kripke, 1976).

(4) The generality of '($\forall p$)' is something which intuitively we need. We find ourselves wanting to say of any moderately reflective member of our speech community that he or she knows that, if any sentence means something, then the sentence got by prefixing that sentence with 'It is not the case that' means the negation of what that sentence means.

To the extent that these considerations tell against the view that the '($\forall p$)' and '($\forall q$)' quantifiers are illegitimate, the worries about wrestling and violence are not well grounded. (For theories$_1$ of meaning for less simple languages, see Section V.1 and the penultimate paragraph of Section VI.1. See also Appendix 2.)

4   TRUTH CONDITIONS AND SEMANTIC THEORIES

We have been considering a false doctrine and a not obviously well grounded worry. Had the doctrine been true it would have provided a reason for considering (in the generality appropriate to a philosophical account of meaning) theories$_1$ of truth rather than theories$_1$ of meaning. Had the worry been well grounded it would have provided a reason for constructing recursively structured theories$_1$ of truth rather than engaging in a violent attempt at constructing a recursively structured theory$_1$ of meaning. As it is, we still have a reason for considering (in generality) theories$_1$ of truth; the reason, namely, that by so doing (and perhaps only by so doing) we can provide a theory$_2$ of truth and thus establish what are the marks of truth. But we lack a reason for engaging ourselves in the detailed construction of theories$_1$ of truth for particular languages.

The (vague) thought that the meaning of a sentence depends upon the meanings (more generally, upon the semantic properties) of its parts may encourage an attempt to reveal, in detail, how the meanings of sentences involving certain particular constructions depend upon the semantic properties of the inputs to those constructions; to answer Davidson's (1969, p.160) question, 'What are these familiar words doing here?' And a philosopher can be reasonably confident that he will find this project, of constructing theories$_1$ of meaning for fragments of particular natural languages or for idealized languages which reproduce (some of) the features found in natural languages, 'a fruitful source of a kind of question and answer which he characteristically prizes' (Strawson, 1969, p.148).

This (vague) thought is naturally accompanied by another, namely that the conditions under which a sentence is true also depend upon the semantic properties of its parts. This second thought may be developed a little. Since a sentence's (material or strict) truth conditions amount to less than its meaning it might be expected that, at least in some cases, a sentence's truth conditions will depend upon some relatively restricted semantic properties of its parts; and if in some cases this is so then it might be expected that some light will be shed by distinguishing cases in which it is so from cases in which it is not (in which, for example, the (material or strict) truth conditions of complex sentences involving a certain construction depend upon nothing less than the meanings of the sentences which are the inputs to that construction).

The second thought, thus developed, provides a modest but sound reason for attempting to construct theories$_1$ of truth in the style of $T\theta$ rather than merely adding rule (T) to a theory$_1$ of meaning in the style of $M\theta$. It does not yet provide a reason for attempting specifically to construct interpretational theories$_1$ of truth, but such a reason is not hard to find. Tracing, through a canonical proof, the impact upon an interpretational truth condition specification of the assignment to an expression of a relatively restricted semantic property must throw some light upon the question as to what richer semantic properties may be assigned to that expression, and (via the actual language relation) upon the question as to what relation members of a population must stand in to a particular expression if the language for which the theory is interpretational is to be the actual language of that population.

These highly general claims need to be backed up by fully worked out examples (see Chapters V-IX.) But perhaps the claims will gain plausibility if we consider a very simple case. Suppose that we add to the propositional calculus language L_1 the expression 'John believes that'. (Call the extended language 'L_2'.) This expression takes a sentence to make a sentence, and so is of the same syntactic kind as '$\sim$'. An expression which takes an expression of syntactic category X to make an expression of syntactic category Y is said to be of category Y/X. S is the category of sentences. So 'John believes that' and '$\sim$' are of category S/S. It is not difficult to state how 'John believes that' contributes to the meanings of sentences in which it occurs.

(M5) $(\forall \sigma)(\forall p)$ [(σ means (in L_2) that p) $\rightarrow$
       ($^\ulcorner$John believes that $\sigma^\urcorner$ means (in L_2) that John believes
       that p)]

This axiom (M5) is formally analogous to that for '$\sim$',

(M4) $(\forall \sigma)(\forall p)$ [(σ means (in L_2) that p) $\rightarrow$
       ($^\ulcorner \sim \sigma^\urcorner$ means (in L_2) that $\sim p$)]

and that formal analogy reflects the fact that this theory$_1$ of meaning treats 'John believes that' as a (unary) sentence operator: an expression which, like '$\sim$', takes an input sentence to yield a sentence whose meaning depends systematically upon the meaning of the input sentence. The system is fixed by the semantic property assigned to the operator (e.g. by (M4) or (M5)). This definition of a sentence operator is intended to exclude expressions which are of category S/S, but which take a sentence to make a sentence whose meaning depends not upon the meaning of the input sentence, but upon its syntactic form. Thus, for example, the expression

‘ . . . ’ is a long sentence

is excluded. The definition is also intended to exclude expressions which take a sentence to make a sentence whose meaning depends in part upon the meaning of the input sentence, and in part upon the particular form of words in the input sentence. Thus, for example, the expression 'Charles swore that' as it occurs in

Charles swore that by Jove he'd get to the top of that
jolly old mountain if it was the last thing he did

is excluded. (This example is borrowed from Bigelow, 1978, p. 116). Expressions of the first kind might be called *quotational* and expressions of the second kind *semi-quotational*.

That the theory treats 'John believes that' as what it intuitively seems to be is, as Wallace (1978, p. 53) points out, a positive virtue of the theory. But the virtue has a price. For there is nothing in this theory to reflect the deep semantic difference between 'John believes that' and '$\sim$'. The truth value of $\ulcorner \sim s_1 \urcorner$ depends just upon the truth value of s_1 (or, equivalently for present purposes, the material truth conditions of $\ulcorner \sim s_1 \urcorner$ depend just upon the material truth conditions of s_1; all materially equivalent sentences — sentences with the same truth value — have the same material truth conditions). The strict truth conditions of $\ulcorner \sim s_1 \urcorner$ depend just upon the strict truth conditions of s_1. And the meaning of $\ulcorner \sim s_1 \urcorner$ depends just upon the meaning of s_1. But even the truth value of 'John believes that s_1' depends upon nothing less than the meaning of s_1. (To say that the truth value of $\ulcorner \sim s_1 \urcorner$ depends just upon the truth value of s_1 is, in this context, merely to say that one cannot change the truth value of the complex sentence by substituting for s_1 another sentence with the same truth value. Thus, if we were to consider the operator $\ulcorner s_2 \ \& \ . . . \urcorner$, we should say that the truth value of $\ulcorner s_2 \ \& \ s_1 \urcorner$ depends just upon the truth value of s_1. This would not be to deny the obvious fact that the truth value of the complex sentence would be different if the earth were not to move.)

This deep semantic difference becomes very clear if we try to construct for L_1 and for L_2 (interpretational) theories₁ of truth yielding a material truth condition specification for each sentence. For '$\sim$' can be treated as a sentence operator in such a theory (e.g. $T\theta$). A sentence s contributes to the material truth conditions of $\ulcorner \sim s \urcorner$ precisely by its own material truth conditions; tracing through the canonical derivation of a material truth condition specification for a negated sentence reveals how this is so. But 'John believes that' cannot be treated analogously. A theory such as $T\theta$ does not state enough about, say, s_1 to yield any consequences at all for the material truth conditions of $\ulcorner$John believes that $s_1 \urcorner$. Any attempt to deal with 'John believes that' in a theory extending $T\theta$ is virtually bound to founder on the patent falsehood

$\ulcorner$John believes that $s_1 \urcorner$ is true (in L_2) $\leftrightarrow$
John believes that s_1 is true (in L_2).

In general, we can distinguish three kinds of (unary) sentence operator. An operator O is *extensional* just in case the truth value of $\ulcorner Os \urcorner$ depends just upon the truth value of s (that is, O admits substitution of material equivalents *salva veritate*) and the strict truth conditions and the meaning of $\ulcorner Os \urcorner$ depend just upon the strict truth conditions and the meaning of s, respectively. O is *intensional* just in case the truth value of $\ulcorner Os \urcorner$ depends not merely upon the truth value but upon the strict truth conditions of s (that is, O only admits substitution of strict equivalents – broadly logical equivalents – *salva veritate*) and the strict truth conditions and the meaning of $\ulcorner Os \urcorner$ depend just upon the strict truth conditions and the meaning of s, respectively. O is *hyperintensional* just in case the truth value of $\ulcorner Os \urcorner$ depends not merely upon the truth value, nor even upon the strict truth conditions, but upon the meaning of s (that is, O only admits substitution of synonyms *salva veritate*) and the strict truth conditions and the meaning of $\ulcorner Os \urcorner$ depend just upon the meaning of s. Thus '$\sim$' is extensional, 'John believes that' is hyperintensional, and the standard modal operators '$\Box$' and '$\Diamond$', expressing broadly logical necessity and possibility, are intensional. (For a discussion of hyperintensional sentence operators, as defined here, and of quotational and semi-quotational expressions, see Bigelow, 1978.)

With this three-way distinction in mind we can see that intensional and hyperintensional operators will resist treatment in a theory$_1$ of truth which delivers only material truth condition specifications, and hyperintensional operators will resist treatment even in a theory which yields strict truth condition specifications. In cases of these kinds a question which can be asked (with varying degrees of profit) is: What revision of our pre-theoretical view that this expression is a sentence operator is needed to bring the expression within the scope of a theory$_1$ of truth delivering material or strict truth condition specifications? In the particular case of 'John believes that' it has been suggested (by various authors adapting a suggestion of Davidson, 1969) that a sufficient revision is to regard 'John believes that' as a (context dependent) sentence in which 'believes' is a two-place predicate and 'that' is a demonstrative; in a context of utterance 'that' refers to the utterance which follows the utterance of 'John believes that'. (This is called the *paratactic* analysis of belief sentences.)

Certain operators resist treatment in certain kinds of theories. This resistance can, as we shall now see, sometimes be broken down. But breaking it down does not afford the illumination at which the general project aims. We noted earlier (at the end of Section II.1) that a rule of proof (from the proper axioms) could be used in the derivations of truth condition specifications. In some cases adding a rule of proof to a theory$_1$ of truth which yields only material truth condition specifications may (at least superficially) bring an intensional operator within the scope of that theory.

48

Suppose that 'Z' is an intensional operator added to L_1 to form L_3 and that we add to $T\theta$ (with 'L_1' replaced by 'L_3' throughout) an axiom

$$(\,\forall\sigma)\,[\ulcorner Z\sigma\urcorner \text{ is true (in } L_3) \leftrightarrow Z\,(\sigma \text{ is true (in } L_3))]$$

and the rule of proof

$$\frac{\vdash A \leftrightarrow B}{\vdash Z(A) \leftrightarrow Z(B)}$$

where '$\vdash$' is read 'there is a proof from the proper axioms of'. Then since

$$\vdash s_1 \text{ is true (in } L_3) \leftrightarrow \text{snow is white}$$

we have, by the rule of proof,

$$\vdash Z\,(s_1 \text{ is true (in } L_3)) \leftrightarrow Z\,(\text{snow is white}).$$

And since

$$\vdash \ulcorner Zs_1 \urcorner \text{ is true (in } L_3) \leftrightarrow Z\,(s_1 \text{ is true (in } L_3))$$

it follows that

$$\vdash \ulcorner Zs_1 \urcorner \text{ is true (in } L_3) \leftrightarrow Z\,(\text{snow is white}).$$

But notice that the addition of a true axiom, say

$$s_1 \text{ is true (in } L_3) \leftrightarrow 2 + 2 = 4$$

yields, via this rule of proof, what may be a false theorem (depending on the meaning of 'Z')

$$\ulcorner Zs_1 \urcorner \text{ is true (in } L_3) \leftrightarrow Z\,(2 + 2 = 4).$$

The explanation of this fact is that the rule of proof was originally acceptable only because every biconditional provable from the proper axioms is not merely true but necessarily true; the provable biconditionals remain true if '$\leftrightarrow$' is rewritten as a connective expressing strict equivalence. And of course 'Z', being an intensional operator, admits substitution of strict equivalents *salva veritate*. The additional axiom, on the other hand, is only contingently true.

Once we have this explanation it becomes clear how a firmer grasp can be gained on the way in which the semantic properties (material and strict truth conditions and meaning) of sentences depend deductively upon the semantic properties of their parts. In the case of a sentence operator, for example, we should construct a theory in which a semantic property is assigned to the operator (by a proper axiom) in such a way that from that axiom, and an axiom or theorem specifying the truth conditions or the meaning of an input sentence, there follows by the *ML* logic alone a theorem specifying the truth conditions or the meaning of the resulting complex sentence. (The background logic of the *ML* must be clearly specified, and in fact some set theory or arithmetic may have to be included. This logical system may include rules of proof, but they will be rules of proof from the logical axioms.) What is misleading about the theory in the example is that the theorem for $\ulcorner Zs_1 \urcorner$ is not a consequence, by the *ML* logic alone, of the axiom assigning a semantic property to Z and the axiom assigning a semantic property to s_1.

It serves clarity to notice that the derivations in a theory of material truth conditions (such as $T\theta$) depend upon a very weak rule of proof which is a derived rule in the presence of the usual logic of the *ML*. It would serve only unclarity to add to a theory of material truth conditions a rule of proof which would be a derived rule only in a theory of strict truth conditions (cast in a *ML* with a correspondingly stronger background logic) and then to claim to have brought an intensional operator within the scope of a theory of material truth conditions.

So finally, our reason for constructing theories$_1$ of truth is not primarily that by doing so we avoid violence, but rather that by doing so we gain insight into the way particular constructions work. And we might hope that a general account of the constraints under which such a project proceeds might aid understanding of our own mastery of a structured language.

NOTES

The rule (T) is a descendant of Tarski's *Convention T*, for which see his 'The concept of truth in formalized languages' (1956). The idea that the concept of truth is to be illuminated by relating it to the use of language has its clearest statement in the final two sentences of Strawson's Inaugural Lecture (1970a, p. 189): 'We connect meaning with truth and truth, too simply, with sentences; and sentences belong to language. But, as theorists, we know nothing of human *language* unless we understand human *speech*'. Much of the interest in theories$_1$ of truth is attributable to Davidson's many papers. Two which are not mentioned in the text are (1973b) and (1977a). The first few pages of

McDowell (1976) contain what is, perhaps, the best brief statement of Davidson's project and of its relation to Frege. Gareth Evans impressed upon me the importance of the evaluative TRUTH predicate of utterances.

The 'plausible' argument against the possibility of providing a structured theory$_1$ of meaning is one that I advanced in my doctoral thesis; Ralph Walker persuaded me to think again. For similar views on some of the topics of this chapter, see Sainsbury (1980).

III

STRUCTURE

---

1   STRUCTURAL CONSTRAINTS

A theory$_1$ of meaning (henceforth: theory of meaning) for a particular language L can play a role in the interpretation of the speech of members of a population G which has L as its actual language. Since members of such a population can themselves interpret the speech of other members, a theory of meaning for L can form part of a theoretical description of the linguistic competence of actual L-speakers. For actual L-speakers can do something which could also be done by someone who knew all that a theory of meaning for L states, and all that a theory of force states, and the fact that L is the actual language of G.

For all that has been said so far, it is only by its output of meaning specifications for the sentences of L that a theory of meaning for L contributes to a theoretical description of the competence of L-speakers; different theories with the same output would serve equally well. And there is something right about this. Suppose, for example, that a certain language has only finitely many sentences. There may be two speakers of this language, one of whom achieved mastery of the sentences of the language one by one, and the other of whom achieved mastery of all the sentences as a result (a causal result) of achieving mastery of just a few sentences. Yet these two speakers have, in one good sense of the word 'competence', the same competence. So a theoretical description of the competence which the two speakers share need reflect neither the unstructured nature of the first speaker's mastery of the sentences of the language, nor the structured nature of

52

the second speaker's mastery. But although this much is right, it also cannot be denied that in another good sense of the word 'competence' the two speakers have very different competences: competences with very different causal structures. The first speaker, it seems, has a competence which comprises a causally distinct subcompetence for each sentence of the language. Further evidence of this suspected causal distinctness would be provided by the discovery that his belief about the meaning of any one sentence could be undermined without any concomitant uncertainty arising with regard to other sentences. The second speaker, it seems, has a competence whose subcompetences are causally interrelated. Further evidence would be provided by concomitant variations in his beliefs about the meanings of various sentences.

If someone regarded the theoretical description of linguistic competence as a step *en route* to a psychological theory, then he would surely wish to impose a constraint upon theories of meaning regarded as a part of such theoretical descriptions. Such a constraint ought to ensure that the structure of the theory (that is, the pattern of the derivations of the meaning specifications) mirrors the structure of the competence described. In order to describe the structure of a man's competence let us introduce some terminology. Let us say that in cases where a speaker is able to know what a sentence s means without any further exposure or training after having been taught what the sentences $s_1, \ldots, s_n$ mean, and in cases where a speaker's revision of his belief as to what s means would involve him in revision of his beliefs as to what $s_1, \ldots, s_n$ mean, the speaker's knowing what s_1 means, ..., knowing what s_n means (jointly) *c-determine* his knowing what s means. And in order to describe the structure of a theory let us say that in case the derivations of meaning specifications for $s_1, \ldots, s_n$ employ resources (principally, proper axioms) already sufficient for the derivation of a meaning specification for s, the meaning specifications for $s_1, \ldots, s_n$ (jointly) *d-determine* the meaning specification for s. Then, armed with these two pieces of terminology, we can state a constraint upon theories of meaning for L considered as part of a theoretical description of the competence of a particular L-speaker S: the *mirror constraint* (*MC*).

If, but only if, S's knowing what $s_1, \ldots, s_n$ mean c-determines his knowing what s means then the meaning specifications for $s_1, \ldots, s_n$ should d-determine the meaning specification for s.

To fix ideas, let us consider the theory of meaning $M\theta$ for the very simple language L_1. It is very likely that if a man has L_1 as his actual language then his knowing what $\ulcorner{\sim}s_2\urcorner$ means and what $\ulcorner s_1 \ \& \ s_3\urcorner$ means will c-determine his knowing what $\ulcorner{\sim}s_1\urcorner$ means. (We might say: it is likely that he will realize that the meaning of $\ulcorner{\sim}s_1\urcorner$ depends upon the meaning of s_1 and the semantic properties of '$\sim$', and that he will realize that these syntactic constituents of $\ulcorner{\sim}s_1\urcorner$ occur also in $\ulcorner{\sim}s_2\urcorner$ and $\ulcorner s_1 \ \& \ s_3\urcorner$. But this description of the situation is epistemologically too heavy-handed to be accepted uncritically: see Section IV.2.) The theory $M\theta$ does mirror the structure of such a man's competence (at least in this respect) for the resources used in derivations of meaning specifications for $\ulcorner{\sim}s_2\urcorner$ and $\ulcorner s_1 \ \& \ s_3\urcorner$ are the proper axioms $(M4)$ for '$\sim$', $(M1b)$ for s_2, $(M1a)$ for s_1, $(M2)$ for '&', and $(M1c)$ for s_3, and the first and third of these are already sufficient for the derivation of a meaning specification for $\ulcorner{\sim}s_1\urcorner$. And this fact might render plausible certain psychological hypotheses about such a man.

In Section II.4 we noted that the (vague) thought that the meaning of a sentence depends upon the semantic properties of its parts might encourage an attempt (on the part of a semantic theorist) to reveal how the meanings of sentences involving particular constructions depend upon the semantic properties of the expressions which are the inputs to those constructions. Now it might seem that *MC* captures that thought (by speaking of one piece of knowledge being c-determined by others) and precisely relates it to the revelation about the workings of particular constructions which is furnished by a properly structured theory of meaning. But that is not quite right. The project which the mirror constraint governs is not the project of the semantic theorist. His project is, surely, that of providing the structurally most revealing theory of meaning for a particular language, and not that of providing the structurally most revealing description of a particular speaker's competence with that language. That *MC* cannot properly govern the project of the semantic theorist is shown by the facts that if a language has no actual speakers then *MC* provides no guidance at all, if a language has two groups of actual speakers with differently structured competences then *MC* guides in two directions which are incompatible for the semantic theorist, and if a language has actual speakers all of whom are dim-witted then *MC* would guide the semantic theorist in such a way as to prevent him from stating in what that dim-wittedness consists.

What the semantic theorist needs is something different from *MC* but (since the thought that the meanings of sentences depend upon the semantic properties of their parts is not entirely unrelated to the fact that speakers are often able to know the meanings of previously unmet sentences on the basis of prior acquaintance with their parts occurring in other sentences) not too different. The rough idea is that a structurally revealing theory of meaning for a language should be such that the meaning specification for s is d-determined by the meaning specifications for $s_1, \ldots, s_n$ if, but only if, it would be possible to come to know what s means on the basis of prior knowledge what $s_1, \ldots, s_n$ mean. A semantic theorist should aim to reveal the maximum structure in a language; he will then be able to say that the dim-wittedness of some speakers consists in their being blind to some of the structure in their actual language. But he should be careful to distinguish his project from that of a linguist who constructs psychological theories about speakers. It would be absurd to try to settle a question about what goes on in the heads of speakers who have L as their actual language solely by appeal to facts about the (semantic) structure of the language L. For it is at least a theoretical possibility that speakers could have L as their actual language while being blind to some of L's semantic structure. The relation between the projects is rather that the semantic theorist sets an upper limit for the linguist. To the extent that a speaker is sensitive (in a sense which will be made clear by Section IV.1) to the semantic structure of his actual language he is a *full understander* of that language. But not every speaker who has a language as his actual language need be a full understander of that language; whether a speaker is a full understander of his actual language is a further empirical question.

We must now make a little more precise the rough idea about the semantic theorist's project. It is difficult to deny that for any sentences $s_1, \ldots, s_n$ and any sentence s it is possible that someone should come to know what s means as a causal result of knowing what $s_1, \ldots, s_n$ mean. For it seems that a man could be wired up so that knowing what $s_1, \ldots, s_n$ mean would trigger knowing what s means. (There may be some doubt whether the triggered state would really be knowledge. Knowing what s means might be a product of a triggered belief as to what s means together with knowledge about the reliability of this way of acquiring beliefs.) We need to exclude this kind of possibility from any constraint upon the semantic theorist's project. The possibilities which matter for that project are possibilities of reasoning from knowing what $s_1, \ldots, s_n$ mean to knowing what s means. Given a language (a set of sentences and a set of meaning specifications), a semantic theorist may notice that there is a systematic similarity of meaning specifications amongst sentences which are syntactically similar. And he may judge that these similarities are such as to enable a rational agent (relevantly like himself) to reason inductively from knowing what certain sentences mean to knowing what other syntactically similar sentences mean. (He need not hold it to be a matter of logical necessity that all rational agents should be struck by just these similarities.) It is this judgment about the possibility of self-conscious, reflective projection of meanings which encourages the attempt to provide a theory of meaning which not only delivers the correct meaning specifications but also reveals how the meanings of sentences depend upon the occurrence of particular syntactic constituents (roughly: words and ways of putting expressions together). So we can state a constraint upon theories of meaning for *L* considered not as part of a theoretical description of the competence of particular *L*-speakers, but rather as revealing the semantic structure of the language *L*: the *structural constraint* (*SC*).

If, but only if, it would be possible for someone to proceed by rational inductive means from knowing what $s_1, \ldots, s_n$ mean to knowing what s means then the meaning specifications for $s_1, \ldots, s_n$ should d-determine the meaning specification for s.

(The expression 'rational inductive means' simply labels the way in which rational agents relevantly like us in their judgments about similarity, for example, reason explicitly about meanings. It excludes bringing to bear general non-semantic knowledge.)

This constraint speaks of the possibility of explicit, self-conscious, reflective projection of meanings. But, notoriously, most natural language users are utterly unreflective and inexplicit in projecting to the meanings of previously unmet sentences. So it might be suggested that a structural constraint upon theories of meaning should speak rather of the possibility of unreflective projection of meanings by speakers relevantly like us. If this suggested revision is to be evaluated we must consider whether it is possible either that the possibilities of unreflective projection should exceed those of reflective projection, or that the possibilities of reflective projection should exceed those of unreflective projection. First, the possibilities of unreflective projection must be narrowed sufficiently to exclude mere possibilities of wiring up, and it is difficult to see how a satisfactory narrowing could be achieved without, in effect, requiring that the possibilities of unreflective

56

projection not exceed those of reflective projection. Second, the possibilities of unreflective projection must be idealized sufficiently to prevent mere memory limitations from distorting the constraint. But even taking that idealization into account we can perhaps imagine, as a bare possibility, a language containing a construction the significance of which could be worked out explicitly even though no speaker relevantly like us could master it unreflectively. In the face of this imagined possibility we can reject the suggested revision to *SC* while making two concessions to the thought behind that suggestion. First, we can concede that, in such a case as the one imagined, the upper limit set by a semantic theorist would be a limit to which no speaker investigated by a linguist could attain; so that the recognition of semantic structure by the theorist would have no role to play in explaining the use of the construction in question by ordinary speakers. And, second, we can concede that, for this very reason, the notion of semantic structure governed by *SC* in its original form is a somewhat idealized or theoretical notion, and so, that the semantic theorist's project is itself a somewhat idealized project.

This response to the suggested revision is not a matter of great moment. In all actual cases we can use *SC* in its original or its revised form. And this is not altogether surprising, for a theorist's explicit projections are in part the result of his considering self-consciously how he would project unreflectively.

2   FINITENESS AND SEMANTIC PRIMITIVES

The constraint *SC* has the intuitively pleasing consequence that if L is a learnable language then a theory of meaning for L which meets *SC* can have only finitely many proper axioms. In order to show that this is a consequence, and to show that the requirement that a theory of meaning should have only finitely many proper axioms cannot itself do the work for which *SC* is intended, we need to introduce some more pieces of terminology.

Consider again the theory of meaning $M\theta$ for the language L_1, and consider in particular the axioms

(*M1a*) s_1 means (in L_1) that snow is white
(*M2*) $(\forall\sigma)(\forall\tau)(\forall p)(\forall q)[((\sigma$ means (in L_1) that p) & $(\tau$ means (in L_1) that $q)) \rightarrow$ $(\ulcorner\sigma$ & $\tau\urcorner$ means (in L_1) that p & $q)]$

and the theorem

> $\ulcorner s_1 \,\&\, s_2 \urcorner$ means (in L_1) that snow is white and the earth moves.

Axiom (*M1a*) specifies, in non-semantic terms, the meaning of the sentence s_1. Axiom (*M2*) specifies, in non-semantic terms (namely, by using the *ML* conjunction), and in full generality, the way in which the sub-sentential item '&' contributes to the meanings of sentences in which it occurs. The theorem specifies, in non-semantic terms, the meaning of the sentence $\ulcorner s_1 \,\&\, s_2 \urcorner$. In contrast, the theorem

> $(\forall p)\,(\forall q)\,[\,(\,(s_1 \text{ means (in } L_1) \text{ that } p)\,\&$
> $(s_2 \text{ means (in } L_1) \text{ that } q)\,) \rightarrow$
> $(\ulcorner s_1 \,\&\, s_2 \urcorner \text{ means (in } L_1) \text{ that } p \,\&\, q)\,]$

does not specify the meaning of $\ulcorner s_1 \,\&\, s_2 \urcorner$ in non-semantic terms, but only in terms of the meaning of s_1 and the meaning of s_2. And this theorem does not specify in full generality the way in which '&' contributes to the meanings of sentences in which it occurs, but only the way in which it contributes to the meaning of the sentence $\ulcorner s_1 \,\&\, s_2 \urcorner$. Let us introduce a (rather inelegant) piece of terminology and say that the axioms (*M1a*) and (*M2*), and the first theorem, *deal non-semantically with* s_1, '&', and $\ulcorner s_1 \,\&\, s_2 \urcorner$ respectively.

In general, an axiom or theorem deals non-semantically with a sentence just in case that axiom or theorem explicitly specifies, in non-semantic terms, what that sentence means. An axiom or theorem deals non-semantically with a sub-sentential expression (for example, a connective) just in case that axiom or theorem explicitly specifies a semantic property of that expression by specifying, in non-semantic terms and in full generality, the way in which that expression contributes to the meanings of sentences in which it occurs. In the case of an expression of category S/S, the full generality is achieved by quantifying over all input sentences (as in the axiom for '$\sim$' in $M\theta$). In the case of an expression of category Y/X, where both Y and X are categories of sub-sentential expressions, the full generality is achieved by quantifying over all expressions of category X. What is specified, in such a case, is the way in which the expression contributes to the contributions to sentence meanings which are made by expressions of category Y within which it occurs. The case of a sub-sentential expression which is of a basic category Z is a little more complicated. (Z is a basic category if there are no categories X and Y

such that Z is the category Y/X. For example, S is a basic category.) In such a case the full generality is achieved indirectly. What is specified is a semantic property of the expression which meshes with the semantic properties which are assigned to all expressions of category S/Z. (For such a case, see the discussion of subject-predicate sentences in Section V.1.)

The derivation in $M\theta$ of the theorem which deals non-semantically with $\ulcorner s_1 \ \& \ s_2 \urcorner$ employs three axioms, and those axioms can be employed in the derivations of meaning specifications for sentences other than $\ulcorner s_1 \ \& \ s_2 \urcorner$ (and not containing $\ulcorner s_1 \ \& \ s_2 \urcorner$). Thus the meaning specification for $\ulcorner s_1 \ \& \ s_2 \urcorner$ is d-determined by meaning specifications for sentences not containing $\ulcorner s_1 \ \& \ s_2 \urcorner$ (and not identical with it; let us allow identity as a limiting case of containment). In general, if a theorem which is not an axiom deals non-semantically with an expression ρ then there is a sentence s containing ρ and sentences $s_1, \ldots,$ s_n not containing ρ such that the meaning specification for s is d-determined by the meaning specifications for $s_1, \ldots, s_n$. In contrast, if an axiom deals non-semantically with ρ then there are no such sentences s containing ρ and $s_1, \ldots, s_n$ not containing ρ.

Let us say that ρ is a *semantic primitive* according to a theory θ just in case an axiom of θ deals non-semantically with ρ. And let us say that ρ is a *semantic primitive* of a language L just in case ρ is a semantic primitive according to some theory of meaning for L which meets *SC*. Then ρ is a semantic primitive of L just in case it is not possible to come to know the meaning of any sentence of L which contains ρ simply by projecting from the meanings of sentences not containing ρ. And this is just what we want of the notion of a semantic primitive (cf. Davidson, 1965, p. 338).

Similarly, ρ is *semantically complex* according to θ just in case a theorem of θ which is not an axiom deals non-semantically with ρ. And ρ is semantically complex in L just in case ρ is semantically complex according to a theory for L which meets *SC*. Similarly again, ρ is a *semantic constituent* of μ according to θ just in case the derivation in θ of the theorem which deals non-semantically with μ employs an axiom or theorem which deals non-semantically with ρ. If r_1 and r_2 are sentences and r_1 is a semantic constituent of r_2 in L then knowing what r_2 means is sufficient for knowing what r_1 means.

If we restrict attention to speakers whose linguistic competence is the product of training and projection, and not for example of magic, then we can say that if a speaker knows what a sentence s means then he must have had some training with sentences containing each of the semantic primitives which are semantic constituents of s. Thus if a language L is learnable (that is, if it is possible to come to know the meanings of all the sentences of L by way of exposure and projection) then there must be a finite set of sentences of L containing as semantic constituents all the semantic primitives of L. And since each sentence contains only finitely many semantic primitives it follows that a learnable language has only finitely many semantic primitives. What is more, if a theory of meaning θ for L meets SC then (in effect) a single proper axiom of θ deals non-semantically with each semantic primitive for L. For suppose that θ has two proper axioms which deal non-semantically with an expression ρ. Then either the two axioms are always employed together in the derivations of meaning specifications for sentences containing ρ as a semantic constituent or else there is an axiom which is employed in the derivations of meaning specifications for some but not all sentences containing ρ. In the latter case, since θ meets SC, there are two batches of sentences containing ρ such that a further course of exposure is needed to enable one to proceed from one batch to the other. But this is just to say that ρ is ambiguous; it plays some (perhaps rather subtle) variation on the 'bank'/'bank' theme. And in such a case of lexical ambiguity we should count ρ as two semantic primitives (or perhaps as one semantic primitive and one semantically complex expression); as theorists we should play some variation on the 'bank$_1$'/'bank$_2$' theme. So we only need to consider the former case, and here the two proper axioms might as well be conjoined into a single axiom. (This was the reason for the parenthetical 'in effect'.)

Let us assume that if θ meets SC then any axioms which can be conjoined (without infringing SC) are conjoined. Then it follows that a theory of meaning for a learnable language, which meets SC, has only finitely many proper axioms. Thus, as was claimed at the beginning of this section, the finite axiomatization constraint (FAC) is a consequence of SC.

Sometimes it has been suggested that FAC can do the work for which SC is intended. Davidson (1970, p. 19), for example, considered the possibility that one take as axioms of a theory of meaning just the meaning specifications for all the sentences of the OL and wrote:

> Such a theory would yield no insight into the structure of the
> language. . . . We could block this particular aberration by
> stipulating that the nonlogical axioms be finite in number; . . .

though it may be that other ways exist of ensuring that a [theory of meaning] has the properties we want.

(Cf. Davidson, 1965 and footnote 2 of Davidson, 1973a.) Wallace (1972, p. 224) made a similar claim: 'A recursion we want; the shape or strategy of the recursion we want to leave open. The demand for a finite theory seems a — perhaps crude — way of satisfying both desires.' But *FAC* does not really go to the heart of the semantic theorist's project. For it is very easy to imagine languages with only finitely many sentences but with just the kind of structure which the semantic theorist should seek to uncover. The simplest examples are provided by subject-predicate languages. Suppose that L_4 is a language with just a hundred sentences constructed from ten names 'm_1', ..., 'm_{10}' and ten predicates 'P_1', ..., 'P_{10}'. Then it is trivially easy to provide a theory meeting *FAC*, namely the theory whose axioms are the hundred meaning specifications for L_4. But this theory 'would yield no insight into the structure of the language'. It is possible for someone who knows what '$P_1 m_1$', '$P_1 m_2$', '$P_1 m_3$', '$P_2 m_4$', '$P_3 m_4$' and '$P_4 m_4$' mean to come to know (by explicit or by unreflective projection) what '$P_1 m_4$' means. Such facts, together with *SC*, oblige the semantic theorist to provide a theory in which the derivations of meaning specifications for the ten sentences '$P_1 m_1$', ..., '$P_1 m_{10}$' employ a common axiom which states the semantic property of 'P_1' upon which the meanings of those ten sentences (partially) depend; and similarly for each other predicate and each name. Here, clearly, it is *SC* and not *FAC* which should guide the semantic theorist.

Let us extend L_4 to an infinite language by adding the connectives '&', 'v', and '∼'. Then both *FAC* and *SC* rule out certain theories. But a theory with 103 axioms (one for each subject-predicate sentence and one for each connective) and a theory with 23 axioms (one for each name, one for each predicate, and one for each connective) equally meet *FAC*, whereas only one of them meets *SC*. And it is obviously the theory which meets *SC* which yields the greater insight into the structure of the language.

Finally we should observe that there are two slightly non-standard formal devices which, if employed, seem to trivialize *FAC*. The first is infinitary conjunction. If we allow ourselves to conjoin infinitely many sentences then we can conjoin infinitely many meaning specifications into a single axiom. The resulting theory yields no insight into structure, and of course it infringes *SC* (since the axiom employed in the derivation of a meaning specification for any one sentence is already sufficient for the derivation of meaning specifications for all other sentences of the *OL*). But the theory is certainly finitely axiomatized. It would be precipitate to rule out this theory simply by banning infinitary conjunction, for there are cases where infinitary conjunction seems to be needed and where a theory employing infinitary conjunction in its axioms meets *SC*. (For an example and a discussion of the present point, see Peacocke, 1978, p. 489.) The second formal device is substitutional quantification 'in and out of quotes'. Suppose that the *OL* is part of the *ML* and that the *ML* contains a quotation functor which takes any *OL* sentence to form a name of that sentence. Then a theory can be provided with a single proper axiom

$(\forall p)$ ('p' means that p).

From this axiom, all instances of the schema

'A' means that A

follow, where an *OL* sentence fills the place of 'A'. As was indicated at (2) at the end of Section II.3, the use, in a theory of meaning, of this kind of quantification 'in and out of quotes' is controversial. And as we shall see in Appendix 6 (which develops Section VI.4) there is an objection to the use of this universally quantified axiom in a theory of meaning, on the grounds that it does not state something knowledge of which suffices for knowing what each sentence of the language means. But, ahead of any detailed investigation of quantification 'in and out of quotes', this axiom is allowed by *FAC*, but is ruled out by *SC* for just the same reason that the infinitary conjunction is ruled out (cf. Kripke, 1976, pp. 365-8).

3   TRUTH THEORIES AND STRUCTURE

The semantic theorist who sets himself to construct theories₁ of truth (henceforth: truth theories, theories of truth, or theories of truth conditions) should be guided by a constraint similar to *SC*. In order to state a constraint upon interpretational truth theories we need to make use of a notion which corresponds, in the case of a truth theory, to d-determination of a meaning specification by other meaning specifications, in the case of a theory of meaning. By a natural extension of our terminology let us say that the canonical theorems for $s_1, \ldots, s_n$ *d-determine* the canonical theorem for s just in case the canonical derivations of truth condition specifications for $s_1, \ldots, s_n$ employ resources (principally, proper axioms) already sufficient for the canonical derivation of a truth condition specification for s.

If a truth theory is to yield insight into structure, under what conditions should the canonical theorem for s be d-determined by the canonical theorems for $s_1, \ldots, s_n$? One initially plausible answer is: if, but only if, it would be possible for someone to proceed by rational inductive means from knowing under what conditions $s_1, \ldots, s_n$ are true to knowing under what conditions s is true. But this answer is incorrect since, in general, it is not possible to project from the truth conditions of sentences to the truth conditions of syntactically similar sentences. There are two cases, according as we consider material or strict truth conditions. Suppose first that a rational agent knows that 'Stockholm is pretty' is true (in English) iff (materially) snow is white, and that 'Oslo is a capital' is true (in English) iff (materially) coal is black. No amount of reasoning will yield this man any knowledge as to the material truth conditions of 'Oslo is pretty'. It might be replied that the rational agent would be better placed if he knew that 'Stockholm is pretty' is true (in English) iff (materially) Stockholm is pretty, and that 'Oslo is a capital' is true (in English) iff (materially) Oslo is a capital; but this reply would be mistaken. One is no better off in the second case than one is in the first. One would, of course, be well placed if one knew that 'Stockholm is pretty' is true (in English) iff (materially) Stockholm is pretty and that this way of stating the material truth conditions is interpretational, and similarly for 'Oslo is a capital'. For then one would know what those sentences mean (via the definition of 'interpretational'), and so could project to the meaning of the syntactically similar sentence 'Oslo is pretty' and thence (via rule (T)) to the truth conditions of that sentence.

We cannot cast a structural constraint upon theories of material truth conditions in terms of projecting material truth conditions. Nor can we cast a structural constraint upon theories of material or strict truth conditions in terms of projecting strict truth conditions. For consider the situation of someone informed by a well-meaning essentialist that 'Cicero is human' is true (in English) iff (strictly) Cicero exists, and that 'Fido is canine' is true (in English) iff (strictly) Fido exists. Such a person is not able to come to any knowledge about the strict truth conditions of 'Cicero is canine'. Or consider a person who knows that '2 is even' is true (in English) iff (strictly) 3 is prime, and that '4 is a square' is true (in English) iff (strictly) 8 is composite. Such a person is not able to come to any knowledge about the strict truth conditions of '4 is even'.

The only conclusion to draw from all this is that a structural constraint upon truth theories should follow the structural constraint upon theories of meaning in speaking of projecting meanings. The constraint upon theories of truth (which we shall call '*SC*' also) is as follows:

> If, but only if, it would be possible for someone to proceed by rational inductive means from knowing what $s_1, \ldots, s_n$ mean to knowing what s means then the canonical theorems for $s_1, \ldots, s_n$ should d-determine the canonical theorem for s.

This has the (intuitively pleasing) consequence that a theory of meaning meeting *SC* and a theory of truth (for the same language) meeting *SC* will, in general, exhibit the same pattern of (canonical) derivations. But it should be noted that given a theory of meaning meeting *SC* (as, for example, the theory of meaning for the language L_2 containing 'John believes that') it may not be possible to provide a truth theory meeting *SC* and exhibiting the same pattern of derivations as the theory of meaning. It may, indeed, not be possible to provide a truth theory meeting *SC* at all; this would be the product of ineliminable hyperintensionality in the *OL*. Or it may be possible to provide a truth theory meeting *SC* by revising one's judgments about the syntactic form of certain *OL* sentences (as, for example, by adopting the paratactic analysis of belief sentences) and then to provide a theory of meaning exhibiting the same pattern of derivations. But such syntactic revisions would have to meet whatever constraints are imposed by syntactic theory. There is no good semantic reason why hyperintensionality must always be eliminable.

4   STRUCTURE AND SURFACE SYNTAX

The constraint *SC* has two parts: the 'if' part and the 'only if' part. The 'if' part obliges the semantic theorist to discern sufficient structure in *OL* sentences to account for the facts about the possibility of projecting (explicitly or unreflectively) to the meanings of previously unmet sentences. The 'only if' part is what rules out the employment of the non-standard formal devices of infinitary conjunction and quantification 'in and out of quotes', but principally the 'only if' part prohibits the wanton ascription of structure to *OL* sentences. It may be asked, however, exactly what would constitute wanton ascription of structure. For if a theorist can show meaning specifications for *OL* sentences to flow deductively from axioms which assign semantic properties to expressions which are literally syntactic constituents of those sentences, then surely it should be possible for someone to project from the meanings of previously met sentences to the meanings of previously unmet sentences built from the same syntactic constituents. And so, surely, the 'only if' part will always be met.

This is an important query. In order to respond to it, we need to mark a distinction which we have so far ignored. This is the distinction to which the expressions 'grammatical form' and 'logical form', 'surface structure' and 'deep structure', bear testimony; the distinction, namely, between sentences as they are found in natural languages and sentences as they are appropriate objects for a systematic semantic theory. To the extent that a theory of meaning, or a theory of truth conditions, applies directly to the sentences of the language in question, the 'only if' part of *SC* is bound to be met (provided that there is no use of those non-standard formal devices). But it is a familiar idea that, in the case of natural languages, a theory of meaning or of truth conditions cannot apply directly to the sentences of the language in question (that is, to *surface* sentences). Rather, according to that idea, such a theory must apply to sentences which are 'regimentations' of those surface sentences (see e.g. Quine, 1960, pp. 157–61). The regimented sentences to which a theory directly applies (that is, the sentences at the *level of input* to the theory) are, at least, unambiguous, and so are different from the unregimented surface sentences. It is the opening of this gap between the surface and the level of input to a theory of meaning, or of truth conditions, that provides the opportunity for wanton ascription of structure.

Given this distinction and this (potential) gap, we need a firm grasp upon the application of *SC* in the case of natural languages. For we cannot simply insist that this gap must never be allowed to open, and that the level of input to a theory must always be the level of surface sentences. Nor can we simply allow, at the other extreme, that if the level of input to a theory is removed from the level of surface sentences, then the theory thereby gains immunity against all structural objections.

Suppose that we set out to construct a semantic theory (a theory of meaning or of truth conditions) for a fragment of English. We should very soon be confronted with the irregularities of plurals, tenses, negative prefixes, and feminine and diminutive suffixes; and each of these presents a problem for the semantic theorist. For knowledge of the meanings of sentences containing 'kiss', 'kissed', 'jump', 'jumped', and 'kill' clearly enables a rational agent to work out the meanings of sentences containing 'killed', and this fact obliges the theorist to assign a semantic property to '-ed' by which it contributes uniformly to the contributions made to sentence meanings by 'kissed', 'jumped', 'killed', and the rest. But while pursuing this policy will enable the theorist to construct a theory meeting *SC*, the language for which this is a theory will not, strictly speaking, be a fragment of English; for the sentences for which meaning (or truth condition) specifications will be delivered will not be all and only the sentences of a fragment of English.

The theory will not be a theory for (a fragment of) English because there are no sentences of English containing past tense verbs 'run(n)ed' or 'swim(m)ed'; but the theory will meet *SC* because one can come to know the meanings of sentences containing those past tense verbs by projecting from the meanings of sentences containing 'kiss', 'kissed', 'jump', 'jumped', and 'run' and 'swim'. The problem for the semantic theorist is that of incompatibility between *SC* and the aim of providing a semantic theory for the language which people actually speak and not just for a language which people might have spoken but do not.

But this incompatibility should not be thought to doom the semantic theorist's project, nor to raise insuperable difficulties for *SC*. What it shows is only that, in the case of natural languages, a semantic theory must be accompanied by a syntactic theory. There is nothing more for a semantic theory to say about 'swam' and 'ran' than what the imagined semantic theory says about 'swimmed' and 'runned'. Rather, the imagined semantic theory needs to be accompanied by a syntactic theory which relates 'swimmed' to 'swam' and 'runned' to 'ran'. And (what is the same fact again, but described now in terms of the possibility of projecting meanings) there is nothing more about meaning that someone must learn to become a speaker of English rather than of the language for which the imagined theory is provided; such a person merely needs the purely syntactic information that one utters not 'swimmed' but 'swam', not 'runned' but 'ran'.

A syntactic theory relating surface sentences to sentences at the level of input to a semantic theory should itself be subject to a constraint analogous to *SC*. The extent to which rational agents do not need to be given syntactic information case by case is some measure of the possibilities for projection in syntax as in semantics; and because of these possibilities a syntactic theory will state (learnable) rules of syntax. But these rules will no more yield immediate consequences for a psychological theory than will the rules of a semantic theory meeting *SC*. It is a further empirical question whether any particular speaker has full grammatical mastery of his language (as against, for example, mere knowledge case by case). And it is a further philosophical question how we should describe the relation between someone who does have full grammatical mastery and a structurally adequate syntactic theory or, for that matter, between someone who has less than full mastery and a theory which is less than adequate but whose structure mirrors the structure of that person's grammatical competence. (For this question, see Chapter IV.)

The past tense in English exhibits *surface syntactic irregularity* which simply forces the level of input to a semantic theory apart from the level of surface syntax. The semantic theorist has done his job once he has provided a theory meeting *SC* for a language free of surface syntactic irregularity (containing a single past tense suffix '-ed' or, more neutrally, *'PAST'*) provided that this language is related to English by a syntactic theory meeting whatever constraints can reasonably be imposed upon such theories. The failure of 'swim' and of '-ed' literally to appear as syntactic constituents of 'swam' has to be regarded as 'so much misleading surface structure'. (The phrase is borrowed from Evans, 1977, p. 489.)

A phenomenon very similar to surface syntactic irregularity is *surface syntactic impoverishment*; indeed cases of the former can be redescribed as cases of the latter. Thus consider a fragment of English in which we find three different negative prefixes. One way to provide a theory meeting *SC* is to take as the level of input to a semantic theory a language with a single negative prefix (perhaps 'un-' or, more neutrally, *'NEG'*) and to relate this language to surface English by syntactic rules which account for the irregularities. Another way to provide a theory meeting *SC* is to take as the level of input a language in which each adjective has three negative versions. In this case the accompanying syntactic theory would have to block the passage to the surface of some of the sentences at the level of input to the semantic theory. Thus, the surface language would be impoverished relative to the language to which a semantic theory directly applies. The choice between these two ways would have to be made on grounds provided by general constraints upon syntactic theories. In fact, it is hard not to believe that the first way is preferable, but we can easily imagine cases which are more finely balanced and clear cases of impoverishment without irregularity.

Clear examples of impoverishment are provided by languages which do not contain all the sentences which can be built from their semantic primitives, that is languages whose sets of sentences are not closed under possible projection of meanings. It is impossible to provide a semantic theory meeting *SC* for such a language. Given such an impoverished language L, the semantic theorist must provide a theory for the smallest language which contains L and is closed under possible projection of meanings. There is nothing for a semantic theory to say about the way in which the meanings of sentences of L depend upon the semantic properties of their parts other than what it says about the larger language; a syntactic theory must mark out the grammatical sentences of L. And (what is that last fact again, but described now in terms of the possibility of projecting meanings) there is nothing more about meaning that someone must learn to become a speaker of L rather than of the larger language for which a semantic theory is provided; such a person merely needs the purely syntactic information that certain sentences are not grammatical. And this information may not have to be imparted case by case. Projection of grammaticality is, in general, just as possible as projection of meanings. (See Appendix 3.)

The phenomena of irregularity and impoverishment excuse the semantic theorist who fails to provide a theory both meeting *SC* and dealing with all and only the grammatical sentences of (a fragment of) a natural language. For those phenomena make the provision of such a theory impossible. But from the fact that provision of such a theory is sometimes impossible it clearly does not follow that failure to provide such a theory is always excusable.

Consider, for example, a propositional calculus language L_5 whose atomic sentences are just those of L_1 and whose only connective is exclusive disjunction '$\veebar$'. It ought to be intuitively plausible that this is not an impoverished language and that this is not an irregular language. So it ought to be intuitively plausible that a semantic theory should apply directly to the sentences of L_5. And it is not difficult to provide, for example, a theory of truth conditions for L_5, meeting *SC*. We simply add to the axioms *(T1a)*, *(T1b)* and *(T1c)* for the atomic sentences s_1, s_2 and s_3 the axiom

$$(\forall \sigma) (\forall \tau) [\ulcorner \sigma \veebar \tau \urcorner \text{ is true (in } L_5) \leftrightarrow$$
$$(\sigma \text{ is true (in } L_5) \veebar \tau \text{ is true (in } L_5))]$$

68

This axiom deals non-semantically with '$\veebar$'. The semantic primitives of L_5, according to this theory, are precisely s_1, s_2, s_3, and '$\veebar$'. The theory clearly meets SC. And L_5 is itself the smallest language containing those semantic primitives and closed under possible projection of meanings.

This theory should be compared with two others. Consider first a theorist who is impressed by the two facts that '$\veebar$' is a relatively un-familiar connective and that he already has a theory for the language L_1, and who therefore proposes to 'preprocess' each sentence $\ulcorner \sigma \veebar \tau \urcorner$ of L_5 into the form

$$(\sigma \vee \tau) \mathbin{\&} \sim (\sigma \mathbin{\&} \tau)$$

at the level of input to a truth theory, and then to bring to bear the antecedently available truth theory $T\theta$ (with 'L_5' for 'L_1') as follows. (Let us, for brevity, omit 'in L_5'.)

> $\ulcorner(s_1 \vee s_2) \mathbin{\&} \sim (s_1 \mathbin{\&} s_2)\urcorner$ is true $\leftrightarrow$
> ($\ulcorner s_1 \vee s_2 \urcorner$ is true $\mathbin{\&}$ $\ulcorner \sim (s_1 \mathbin{\&} s_2)\urcorner$ is true)

by the axiom *(T2)* for '$\&$', and thence by *(T3)*, *(T4)*, and *(T2)* again and by the axioms for the atomic sentences s_1 and s_2:

> $\ulcorner(s_1 \vee s_2) \mathbin{\&} \sim (s_1 \mathbin{\&} s_2)\urcorner$ is true $\leftrightarrow$
> ((snow is white $\vee$ the earth moves) $\mathbin{\&}$
> $\sim$ (snow is white $\mathbin{\&}$ the earth moves)).

According to this proposal the sentences $\ulcorner s_1 \vee s_2 \urcorner$, $\ulcorner s_1 \mathbin{\&} s_2 \urcorner$ and $\ulcorner \sim (s_1 \mathbin{\&} s_2)\urcorner$ are semantic constituents of the sentence which appears in surface syntax as $\ulcorner s_1 \veebar s_2 \urcorner$. The failure of these sentences literally to appear as syntactic constituents of $\ulcorner s_1 \veebar s_2 \urcorner$ is, according to this pro-posal, 'so much misleading surface structure'. Judged by the standard set by SC for theories for L_5 this proposal is inadequate, since the resources employed in the canonical derivation of a theorem for $\ulcorner s_1 \veebar s_2 \urcorner$ are already sufficient for the canonical derivation of a theorem for $\ulcorner s_1 \mathbin{\&} s_2 \urcorner$, whereas it is not possible to project from the meaning of $\ulcorner s_1 \veebar s_2 \urcorner$ to the meaning of $\ulcorner s_1 \mathbin{\&} s_2 \urcorner$. Nor is the proposal readily defended by appeal to a syntactic theory. No plausible story about irregularity can be told to account for the fact that it is impossible to project to the meaning of $\ulcorner s_1 \mathbin{\&} s_2 \urcorner$. And the concept of impoverish-ment does not help either, for although one could devise a syntactic theory which would block the passage of the sentence $\ulcorner s_1 \mathbin{\&} s_2 \urcorner$ from the level of input to a truth theory (the language L_1) to the surface language L_5, and which would permit the passage (and the abbreviation) of $\ulcorner (s_1 \lor s_2) \mathbin{\&} \sim (s_1 \mathbin{\&} s_2) \urcorner$, the proposal would still leave it utterly mysterious why L_5-speakers who knew the meaning of $\ulcorner s_1 \mathbin{\underline{\lor}} s_2 \urcorner$ would not, we may reasonably suppose, need the syntactic information that $\ulcorner s_1 \mathbin{\&} s_2 \urcorner$ is not a grammatically acceptable sentence of L_5. This proposal cannot be justified within the project described in the present chapter, even though it may find a place within some other project. Within the present project such a proposal would only be justified in case '$\underline{\lor}$' was added to a language like L_1 as an explicitly abbreviatory device. (Cf. Davidson, 1977a, p. 247:

> We know how to give a theory of truth for the formal
> language; so if we also knew how to transform the sentences
> of a natural language systematically into sentences of the
> formal language, we would have a theory of truth for the
> natural language.

Cf. also Sainsbury, 1977 and 1979, pp. 149–60.)

It is of the utmost importance to appreciate that it is not the fact that on this first proposal one does not use '$\underline{\lor}$' in the *ML* to state the truth conditions of *OL* sentences containing '$\underline{\lor}$' that renders the proposal unacceptable. A semantic theory which, for each *OL* expression (in particular, each sentence), uses just that same expression (sentence) in the *ML* in the specification of its own semantic properties is said to be *homophonic*. The theory $T\theta$ is homophonic in its treatment of the connectives '&', '$\lor$', and '$\sim$', and the obviously adequate theory for L_5 is homophonic in its treatment of '$\underline{\lor}$'. If there is a gap between surface syntax and the level of input to a semantic theory then, of course, a theory which is homophonic with respect to the language at the level of input is not homophonic with respect to the language at the surface. But this departure from homophony need not mark an inadequacy. And even if there is no gap between surface syntax and the level of input to a semantic theory a non-homophonic (heterophonic) theory may be adequate.

To see this last point consider now a second deviation from the original, obviously adequate, theory for L_5. Consider, in particular, a theorist who likes to use familiar vocabulary in the *ML* and therefore proposes as an axiom for '$\underline{\lor}$'

$$(\forall \sigma)(\forall \tau)\,[\ulcorner \sigma \mathbin{\underline{\lor}} \tau \urcorner \text{ is true} \leftrightarrow$$
$$((\sigma \text{ is true v}\tau \text{ is true}) \mathbin{\&} \sim(\sigma \text{ is true } \& \ \tau \text{ is true}))]\,.$$

This axiom specifies, in non-semantic terms (namely, by using the *ML* conjunction, inclusive disjunction, and negation), and in full generality, the way in which the sub-sentential item '$\veebar$' contributes to the truth conditions of sentences in which it occurs; that is, the axiom *deals non-semantically with* '$\veebar$'. (We carry over this and related pieces of terminology from the case of theories of meaning.) From this axiom and those for s_1 and s_2 a canonical derivation yields

> $\ulcorner s_1 \veebar s_2 \urcorner$ is true $\leftrightarrow$
> ((snow is white v the earth moves) &
> $\sim$ (snow is white & the earth moves)).

It might perhaps be complained that this departure from homophony renders the theory no longer interpretational. But whether or not this complaint is justified (and departure from homophony does not always result in a non-interpretational theory), the important point is that the departure from homophony introduces no structural inadequacy. Homophony is not the same as structural adequacy, and it would be wrong to say that it is the first deviant proposal's departure from homophony which constitutes its treating the structure of L_5 as 'so much misleading surface structure'.

Homophony is not the same as structural adequacy. (There are homophonic theories which infringe *SC*, and, as we have just seen, heterophonic theories which meet *SC*.) But still, homophony is quite closely related to structural adequacy. Consider again the theory resulting from the second deviant proposal about '$\veebar$'. If, throughout this theory, we replace the complex *ML* expression

$$(\dots v \text{ ——}) \& \sim (\dots \& \text{——})$$

by a new simple *ML* expression (which we might as well write as '$\veebar$'), and if we provide enough *ML* logic for '$\veebar$' to ensure that it has the same substitution properties as the complex expression which it replaces, then the result is a theory which treats '$\veebar$' homophonically, and exhibits exactly the same pattern of derivations. Thus, if there is a theory whose level of input is the level of surface syntax and which meets *SC*, then there is a similar theory which is homophonic with respect to the surface language. Enforced departure from homophony with respect to the surface language is a sign of the enforced introduction of a gap between surface syntax and the level of input to a semantic theory (enforced by *SC*).

Evans's (1977, pp. 488-9) phrase 'so much misleading surface structure' occurred in the following context:

> I come to semantic investigations with a preference for *homophonic*
> theories; theories which try to take serious account of the semantic
> and syntactic devices which actually exist in the language. . . . The
> objection [to a heterophonic theory] would not be that such truth
> conditions are not correct, but that, in a sense which we would
> all dearly love to have more exactly explained, the syntactic shape
> of the sentence is treated as so much misleading surface structure.

It does not seem altogether unreasonable to hope that the sort of
explanation for which Evans here expresses our desire might be provided by considerations such as those of the last few pages.

NOTES

My first thoughts on the topics of this chapter were prompted by the
following sentence from Evans (1975, p. 344):

> [I] f (but only if) speakers of the language can understand certain
> sentences they have not previously encountered, as a result of
> acquaintance with their parts, the semanticist must state how
> the meaning of these sentences is a function of the meanings of
> those parts.

I subsequently learned a great deal from many conversations with
Gareth Evans on these topics, and several points in the chapter, including the distinctions between finiteness and structural adequacy and
between homophony and structural adequacy, are attributable to him.

Christopher Peacocke persuaded me to focus upon *SC* rather than
MC. I discussed both constraints in 'Meaning and structure' (forthcoming),
where I compared the 'only if' part of *SC* with a constraint based upon
the following sentences from Wallace (1972, p. 225):

> If we are thinking of translating natural languages, and of applying
> truth theory to natural languages, it seems reasonable to require
> that every sentence built from vocabulary that occurs in
> translations be a translation. Formally, if $s_1, \ldots, s_n$ are sentences
> of L_2 that translate some sentences of L_1, and if s_{n+1} is a
> sentence of L_2 built from vocabulary that occurs in $s_1, \ldots, s_n$
> then s_{n+1} translates some sentence of L_1.

I discussed *SC* further in 'Meaning, structure and understanding'
(1981).

IV

UNDERSTANDING

1 FULL UNDERSTANDING OF A LANGUAGE

A semantic theorist can engage upon the project of constructing the best theory of meaning, or the best theory of truth conditions, for a particular language without entering any remotely controversial psychological hypotheses about particular speakers of that language. It is quite uncontroversial that any speaker who has that language as his actual language, at a certain time t, is psychologically so constituted at t as to be able to interpret utterances in that language. That is, abstracting harmlessly from considerations of mood and force, he is psychologically so constituted at t that for each sentence s of his actual language he is able, at t, to come to know the meaning of s if a token of s is presented to him.

Let us focus upon the language L_4 with a hundred sentences. At any time, anyone who has L_4 as his actual language is in a state of a complex psychological type, the same psychological type for each speaker and each time. What is more, at any time t, anyone who has L_4 as his actual language is, for each sentence s of L_4, psychologically so constituted at t that he is able, at t, to come to know the meaning of s if a token of s is presented to him. For each sentence s of L_4 there is a psychological state type such that at any time, anyone who has L_4 as his actual language is in a state (token) of that psychological type; let us say, of the $<s, L_4>$ *semantic state* type. We can go further. For each semantic primitive of L_4, anyone who has L_4 as his actual language is able to come to know the meaning of any sentence of L_4 which contains that primitive, if a token of that sentence is presented to him. So

73

for each semantic primitive ρ, there is a psychological state type such that at any time, anyone who has L_4 as his actual language is in a state (token) of that psychological type; let us say, of the $<\rho, L_4>$ *semantic state* type.

It is crucially important to notice two things at this stage. The first is that, for all that can uncontroversially be said, the only states (state types) which all speakers of L_4 are in at all times are psychological states. It does not follow that there is any physical state (type) which everyone who is in the $<'P_1 m_1', L_4>$ semantic state at t is in at t. Nor does it follow that if someone is in the $<'P_1 m_1', L_4>$ semantic state at t and at t' then there is some physical state (type) which that person is in at t and at t'. The second thing to notice is that one cannot uncontroversially move from the mere fact that a speaker has L_4 as his actual language to the claim that there is some particular theory of meaning for L_4 of which that speaker has implicit (or tacit) knowledge, unless implicit knowledge is defined in such a way as to make it a quite uninteresting notion. For that move is only uncontroversial if it is a sufficient condition for implicit knowledge of all that is stated by a theory of meaning that a person should merely be able to come to know the facts stated by the meaning specifications which the theory yields as its output. And if this is a sufficient condition for implicit knowledge then, although one can certainly attribute to anyone whose actual language is L_4 implicit knowledge of all that is stated by the best theory of meaning for L_4 (the one meeting *SC*), one can equally attribute implicit knowledge of all that is stated by the indefinitely many other theories which yield the same output. (Similarly, from the fact that a speaker recognizes as grammatical sentences just the strings of symbols which are certified as grammatical by some particular syntactic theory one cannot move uncontroversially to the claim that the speaker has implicit knowledge of that theory, unless one so defines the notion of implicit knowledge that it does not differentiate amongst theories which certify the same strings as grammatical. And if one does so define it, then the notion is rendered quite uninteresting.)

This second point is important, but it does not follow from it that there can be no reasonable notion of implicit knowledge upon which we may sometimes be in a position to attribute to a speaker of L_4 implicit knowledge of the best theory of meaning for L_4. What follows, rather, is that we need to distinguish amongst speakers all of whom have L_4 as their actual language. And to make that distinction we can employ the notion of a *full understander* (a speaker who is sensitive to

Understanding

the semantic structure of his actual language) which was briefly introduced in Section III.1. That notion itself deserves clarification. As a
first attempt we might say that a speaker of a language is a full understander just in case his knowing what s means is c-determined by his
knowing what $s_1, \ldots, s_n$ mean in all those cases in which, in the best
theory of meaning for the language, the meaning specification for s
is d-determined by the meaning specifications for $s_1, \ldots, s_n$. That is,
S is a full understander of L just in case the theory of meaning for L
which meets SC also meets the mirror constraint with respect to S.

We allowed (in Section III.1) two cases in which a speaker's knowing
what s means is c-determined by his knowing what $s_1, \ldots, s_n$ mean. In
the first case a speaker may come to know what s means without any
further exposure or training after having been taught what $s_1, \ldots, s_n$
mean. In the second case a speaker may be such that revision of his
belief as to what s means would involve him in revision of his beliefs
as to what $s_1, \ldots, s_n$ mean. Of these two cases the first, which has to
do with the order of acquisition of pieces of semantic knowledge, does
not really go to the heart of the matter. One reason is that, if we are
considering speakers who now know the meanings of all the sentences
of their language, then the past order of acquisition is only marginally
relevant. For it has no immediate consequences for their present
sensitivity to, or blindness to, the semantic structure of their language.
The second case is the more important.

So let us use the second case of c-determination in a further attempt
at defining full understanding. (Intuitively, a full understander's competence has the finest structure consistent with the structure of the
language.) A speaker S is a full understander of L just in case, whenever
s is a sentence built from the semantic primitives discerned in $s_1, \ldots,$
s_n by the best theory of meaning for L, S is such that if he were to
revise his belief as to what s means then he would revise his beliefs
about $s_1, \ldots, s_n$ in a corresponding way. This last phrase 'in a corresponding way' can be spelled out as follows. If S were to revise his
belief about the meaning of s, in that respect of the meaning which is
revealed in the best theory of meaning for L as a deductive consequence
of the occurrence in s of the semantic primitive ρ with semantic property Π, and if S's revised belief about s were to be the deductive consequence of assigning to ρ the property Π' rather than Π, then S would
revise his beliefs about the meanings of $s_1, \ldots, s_n$ in such a way as
would be the deductive consequence of the assignment to ρ of Π'
rather than Π.

75

It is a consequence of this definition of full understanding that if S is a full understander of L_4, for example, then if S were to revise his belief as to what '$P_1 m_1$' means, and if the revision were to concern that respect of the meaning which a semantic theorist associates with the occurrence of 'P_1', then S would correspondingly revise his beliefs about the meanings of '$P_1 m_2$', ..., '$P_1 m_{10}$'. As a limiting case, if S's belief about '$P_1 m_1$' were to be totally undermined (while he continued to have correct beliefs about '$P_2 m_1$', ..., '$P_{10} m_1$'), then his beliefs about '$P_1 m_2$', ..., '$P_1 m_{10}$' would be correspondingly undermined; he would then have as his actual language a language with just ninety sentences. Let us summarize this consequence of the definition by saying that if S is a full understander of L_4 at t then S is, at t, in a psychological state of the 'P_1' *differential state* type. In general, to be a full understander of a language L is to have L as one's actual language and to be such that, for each semantic primitive ρ of L, one is in the ρ differential state.

Corresponding to the first point after the introduction of semantic states we should notice here that, for all that can uncontroversially be said, the only states (state types) which all full understanders of L_4 are in at all times are psychological states. It does not follow that there is any physical state (type) which everyone who is in the 'P_1' differential state at t is in at t, nor that for each speaker there is a physical state (type) which he is in at all times at which he is in the 'P_1' differential state.

This definition of differential states, and correspondingly the second attempt at defining full understanding, makes crucial use of counter-factual conditionals: if S were to change one belief he would change certain other beliefs. And, as is often the case with counterfactual definitions, it can reasonably be objected that the counterfactual condition's obtaining is neither necessary nor sufficient for the obtaining of the condition which we are out to define, and of which we have some antecedent intuitive grasp. In the case of full understanding the counterfactual condition is not necessary, because we can imagine a situation in which a speaker who is intuitively a full understander (of L_4, say) is so wired up that if he were to revise any of his semantic beliefs about sentences then his full understanding would be wiped out and replaced by mere phrasebook knowledge for each sentence (of L_4) as to what it means, so that he would not make corresponding revisions in his semantic beliefs about other sentences. Similarly, the counterfactual condition is not sufficient, because we can imagine a situation in which a speaker who is intuitively not a full understander is so wired up that if he were to revise any of his semantic beliefs about sentences then he would come to full understanding, so that he would make corresponding revisions in his semantic beliefs about other sentences.

We can go some way towards overcoming the inadequacy of the counterfactual definition by employing the notion of a state's contributing to a causal explanation. Thus, a speaker S is a full understander of L at t just in case, for each semantic primitive ρ of L there is a state (token) $\Sigma(\rho)$ of S such that

(1) $\Sigma(\rho)$ is causally operative at t;
(2) for any sentences s and s' containing ρ as a semantic constituent, S's being in $\Sigma(\rho)$ at t and $\Sigma(\rho)$'s being causally operative at t and S's revising at t his belief about s (in that respect of the meaning associated with the presence of ρ) together suffice for a causal explanation of S's revising at t his belief about s' in a corresponding way.

What follows 'for each semantic primitive ρ of L' in this definition itself provides a new definition of 'S is in the ρ differential state'.

Upon many views in the philosophy of mind the state (token) $\Sigma(\rho)$ will be a state of a physical type, and it may be only under a physical description of $\Sigma(\rho)$ that S's being in $\Sigma(\rho)$ contributes to a causal explanation. On many views, also, the state (token) of the physical type is identical with the state (token) of the psychological (ρ differential) type. But it is sufficient, for present purposes, to maintain only that the physical and psychological state tokens stand in all the same causal relations. We can then say, rather neutrally, that the ρ differential state is *realized* in S at t by a state (token) $\Sigma(\rho)$ of a physical type. Such views in the philosophy of mind are not the only ones possible, but it is hard to see how there could be a view upon which no account of full understanding could be given along the lines sketched in the previous paragraph. (For example, it would make no important difference if one held that psychological states are realized by states of an immaterial substance.)

It would be extremely hasty to claim that this last definition captures just the notion of full understanding that we want. Nor is this the place to offer much in the way of further refinement. The aim of the present section is just to examine the idea that some speakers of a language (the full understanders) stand in an interesting relation (a relation which linguists express using the phrase 'implicit knowledge') to the best theory of meaning for their language. But we can consider one further clause which might be added to the definition.

(3) for any sentence s containing ρ as a semantic constituent, S's being in $\Sigma(\rho)$ at t and $\Sigma(\rho)$'s being causally operative at t contribute non-redundantly to the causal explanation of S's actual belief at t about the meaning of s (in particular, in that respect of the meaning associated with the occurrence in s of ρ).

For some such clause as this is needed properly to rule out the case of a speaker who is intuitively not a full understander but is so wired up that if he were to revise any of his semantic beliefs about sentences then he would come to full understanding. The states, of such a speaker, which meet clause (2) will presumably be causally operative in some way, but not in the way required by clause (3). It should not be objected to this clause that S might have come to know what some such sentence s means long before he came to be in any state which realized the differential state. For this clause does not speak of the causal ancestry of S's first coming to know what certain sentences mean; it only speaks of the causal explanation of S's present belief (knowledge) state. For all that this clause states, the causal ancestry of S's first coming to know the meanings of some sentences containing ρ traces back to a training programme to which also the causal ancestry of $\Sigma(\rho)$ traces back.

We can now define a structural feature of a speaker's competence. Let us say that S's belief about the meaning of s is *differentially determined* by his beliefs about $s_1, \ldots, s_n$ just in case (i) the causally operative states of S which contribute non-redundantly to the causal explanation of S's belief about s are among the causally operative states of S which contribute non-redundantly to the causal explanations of his beliefs about $s_1, \ldots, s_n$, and (ii) those first causally operative states of S are such that S's being in those states and S's revising his belief about s together suffice for a causal explanation of S's revising his beliefs about $s_1, \ldots, s_n$ in corresponding ways. Then we can state the interesting relation between full understanders of a language and the best theory of meaning for that language (the theory meeting *SC*) as follows. A full understander's semantic belief about s is differentially determined by his semantic beliefs about $s_1, \ldots, s_n$ just in case the meaning specification for s is d-determined by the meaning specifications for $s_1, \ldots, s_n$. The interesting relation is one of isomorphism between a structure of causal explanations and a structure of derivations. The same kind of isomorphism may hold between a speaker who is not a full understander of his actual language and a theory for that language which does not meet *SC*.

If one's main interest is in constructing psychological theories about speakers, then one will collect evidence about the structure of causal explanations concerning a particular speaker (by observing his acquisition and revision of semantic beliefs about sentences) and then incorporate into one's theoretical description of that speaker the theory of meaning for his language which meets, with respect to him, the mirror constraint (now stated in terms of differential determination rather than c-determination).

All this does not quite account for the use of the expression 'implicit knowledge'. But it is not difficult to define implicit knowledge so that we may attribute to someone who has L as his actual language implicit knowledge of that theory of meaning for L whose derivational structure mirrors the structure of that man's competence, and in particular so that we may attribute to a full understander of L implicit knowledge of the best theory of meaning for L. For all we have to do is to elevate this requirement on attributions to a definition. What is stated by an axiom of a theory of meaning for L which is employed in the derivations of meaning specifications for all sentences containing an expression ρ is implicitly known by S (who knows the meanings of those sentences in L) just in case S's semantic beliefs about those sentences share a common partial causal explanation. Thus, if a certain theory of meaning for L has an axiom which assigns to ρ the semantic property Π, then it is not sufficient for implicit knowledge that ρ has Π that a speaker should be in the $<\rho, L>$ semantic state; he must also be in the ρ differential state. And if he is in the ρ differential state and revises his belief about one sentence, and consequently about all sentences, containing ρ then, it may be said, he changes his implicit belief about ρ. This talk about implicit knowledge and implicit belief is harmless, so long as it is appreciated that such talk merely summarizes what can be said in terms of causal explanation. (Similarly, in the case of syntactic theory, if a speaker recognizes as grammatical sentences just the strings of symbols which are certified as grammatical by a certain theory, then we may attribute to that speaker implicit knowledge of a particular grammatical rule provided that the speaker's acts of recognition of the sentences whose grammaticality follows (in part) from that rule, share a common partial causal explanation.)

The example from which we began and to which we have recurred at various points is that of the finite language L_4. In the case of a very small finite language like L_4 we can speak quite straightforwardly of a speaker having a semantic belief about each sentence. In the case of a large finite language, and especially in the case of an infinite language, we must speak more cautiously of a speaker being, for each sentence, in a state adequate to yield a semantic belief (indeed, a piece of knowledge) about that sentence if he is presented with a token of it. For each sentence s of an infinite language L, being in a state of the $<s, L>$ semantic state type amounts to having a potential belief about s. And talk of semantic beliefs, in the foregoing sketch of an account of full understanding, must be extended to cover potential semantic beliefs.

In the case of an infinite language L we do not, typically, recognize that a man has L as his actual language and then go on to ask whether he is a full understander of L. For typically it is only by discerning structure in a man's competence with the finitely many sentences which he actually uses (by observing the pattern of his acquisition and revision of semantic beliefs) that we put ourselves in a position to attribute to that man a potential semantic belief about every sentence of L. We certainly would not allow that a man has L as his actual language just because he knows the meanings of a few sentences of L in which all of L's semantic primitives occur. For perhaps those pieces of semantic knowledge have no common partial explanations. (Perhaps he has mere phrasebook knowledge of the meanings of those few sentences.) If this is so then this man's actual language comprises just those few sentences. If, on the other hand, the man has implicit knowledge concerning the semantic properties of the semantic primitives (and whether he has such implicit knowledge is not an empirically inaccessible matter) then his actual language is L. And there are imaginable intermediate cases.

This shows why the objection to Grice's programme which was mentioned in Section I.2 is groundless. (The objection, from Platts, 1979, turned on the fact that each speaker only uses finitely many sentences.) Suppose that a man knows, for each sentence in some finite set, that there is a convention around him to utter that sentence with certain intentions. If those pieces of knowledge have no common partial explanations, if revision in one belief has no consequences elsewhere, then there is no question of defining what is his actual language in terms of hypothetical intentions. His actual language comprises just the sentences in the finite set. If on the other hand those pieces of knowledge do have common partial explanations then we shall appeal to hypothetical intentions. But there is no problem as to what constrains those hypothetical intentions. Those hypothetical intentions are causally constrained by what causally explains the original knowledge about intentions (see again Loar, 1976, pp. 158–61).

Despite the close connection, in typical cases, between having an infinite language as one's actual language and being a full understander of that language the first is (just as in the case of a finite language) not logically sufficient for the second. And it is by making this conceptual distinction that we are able to find a place for an interesting notion of implicit knowledge.

2   IMPLICIT KNOWLEDGE AND LINGUISTICS

Someone who has syntactic and semantic mastery of a language can tell which strings of symbols, or of sounds, are well-formed sentences, and can tell what sentences mean. Lying behind this fairly readily observable linguistic behaviour there is, according to linguists, implicit knowledge of a syntactic theory and a semantic theory. Thus, in a famous passage Chomsky (1965, p. 8) wrote:

> Obviously, every speaker of a language has mastered and
> internalized a generative grammar that expresses his knowledge
> of his language. This is not to say that he is aware of the rules
> of the grammar or even that he can become aware of them. . . .
> Any interesting generative grammar will be dealing, for the
> most part, with mental processes that are far beyond the level
> of actual or even potential consciousness. . . . Thus a
> generative grammar attempts to specify what the speaker
> actually knows.

And in another place he wrote (Chomsky, 1975, p. 304):

> The linguist's theory is . . . a psychological theory. It is an
> attempt to account for evidence of behavior and introspection
> by ascribing to the language-user a certain system of rules and
> principles that he applies in language use, as a speaker and
> hearer. It is postulated, then, that a person who knows a human

language has internalized, has developed a mental representation of a grammar.

This position, which is regarded as uncontroversial by linguists, has often been attacked by philosophers. Quine pointed to the clear distinction between a rule's fitting a person's behaviour and a rule's guiding that behaviour. Two sets of rules which each certify the same strings as grammatical sentences equally fit the behaviour of a man who recognizes just those strings as grammatical. A set of rules guides someone if he refers to the rules in arriving at his judgments about grammaticality. Quine (1972, pp. 442, 444) went on:

> But now it seems that Chomsky and his followers recognize an intermediate condition, between mere fitting and full guidance in my flat-footed sense of the word. . . . If it is to make any sense to say that a native was implicitly guided by one system of rules and not by another [system with the same output] , this sense must link up somehow with the native's dispositions to behave in observable ways in observable circumstances.

Quine did not actually say that the required link could not be made, and he provided an attractive metaphor in terms of which we can state very briefly how the link can be made. He spoke of two trees with the same 'superficial mass of foliage'; what is demanded of the linguist is that he should explain how, by observing just the foliage, one can learn about the shape of the tree. The reply to this demand which is suggested by Section IV.1 is that one should tug on one piece of foliage and see what else moves.

In a more recent paper, Michael Levin (1977) points to another, similarly motivated, distinction. The axioms of a syntactic theory generate theorems which state that certain strings are grammatical sentences. Speakers of a language recognize certain strings as grammatical, and doubtless these acts of recognition are generated by antecedent events. The crucial distinction is between derivational generation of theorems and causal generation of acts of recognition. For a confusion of two senses of 'generate' would lead to a hasty assumption that a syntactic theory can form part of a psychological theory about speakers. According to Levin (1977, p. 131), 'The whole idea that grammars *explain* comes from smuggling into the idea of an empirically adequate grammar the quite separate assumption of its realization in human speakers.'

It is, perhaps, just possible that some linguists have confused these two notions. It is just possible that some have failed to notice that 'It requires further argument ... to show that the speaker executes processes isomorphic to the [derivational] generation process' (ibid.; but see e.g. Chomsky, 1969, p. 155). But, as we have seen, there is no need to trade upon confusion, for the further argument can be given. Concerning a particular theory and a particular speaker, empirical evidence may make it very plausible that the pattern of causal generation in that speaker is isomorphic to the pattern of derivational generation in that theory (by making it very plausible that the speaker is in psychological states of differential state types as well as psychological states of semantic state types).

There is a reason why linguists sometimes neglect to mention the need for this kind of evidence in particular cases. For there is considerable evidence of uniformity in the patterns of causal generation across speakers of a single language. Thus the syntactic theory which can form part of a psychological theory for one speaker of a language will probably be applicable, also, for most other speakers of that language. What is more, there are formally specifiable characteristics of syntactic theories such that there is some evidence, across a range of languages, that the syntactic theory which is psychologically applicable has those characteristics. Such evidence may, of course, be subjected to critical examination. But admitting that is very far from admitting that the whole discipline of linguistics rests upon a grotesque confusion.

There is a rather different kind of attack which a philosopher might launch. He might accept that there are states of speakers (psychologically characterized but, probably, physically realized) which correspond one by one with axioms of syntactic and semantic theories, but object to the use of the terms 'implicit knowledge' and 'implicit belief'. For, he might say, use of those terms suggests wrongly that being in those states is relevantly similar to having a piece of (explicit, propositional) knowledge or a (conscious) belief.

Chomsky's view on this matter is that while one could choose to separate conscious from implicit knowledge, and to reserve the term 'knowledge' for the former (using, perhaps, 'cognition' to include both), this distinction would not be particularly important psychologically:

It may be expected that conscious belief will form a scattered
and probably uninteresting subpart of the full cognitive
structure. (Chomsky, 1976, p. 163.)

In this usage, what is 'known' will be a rather ill-defined and,
perhaps, a scattered and chaotic subpart of the coherent and
important systems and structures that are cognized. For psychology,
the important notion will be 'cognize', not 'know'. (Ibid. p. 165.)

Clearly, Chomsky's remarks do not settle the philosophical question
whether there is an important conceptual difference between conscious
belief and implicit belief. Nor is this question to be settled easily. But
perhaps it can be made plausible that there might be a distinction worth
preserving.

Consider first, as an example, the case of a 'smart bomb'. On the
basis of the observed behaviour of such a missile we entertain the
(correct) hypothesis that it contains internal physical mechanisms
which guide it onto its target. The question then is whether we should
extend our concept of belief so as to attribute to the missile beliefs
which guide its behaviour. There are two very elementary things which
can be said about belief. One is that beliefs can be expressed by utterances. The other is that beliefs contribute to the explanation of (non-
linguistic) behaviour. The first of these features of belief does not apply
in the case of the 'smart bomb', so if the concept of belief is to be
extended it must be on the grounds of an analogy between the explanation of the missile's behaviour and familiar explanations of human
behaviour in terms of the agent's propositional attitudes. Familiar
propositional attitude explanations involve appeal to beliefs and desires,
so if an analogy is to be made out then we shall have to attribute to
the missile both beliefs about, say, the density of population in various
areas and desires, say, the desire to drop explosives on an area with a
population density of such and such. And this attribution of a desire
seems quite empty; we cannot, for example, make anything at all of
the question why the missile desires that. What is more, the emptiness
of this single desire attribution points to the very close connection
between the beliefs attributed and the behaviour to be explained, a
connection which is disanalogous to the connection between belief
and behaviour in standard cases. For it is an impressive feature of
propositional attitude explanation that no particular pattern of
behaviour is guaranteed by the presence of any particular belief. Thus
it seems that there might be a distinction worth preserving between
implicit beliefs attributed to a 'smart bomb' and conscious beliefs
attributed to a human agent.

Then consider, as a second example, one way of using the 'implicit belief' terminology in the case of a human speaker who has mastered a language. This way of using that terminology begins from the fact that implicit beliefs about, for example, the syntactic properties of certain constructions do not interact with conscious beliefs. There is no felt incompatibility between an implicit belief and a directly contradictory conscious belief (cf. Stich, 1971, p. 489), and, as Chomsky points out, there seems to be no way of bringing the implicit belief to consciousness. One way (although, obviously, not the only way) of responding to this fact about partitioning is to incorporate into one's psychological theory a language faculty to be the holder of the implicit beliefs. The output of the language faculty would be, in respect of grammaticality or ungrammaticality, a recognizable signal to the conscious mind (a mental prod). A speaker would recognize ungrammaticality by recognizing the result of the language faculty's prod. If one describes the psychological situation this way (which does not seem entirely false to the phenomenology of the recognition of ungrammaticality) then one cannot fail to be impressed by the analogy between the language faculty and the 'smart bomb'. To be sure one can award to language faculties an unmotivated desire to signal grammaticality corresponding, perhaps, to the unmotivated desire to protect themselves that most people have. But there is still too close a connection between a language faculty's beliefs and its behaviour, and again it seems that there might be a distinction worth preserving between implicit beliefs attributed to a language faculty and conscious beliefs attributed to a human agent. And how could such a distinction be obliterated merely by attributing the implicit beliefs to the speaker rather than to his language faculty?

Perhaps this last, rhetorical, question is too hasty. For there are relevant differences between the two descriptions of the psychological situation. If the implicit beliefs are attributed directly to the speaker then we can leave out of the story the prod and the recognition of the prod. Rather, the implicit beliefs simply yield the (conscious) belief that a certain sentence is grammatical, or means such and such. And in standard explanations of beliefs in terms of other beliefs (rather than of behaviour in terms of beliefs) one does not appeal to desires. But even when these differences have been noted, parallels with the other two cases remain. First, in the case of implicit belief there is no expression by utterances. Second, implicit beliefs attributed to speakers do not contribute, with desires, to the explanation of behaviour. Only the resultant conscious beliefs contribute in that way. The explanatory role of the implicit beliefs is exhausted by their yielding conscious beliefs. Third, just as, in standard cases, no particular pattern of behaviour is guaranteed by the presence of any particular belief, so also, no particular distinct belief is guaranteed by the presence of any particular belief. Certainly, the presence of a belief does not guarantee belief in what follows deductively from it (in a syntactic or semantic theory, for example). And if this feature of standard cases is really characteristic of propositional attitude explanation then, as before, it seems that there might be a distinction worth preserving between implicit beliefs attributed to a speaker and conscious beliefs.

NOTES

I am grateful to Christopher Peacocke for advice about avoiding the use of counterfactual conditionals in the definition of full understanding. I have not been concerned with the further constraints which are imposed upon the causal ancestry of semantic beliefs and, in particular, upon the kind of causal explanation involved, by the requirement that the beliefs should constitute knowledge. Attention to this requirement rules out some cases which might otherwise seem to provide examples of speakers who have a language as their actual language without being full understanders of the language. But it does not rule out all such cases.

On the debate between philosophers and linguists see, for example, Fodor (1968), Stich (1971), Graves *et al.* (1973), Stich (1972), Chomsky and Katz (1974). See also Stich (1978). In 'Languages and language', Lewis (1975, p. 20) subscribed to the Quinean view: 'Unfortunately, I know of no promising way to make objective sense of the assertion that a grammar Γ is used by a population P whereas another grammar Γ', which generates the same language as Γ, is not.' In 'Index, context, and content' (1980, p. 81), he was slightly less pessimistic:

> You might insist that a good grammar should be suited to fit into a psycholinguistic theory that goes beyond our common knowledge and explains the inner mechanisms that make our practice possible. There is nothing wrong in principle with this ambitious goal, but I doubt that it is worthwhile to pursue it in our present state of knowledge.

For views essentially the same as mine on the topics of this chapter see Evans (1981).

PART TWO

QUANTIFICATION AND REFERENCE

V

NAMES

1 NAMES AND SEMANTIC THEORIES

In Part One, a (schematic and provisional) description of the semantic theorist's project was offered. A good place at which to begin upon that project is with languages whose sentences exhibit that most basic combination of subject and predicate. In Sections III.2 and IV.1 we considered such a language, namely the language L_4 with just a hundred sentences constructed from ten names and ten predicates. If a semantic theory (a theory of meaning or a truth theory) for L_4 is to meet SC then it must have axioms which specify semantic properties of those names and predicates. Those axioms will not themselves provide philosophical elucidation of the theoretical concepts used in them, any more than meaning specifications provide philosophical elucidation of the concept of meaning or truth condition specifications provide philosophical elucidation of the concept of truth. So a question arises as to how we can elucidate the theoretical concepts used in the axioms. The outline of an answer is provided by the following sentence from McDowell (1978, pp. 122-3):

> [W]e can conceive the deductive shape which the theory assumes,
> in order to meet [the requirement of *system*], as setting up a
> complex of channels by which the impact of [the requirement
> of *psychological adequacy*], bearing in the first instance on
> interpretations of whole utterances, is transmitted backwards,
> through the derivations of theorems licensed by the theory, to
> the premises of those derivations, in which the theory says

what it does about sentence-components and modes of
sentence-construction.

SC requires a certain pattern of derivations of meaning, or truth
condition specifications from axioms. The *PAC*s cast light upon the
concepts of meaning, and of truth, used in the derived theorems.
Thence, via the inverse of that pattern of derivations, light is cast
upon the theoretical concepts used in the axioms.

Suppose that we try, first, to provide a theory of truth meeting
SC for L_4. There is more than one way to do this. We can assign a
semantic property to the syntactic operation of concatenating a name
with a predicate.

AxPred 1 $(\forall \Phi)(\forall \gamma) [\Phi \cap \gamma$ is true $\leftrightarrow Ref(\gamma) \in Ext(\Phi)]$

(Read: for any predicate Φ and name γ of L_4 the sentence made up
of Φ followed by γ is true iff the *reference* of γ is a member of the
extension of Φ. 'in L_4' is suppressed throughout.) Along with *AxPred 1*
we need, for each name, an axiom assigning it a reference and, for each
predicate, an axiom assigning it an extension. Thus, for 'm_1' we might
have

$$Ref('m_1') = n_1.$$

The expression 'n_1' used in this axiom is a name in the *ML* of the
object of which 'm_1' is a name. And for 'P_1' we might have

$$(\forall x)(x \in Ext('P_1') \leftrightarrow Q_1 x)$$

or

$$Ext('P_1') = \{x : Q_1 x\}.$$

In either case a predicate ('Q_1') in the *ML* is used in assigning a semantic property to 'P_1'. From these axioms we can easily derive

$$'P_1 m_1'\text{ is true} \leftrightarrow Q_1 n_1.$$

(Let us suppose that this truth condition specification is interpretational.)

Without infringing *SC* we can provide a theory with one less axiom
by dropping *AxPred 1* and either reformulating the axioms for names
as, for example,

$$(\forall \Phi)[\Phi \cap 'm_1'\text{ is true} \leftrightarrow n_1 \in Ext(\Phi)]$$

or else reformulating the axioms for predicates as, for example,

$$(\forall\gamma)\,[`P_1`\cap\gamma \text{ is true} \leftrightarrow Q_1\,(Ref(\gamma))]\,.$$

So long as we consider only languages in which each predicate takes one name to form a sentence there is nothing to choose between these two ways of doing without *AxPred 1*. But once we consider languages with, for example, some two-place predicates as well, the theory which is formally smoothest is one which avoids both *AxPred 1* and the corresponding axiom for two-place predicates

AxPred 2 $(\forall\Psi)\,(\forall\gamma)\,(\forall\delta)\,[\ulcorner\Psi\,(\gamma,\delta)\urcorner \text{ is true} \leftrightarrow$
$$\langle Ref(\gamma), Ref(\delta)\rangle \in Ext\,(\Psi)]$$

by retaining straightforward axioms for names, for example,

$$Ref(`m_1`) = n_1$$

and employing less straightforward axioms for predicates, for example,

$$(\forall\gamma)\,[\ulcorner P_1\,\gamma\urcorner \text{ is true} \leftrightarrow Q_1\,(Ref(\gamma))]$$

and for a two-place predicate 'R_1'

$$(\forall\gamma)\,(\forall\delta)\,[\ulcorner R_1\,(\gamma,\delta)\urcorner \text{ is true} \leftrightarrow S_1\,(Ref(\gamma), Ref(\gamma))]\,.$$

The fact that such a theory is in general (although not in the case of L_4) smoother than the alternatives is a consequence of a relatively superficial asymmetry between names and predicates: 'subject-terms [names] are distinguished from predicate-terms by the fact that more than one of them may appear in some forms of such [subject-predicate] sentences' (Strawson, 1974a, p. 4). This asymmetry is not, of course, evident in the case of L_4, and that it is not evident there is a symptom of its superficiality.

The concept of reference which is employed in the axioms of the truth theory for L_4 is not itself employed in the truth condition specifications which are derived (canonically) from those axioms; rather, it is internal to the theory. So, it is natural to say, the concept of reference is a primitive theoretical concept whose content is exhausted by the contribution which it makes, via canonical derivations, to the output of the theory. The concept which is employed in the axioms of the truth theory for L_4, is, of course, that of reference in L_4. So it might seem that the illumination of that concept which would come, via the notion of a canonical derivation in that theory, from prior illumination of the concept of truth in L_4 (achieved, in effect, by asking under what conditions L_4 would be the actual language of a population) would be independent of any illumination of reference in languages other than L_4. But this thought would be mistaken. Such illumination of the concept of truth as may have been provided in Chapters I and II is quite general; it is illumination of truth in L for variable L. And the pattern of canonical derivations in the truth theory for L_4 can be specified quite generally and can be exhibited in theories for other languages. So the illumination of the concept of reference will itself be quite general; it will be illumination of reference in L for variable L.

In fact, however, the content of a reference specification is not exhausted by the contribution which that specification makes, via canonical derivations, to truth condition specifications. If the only requirement imposed upon the canonically derived theorems is that they be correct then, even if the canonical proof procedure is held constant, the reference relation is seriously underdetermined. Suppose, for example, that the objects which (intuitively) are named by the ten names in L_4 are located at points on the circumference of a circle, and that X is a function which assigns to each object the object immediately on its left (facing into the circle, say). If we alter the reference specifications so that, for example,

$$Ref(\text{'}m_1\text{'}) = X(n_1)$$

and correspondingly (that is, compensatingly) alter the assignments of semantic properties to the predicates so that, for example,

$$(\forall \gamma)\,[\ulcorner P_1\gamma \urcorner \text{ is true} \leftrightarrow Q_1\,(X^{-1}\,(Ref(\gamma)))]$$

(where X^{-1} is the inverse function of X) then we can derive, by the same canonical proof procedure as before,

$$\text{'}P_1 m_1\text{'} \text{ is true} \leftrightarrow Q_1\,(X^{-1}\,(X(n_1))).$$

This is a correct truth condition specification for '$P_1 m_1$', even if '$\leftrightarrow$' is read as a strict biconditional. (The example is from Wallace, 1977.)

This example does not show that the reference relation must remain seriously underdetermined. What it shows, rather, is that we need to make use of the fact that among equally correct truth theories for L_4 some are interpretational and some are not. More adequate illumination of the concept of reference will come from the notion of an interpretational truth condition specification via the pattern of canonical derivations exhibited in the original theory for L_4. If (as we supposed) the original theory for L_4 is interpretational then the new one (with the same canonical proof procedure) is not. (Using a different canonical proof procedure one can derive the original biconditionals from the altered axioms. But that fact does not, by itself, reveal any inadequacy in the offered illumination of the concept of reference.)

Another way to approach the question of underdetermination of the reference relation is to focus upon theories of meaning rather than interpretational theories of truth, and to ask, in particular, what a theory of meaning for L_4 meeting *SC* would be like. A suitable axiom for the name 'm_1' is

$MRef$ ('m_1', n_1).

The *ML* expression 'n_1' is here used, but the position which it occupies need not admit substitution of co-referring proper names *salva veritate* (in contrast with the position which 'n_1' occupies in a reference specification). That is, even though, say, $n_1 = n_2$ it may not follow from this axiom that

$MRef$ ('m_1', n_2).

A suitable axiom for the predicate 'P_1' is

$(\forall \gamma)(\forall v) [MRef (\gamma, v) \rightarrow (\ulcorner P_1 \gamma \urcorner$ means that $Q_1 v)]$.

The quantifier '$(\forall v)$' used in this axiom is analogous to the '$(\forall p)$' and '$(\forall q)$' quantifiers used in Section II.3. The only property of the '$(\forall v)$' quantifier which is actually needed is that one can proceed from such an axiom (universally quantified in the 'v' place) to its instantiations in which particular *ML* names occupy the 'v' place. For, given that property, we have

$MRef$ ('m_1', n_1) $\rightarrow$ ('$P_1 m_1$' means that $Q_1 n_1$)

from which we can proceed to the desired meaning specification for the sentence '$P_1 m_1$'.

Suppose now that we introduce a rule (R), analogous to the rule (T) at the beginning of Chapter II.

> (R) From: $MRef (c, v)$
> infer: $Ref (c) = v$.

We can achieve the effect of the appeal to the notion of an interpretational truth theory by saying that the more adequate illumination of the concept of reference comes, via the pattern of derivations exhibited in the theory of meaning for L_4 and via the rule (R), from the illumination of the concept of meaning provided by *PAC*s such as those in

Chapter I. (The pattern of derivations is largely determined by the form of the axioms for the predicates; it is there that the connection between meaning and *MRef* is made.)

Let us then recur to the example of the function X and ask whether the concept of reference leaves the reference relation seriously under-determined. To show that the reference relation is left underdetermined one has to show that holding fixed the meanings of complete sentences, the pattern of derivations of meaning specifications, and the rule (R), one can nevertheless vary the reference relation. Suppose, for example, that $X(n_1) = n_3$. Then, there are at least two candidates for the new axiom for 'm_1' in a theory of meaning for L_4, each consistent with a reference relation according to which 'm_1' refers to $X(n_1)$ (that is, to n_3), namely

$$MRef \; ('m_1', X(n_1))$$

and

$$MRef \; ('m_1', n_3).$$

In either case, the new axiom for 'P_1' is

$$(\forall \gamma) \, (\forall \nu) \, [MRef \, (\gamma, \nu) \to (\ulcorner P_1 \gamma \urcorner \text{ means that } Q_1 \, (X^{-1} \, (\nu)))] \, .$$

A derivation in the pattern exhibited yields, in the first case,

$$'P_1 m_1' \text{ means that } Q_1 \, (X^{-1} \, (X(n_1)))$$

and, in the second case,

$$'P_1 m_1' \text{ means that } Q_1 \, (X^{-1} \, (n_3)).$$

These meaning specifications are incompatible with each other and with

$$'P_1 m_1' \text{ means that } Q_1 n_1 \, .$$

(If this is not already obvious, one only needs to consider the beliefs which speakers could be expected to have if they had as their actual language a language in which '$P_1 m_1$' meant one of these things rather than another.) So, once the concept of reference is adequately illuminated the threat of underdetermination of the reference relation is removed.

2   GENUINE SINGULAR REFERENCE

Reference is a relation between expressions and objects. If a name c

refers (in a language L) to a particular object v then the truth of atomic (subject-predicate) sentences containing the name c depends upon how things are with that object v. The kind of illumination of the concept of reference which was gestured towards in Section V.1 yields *inter alia* the consequence that the truth of '$P_1 m_1$', for example, depends upon whether the object n_1 is Q_1. Thus

'$P_1 m_1$' is true $\leftrightarrow Q_1 n_1$

where '$\leftrightarrow$' is read as the strict biconditional. The object assigned as reference to a name 'enters the truth conditions' of atomic sentences containing that name. This, in turn, has a consequence for sentences containing intensional operators such as '$\Box$'. Recall that for any sentence s the truth value and (strict) truth conditions of $\ulcorner \Box s \urcorner$ depend upon the (strict) truth conditions of s, and suppose that 'm_1' and 'm_2' both refer to the same object (that is, that $n_1 = n_2$). Then '$P_1 m_1$' and '$P_1 m_2$' are true under precisely the same conditions and so '$\Box P_1 m_1$' and '$\Box P_1 m_2$' have the same truth value, and indeed the same (strict) truth conditions. Thus, treating names in the way illustrated in Section V.1 has clear consequences for the substitutability of co-referring names *salva veritate* within the scope of intensional operators.

Let us summarize these features of the reference relation by saying that the object which is assigned to a name as its reference is *truth conditionally salient* (*tc-salient*). (The features thus summarized are stressed in e.g. Peacocke, 1975.) Tc-salience of the object assigned to a name has no immediate consequences for the substitutability of co-referring names *salva veritate* within the scope of hyperintensional operators. Even though '$P_1 m_1$' and '$P_1 m_2$' have the same truth conditions it by no means follows that they have the same meaning. So it does not follow from the fact that 'm_1' and 'm_2' refer to the same object that 'John believes that $P_1 m_1$' and 'John believes that $P_1 m_2$' have even the same truth value. That would only follow if the converse of rule (R) were an acceptable rule. And while one should certainly aim to give some account of the circumstances under which two co-referring names do, or do not, make the same contribution to meaning, the onus is all upon the person who holds that the converse of (R) is acceptable to explain why this is so (especially given that the converse of rule (T) is unacceptable).

The semantic property assigned to 'm_1' in a truth theory is not indifferent to the existence or non-existence of the object n_1. Since reference is a relation between expressions and objects, the expression

'm_1' would not have that same semantic property if n_1 were not to exist. So sentences containing 'm_1' would not have the same truth conditions that they in fact have if n_1 were not to exist. Indeed, under those circumstances those sentences would have no truth conditions (save, of course, in other languages). The rule (R) makes a close connection between the contribution which 'm_1' makes to the meanings of sentences and its contribution to truth conditions. The expression 'm_1' would not contribute to meanings as it in fact does if n_1 were not to exist. Indeed, under those circumstances sentences containing 'm_1' would have no meanings (save in other languages). The meanings of sentences containing names are *existence dependent*.

If sentences of L_4 containing 'm_1' could not mean what they in fact mean if n_1 were not to exist, then no population could have that language (containing those sentences with those meanings) as its actual language if n_1 were not to exist. But if the beliefs (and other propositional attitudes) which are involved in having L_4 as one's actual language were themselves indifferent to the existence or non-existence of n_1 then no explanation of this impossibility would be available. So (R) requires, in effect, that those beliefs (and other propositional attitudes) would themselves not survive n_1's non-existence. To assign a name a semantic property by an *MRef* axiom (related by (R) to a reference axiom) is to fit that name to play a role in the expression of beliefs of a distinctive kind, namely singular beliefs concerning a certain object to the effect that it is thus and so, beliefs which it would be impossible to have if that object were not to exist. Beliefs expressed by sentences containing names are existence dependent (McDowell, 1981, Section II):

> If an object's non-existence would not matter for the existence
> of certain thoughts, then the object's relation to those thoughts
> falls short of an intimacy which. . . sometimes characterizes
> the relation of things to thoughts, namely that the thoughts
> would not exist if the things did not. The difference between
> thoughts which have this intimate relation to objects and
> thoughts which do not is sufficiently striking to deserve to
> be marked by the stipulation that only the former should
> count as being in the strictest sense about objects.

Let us summarize these features of the reference relation (the existence dependence of meanings and of beliefs) by saying that the object which is assigned to a name as its reference is *epistemologically salient* (*e-salient*). (The features thus summarized are stressed in e.g. McDowell, 1977.)

A relation between names and objects such that the object which is assigned to a name is both tc-salient and e-salient deserves to be called *genuine singular reference*. It is then an empirical question whether a certain expression of a natural language in use is a genuine singular referring expression; having the syntactic form of a proper name is neither a necessary nor a sufficient condition. A principled answer to this empirical question in any given case requires an answer to the more general question under what conditions it is possible for a person to have a singular belief concerning an object. This is, indeed, a difficult question, but without giving anything like a complete answer one might reasonably adopt two partial answers (one negative, one positive) for the case in which the object is a medium-sized material object (a chair, a cat, or a man). The negative partial answer is that if a person is totally causally isolated from the object then he can have no singular beliefs concerning it. The positive partial answer is that if a person has had frequent perceptual (particularly visual) contact with the object and is able reliably (although perhaps not infallibly) to recognize the object as the same object again then he can have singular beliefs concerning it. Part of the difficulty of the question is that in order to deal with intermediate cases (for which the partial answers are not adequate) one needs to make a motivated extension of the notion of perceptual contact. One very plausible view is that perceptual contact is a central kind of information yielding causal transaction; the extension would then be to causal interactions of a kind suitable for yielding information (and sometimes misinformation) (see Evans, 1973 and McDowell, 1977, pp. 184-5).

Let us say that a genuine singular reference theorist (*GSR* theorist) is someone who accepts at least these partial answers to the difficult question about singular belief, and holds that names of material objects which are not causally remote may have the semantic function of genuine singular reference. A *GSR* theorist stands in contrast to someone who holds that the contribution to meanings made by a name (for short: the meaning of a name) is purely descriptive, and so holds that the meanings of sentences containing a name are indifferent to the existence or non-existence of any object which may (because it fits the description) be assigned to the name as its reference. This latter view about meaning leads to a characteristic view about the beliefs expressed by sentences containing a name, namely that those beliefs are themselves indifferent to the existence or non-existence of any object which may be assigned to the name as its reference. According to such an opponent, a *GSR* theorist faces two difficult cases: (i) empty names and (ii) co-referring names. Let us consider these in turn.

(i)   One consequence of the *GSR* theorist's position is that a person who uses what is syntactically a name in making an utterance which he takes to be an assertion about an object, and an expression of a singular belief concerning an object, may be quite radically mistaken. For if the name has, after all, no reference then the sentence which he uses really has no meaning and there is no such singular belief as that which he takes himself to express. The supposed difficulty is that the possibility of such a radical error goes against the intuition that a man knows what he himself means and knows what he himself believes. If this intuition were correct then genuine singular reference would be possible only for a very restricted range of objects, perhaps oneself or one's present stage, and one's present experiences. And this much in the way of genuine singular reference and so of singular belief may well be allowed by the opponent, whose view would then be that there are hardly any (rather than no) singular beliefs (see e.g. Schiffer, 1978, especially at p. 200).

It is, of course, no part of the *GSR* theorist's position that someone who makes such a radical error (as a result of a name's lacking a reference) has no relevant beliefs at all. Such a person may have plenty of relevant general beliefs, for general beliefs are indifferent to the existence or non-existence of particular objects. What is characteristic of the *GSR* theorist is the claim that not all beliefs are general beliefs; there are, in addition, singular beliefs.

If the intuition that there can be no illusion of understanding and no illusion of belief is to count against the *GSR* theorist, then the intuition must be supported by an argument. Yet it is exceedingly difficult to see how such an argument can be given without simply begging the question against the *GSR* theorist and insisting from the outset that (almost) all beliefs are general beliefs. And the intuition will perhaps seem even less secure if we consider an analogy between illusion and pretence. Suppose that a group of people decide to pretend that there is an object with which they have frequent perceptual contact (perhaps, that there is a man frequently to be seen about the village who has mysterious powers). They pretend to name the object and pretend to make assertions about it and to express beliefs and other propositional attitudes concerning it. (Perhaps they introduce the name

'Alfred' and come out with such utterances as 'I saw Alfred this morning and he looked angry' and 'Alfred has made it rain again'.) It is easy to agree that precisely because their linguistic practice rests upon a pretence, in reality the expression is not a name, in reality they are not making assertions, and in reality they have no such singular propositional attitudes. Suppose that another group of people are under an illusion that there is an object with which they have frequent perceptual contact. They believe that they have named the object and consequently believe that they make assertions about it and express propositional attitudes concerning it. It ought to be equally easy to agree in this case that precisely because their linguistic practice rests upon an illusion, in reality the expression is not a name, in reality they are not making assertions, and in reality they have no such singular propositional attitudes. (Cf. Frege, 1892, pp. 62–3 and McDowell, 1981.)

(ii)   One way of making vivid the idea that singular beliefs are not indifferent to the existence or non-existence of the objects which they concern is to represent the content of such a belief as an ordered pair of an object and a property. The content of a belief that $Q_1 n_1$ would be represented as $<n_1, \text{ being } Q_1>$. This ordered pair would not exist if n_1 were not to exist. (Cf. Donnellan, 1974, p. 225.)

Given that representation it follows that all singular beliefs concerning n_1 to the effect that it is Q_1 have the same content. And if all such beliefs have the same content then one ought to be able to substitute co-referring names within hyperintensional operators (such as 'John believes that') *salva veritate*. So it may seem that the *GSR* theorist can make nothing of the idea that someone might believe that $Q_1 n_1$ but not believe that $Q_1 n_2$ even though $n_1 = n_2$.

This supposed difficulty (as presented) depends upon assimilating genuine singular reference to something rather different which might be called *direct reference*. According to a direct reference theorist meaning cuts no finer than reference in the case of names; (roughly) the meaning is the object referred to. But the *GSR* theorist's opponent may well respond that although genuine singular reference can be distinguished from direct reference, the *GSR* theorist occupies an unstable middle position between the direct reference theorist on one side and the opponent on the other. For, he may say, if two co-referring names are to have different meanings then those meanings must be descriptive. A belief about the object which is assigned to both names as their reference must be a belief about the object thought of as, say, the *F*. But then the (allegedly singular) belief concerning x

(thought of as the F), to the effect that it is thus and so, is nothing other than the belief that the F is thus and so (that is, the belief that whichever object is uniquely F is thus and so). And that is a purely general belief.

The opponent's response will be seen at its best if we focus upon a certain familiar example. 'Hesperus' and 'Phosphorus' might be held by a *GSR* theorist to be two names with the same reference, namely the planet Venus, but with different meanings. The opponent's response, applied to this example, is that once one moves away from the (direct reference theorist's) view that the sentence 'Hesperus is not Phosphorus' has the same meaning as (and so expresses the same belief as) the sentence 'Hesperus is not Hesperus', one must introduce some descriptive meaning for the two names, and say that 'Hesperus' has as a component of its meaning the meaning of a description 'the H' and that 'Phosphorus' has as a component of its meaning the meaning of a description 'the P'. And, the opponent may conclude, once one has introduced those descriptive components one will have to admit that the belief expressed by 'Hesperus is not Phosphorus' is precisely the (purely general) belief that the H is not the P (that is, the belief that whatever is uniquely H is not also uniquely P). Simon Blackburn (1979, pp.30-1) has put the opponent's view very clearly.

> We all know, in these stories, what is going on. The Babylonians were deceived by the separate appearances of Hesperus. . . .
> All we have to do to know what is going on is to incorporate this into our ascription of belief: the Babylonians believed that the thing (appearing in way 1) was not identical with the thing (appearing in way 2).

But although the opponent's view can be stated quite persuasively, there are clearly two points at which his response to the *GSR* theorist would need to be filled out. One is the claim that some descriptive component must be introduced into the meanings of proper names. The other is the claim that if the meaning of a name has a descriptive component then beliefs expressed by sentences containing the name are purely general. Neither of these steps is at all obvious.

If two co-referring names are to differ in meaning then certainly sentences which differ only in which of the two names is used must have different meanings, and so via the actual language relation must be used to express different beliefs (that is, beliefs with different contents). It is intuitively sufficient for two beliefs concerning the same object (to the effect that it is thus and so) to have different contents that having those beliefs should involve thinking about the same object in two different ways. (In this connection, Frege, 1892, spoke of differing *modes of presentation* of the same object.) And it is intuitively sufficient for two beliefs concerning the same object (to the effect that it is thus and so) to involve thinking about the object in two different ways that those beliefs should be systematically sensitive to two different kinds of evidence (involving that same object). So suppose that the two names 'Hesperus' and 'Phosphorus' are associated with two different ways of thinking about the planet Venus (or, perhaps better, with two mutually exclusive ranges of ways of thinking about the planet Venus). Suppose (what is intuitively sufficient for this) that mastery of the two names 'Hesperus' and 'Phosphorus' involves two quite different dispositions to form beliefs; a disposition to form beliefs (which one expresses using 'Hesperus') on the basis of evidence which, as the theorist might put it, involves the planet Venus as seen in the evening, and a disposition to form beliefs (which one expresses using 'Phosphorus') on the basis of evidence which, as the theorist might put it, involves the planet Venus as seen in the morning. Despite the theorist's description of these dispositions, there is no evident reason why having such dispositions should involve having, or bringing to bear, the concepts of evening and morning. So there is no immediate move from the idea that 'Hesperus' and 'Phosphorus' might differ in meaning in this way, to the idea that the meaning of 'Hesperus', for example, should have as a component the meaning of 'the heavenly body which appears in the evening'. In fact there is no reason why, in order to have a disposition of the kind we are considering, one must antecedently have in mind a description and judge the relevance of evidence involving an object according as that object fits or fails to fit that description (see McDowell, 1977, pp. 176-8 and Evans, forthcoming a).

Nevertheless, the opponent might be able to fill the first gap in his response. For if someone has a disposition to form 'Hesperus' expressed beliefs on the basis of evidence involving Venus as seen in the evening, then (it is plausible to hold) that person has all the conceptual apparatus he needs for the introduction of a predicate 'H' which applies to any object according as that object appears in the way in which Venus appears on the occasions which are evidentially relevant to 'Hesperus' expressed beliefs. So there is a description 'the H' which, although it is not antecedently available, is such that thinking about Venus in the 'Hesperus' way is (plausibly) thinking about Venus as the *H*. We shall call 'H' a *WT predicate*.

Let us simply grant that, at least in the case of this familiar example, the opponent has filled the first gap in his response to the *GSR* theorist. Then, to fill the second gap, he must show that believing concerning Hesperus (that is, concerning Venus), as the *H*, that it is thus and so is just believing that the *H* is thus and so. Schiffer (1978, p. 184) claims that, in a case in which the believer believes that there is a unique *H*, this second gap can be filled:

> [S] uppose that Ralph knows that there is just one *H*, and
> believes Venus to be thus and so under the description '*H*'. This
> belief . . . reduces to his belief that *the H is thus and so.*
> I have altered Schiffer's example.)

This is no argument. But perhaps the opponent may advance an argument as follows. To explain how the belief that Hesperus is Phosphorus can be different from the belief that Hesperus is Hesperus one must reveal the information value of the first as different from that of the second. If this difference is a product of the difference between the meanings of the descriptions 'the *H*' and 'the *P*' then surely the content of the first belief is just that the *H* is the *P* (that is, that a single object is both uniquely *H* and uniquely *P*).

To this argument the *GSR* theorist may reply that in general the best way to specify the content of a belief which a man expresses in his use of a certain sentence is to use a sentence which has the same meaning as that man's sentence; to say, 'He believes that . . .' where what fills the gap is a sentence of the reporter's language with the same meaning as the used sentence of the believer's language. Indeed, this is the only way except in those cases where the believer is thinking about an object in some relatively specific way and uses, in the expression of his belief, a proper name which is associated with a less specific way, or a wider range of ways, of thinking about that object. In such a case it might be possible to use an expression (another proper name or perhaps a demonstrative) associated with the more specific way of thinking about the object, in order to specify more finely the content of the man's belief. In either case (unless the question is to be begged against the *GSR* theorist) faithful specifications of singular beliefs expressed using proper names will themselves employ proper names or other genuine singular referring expressions. And this should not create a puzzle unless one is absolutely in the grip of the ordered pair conception of the content of singular beliefs. Once one is free from the grip of that conception (as the *GSR* theorist is free from it) the notion of a way of thinking about an object will account for the possibility that someone may believe that Hesperus is thus and so without believing that Phosphorus is thus and so.

3   DESCRIPTION THEORIES OF NAMES

The *GSR* theorist's opponent is a description theorist. In fact, two kinds of description theorist can be distinguished; the first makes a clear semantic proposal while the second does not. According to a description theorist of the first kind (such as the opponent described in Section V.2) each proper name has the same meaning as some definite description. This is a clear semantic proposal: for any population which has as its actual language a language containing a name of a certain object there is a description which that object uniquely fits, such that the meaning of the name in that population is just the meaning of that description.

A description theorist of this first kind must avoid two putative objections. The first is that the description theorist pays too little respect to the unreflective nature of mastery of a name. The description which is offered as giving the meaning of a name must not be such as to involve the attribution to members of the population of a degree of conceptual sophistication which is clearly not required for mastery of the name. Thus, in the 'Hesperus' case, it would be an error to offer the description 'the heavenly body which appears in the evening'. But at least in this case, the description theorist can avoid this first putative objection by offering a conceptually more modest description, perhaps indeed the description 'the '*H*'' (making use of a predicate furnished by a way of thinking, or range of ways of thinking, about the object named, that is, a *WT* predicate). The second putative objection is that the description theorist pays too little respect to the tc-salience of the object which is assigned to a name as its reference. For almost any description 'the *F*' which the description theorist offers as giving the meaning of a name c, the sentence $\ulcorner \Diamond(c \text{ is not } F)\urcorner$ is clearly true, while $\ulcorner \Diamond(\text{the } F \text{ is not } F)\urcorner$ has a false reading. This objection can be overcome. The technical details must wait until Part Three (see, in particular, Section IX.3), but it suffices for now to imagine that a particular kind of definite description beginning with 'the*' is tailored to have the property that the truth, even with respect to counterfactual situations, of 'the* F is thus and so' turns upon how things are with the object which is actually uniquely F. This has the consequence that if c is a name of an object which is (actually) uniquely F, then $\ulcorner\Diamond (c$ is thus and so$)\urcorner$ has the same truth value as $\ulcorner\Diamond$ (the* F is thus and so$)\urcorner$ and $\ulcorner\Box (c$ is thus and so$)\urcorner$ has the same truth value as $\ulcorner\Box$ (the* F is thus and so$)\urcorner$. Thus, in the case of 'Hesperus' both putative objections can be avoided by offering the description 'the* H' as giving the meaning of the name.

The description theorist's semantic proposal is, nevertheless, not credible. For each name he must provide (even in cases in which members of the population are none too reflective about their own sensitivity to evidence) a description 'the F' which plausibly gives the meaning of the name in the shared language of the population (so that, at least, the named object is uniquely F), and such that members of the population believe that there is a unique F (because if a member of the population did not believe that there is a unique F then he would not believe that the (unique) F is thus and so). He then faces a dilemma. Either he looks to a *WT* predicate, or else he does not. If he does look to a *WT* predicate then he faces the difficulty that, to the extent that mastery of a name requires thinking about the named object in a particular way, that way may be highly unspecific. Consequently, if 'F' is introduced as a *WT* predicate then it is not generally the case that the named object is uniquely F, and it is not generally the case that members of the population believe that there is a unique F. (Concentration upon 'Hesperus' and 'Phosphorus' may obscure this very obvious point. That is why those names provide the description theorist's most favoured case.) If on the other hand he looks to some predicate other than a *WT* predicate then he faces an equally serious difficulty. For if c is a name and 'F' is not a *WT* predicate then, in general, the belief which is expressed by 'c is F' is a belief which could have been incorrect even though some object was uniquely F. The description theorist is unable to say in what that incorrectness would have consisted.

There is a feature of this dilemma which may suggest a line of counterattack for the description theorist. For the difficulty raised in the second horn of the dilemma does not apply to *WT* predicates. Indeed, there are no very obvious difficulties for the description theorist in his most favoured case, when he does look to *WT* predicates. (This is not to say that one must accept the description theorist's proposal in that most favoured case; his argument had a serious gap.) So the description theorist might launch a counterattack by claiming that the first horn is itself disastrous for the *GSR* theorist. For suppose that 'Bert' and 'Harry' are two names of the same man, each associated with the same highly unspecific way, or wide range of ways, of thinking about that man. Then one could believe that Bert is thus and so and fail to believe that Harry is thus and so, by failing to realize that Bert and Harry are the same man. And it seems that the *GSR* theorist is unable to offer any account of the content of the two beliefs which explains how someone can have one belief without the other (cf. Kripke, 1979 and Schiffer, 1978, p. 184).

This is indeed a puzzle, but not a puzzle which is particularly relevant to the *GSR* theorist. 'Bert' and 'Harry' are synonymous names: *ex hypothesi* they have the same meaning. A man may master each of these names (know the meaning of each name) and yet sincerely assent to 'Bert is rich' but sincerely dissent from 'Harry is rich' (not know that they mean the same). This phenomenon, although puzzling, has nothing especially to do with names. In general it is possible to know the meaning of each of two synonymous expressions without knowing that they mean the same. One way of drawing attention to this phenomenon is to point to the apparent failure of substitutivity of synonyms *salva veritate* within such operators as 'John believes that' (cf. Burge, 1978). Some account must be given of this phenomenon as it occurs in general, and whatever account is given can be applied to the case of names. Thus, for example, one might adopt the position that strictly and literally synonyms can be substituted *salva veritate* in belief contexts, but that when someone reports a man's belief using that man's own language it is usually assumed (because it is usually correct to assume) that the man would, if sincere, assent to the sentence used in the specification of the content of the belief. On such an account the man who believes that Bert is rich believes that Harry is rich. He fails to assent to 'Harry is rich' because he fails to realize that the sentence expresses one of his beliefs. In any case, the counterattack by the description theorist of the first kind fails, and his semantic proposal is not credible. (See Appendix 4.)

A description theorist of the second kind is not primarily concerned to make a semantic proposal. His theory is primarily a theory about thought, that is, about the propositional attitudes of individual speakers. His main claim is that there are (almost) no singular beliefs (again an exception may be made for singular beliefs concerning oneself or one's present stage, and one's present experiences).

It may consistently (though perhaps misleadingly) be allowed by such a theorist that a man may be reported as believing, for example, that Whitlam is modest, or even as believing concerning Whitlam that he is modest. Such a report will be correct just in case the man has a general belief that the object (or perhaps, an object) which is . . . is modest, and this belief is related in a certain way to the man Whitlam. The nature of the required relation may be varied to yield various different description theories of thought. One possibility is that the relation should be one of fit: the descriptive material (filling the gap marked by ' . . . ') should fit the man Whitlam. Another possibility is that the relation should be a causal one (a generalization of the information yielding relation involved in perception): the general belief should stand in a certain causal relation to the man Whitlam. Other possibilities lie between these two. In any case, the crucial feature of a description theory of thought is that, even if it allows a certain kind of belief ascription which might be called singular belief ascription, such ascription is not ascription of singular beliefs.

A description theory of thought is not primarily a semantic theory. Blackburn (1979, p. 31) suggests, for example, that semantic questions are questions about a technical notion of belief expression which is quite unrelated to a theory of thought:

> The semantic problem here is to decide whether we should
> attribute a meaning (or a truth-condition) to sentences in which
> the name is used. . . when there is nobody to serve as referent.
> Suppose that we remain faithful to the directly referential
> account. . . and grasp the nettle: sentences using such a name are
> given no truth-condition. [If speakers use such sentences] then they
> literally express no beliefs at all. . . . [T]his solves the semantic
> problem. . . but leaves the philosophy in a very embryonic state.

It is, however, a mistake to hold that a semantic theory and a theory of thought are independent. For suppose that someone decides upon the solution to the semantic problem about empty names which Blackburn countenances. It follows that certain sentences of our language would not have meant what they in fact mean if certain objects had not existed. (Indeed, under those circumstances no sentences would have meant what those sentences of our language in fact mean.) And as we saw in Section V.2 this leads, via any account of the actual language relation in a Gricean spirit, to the conclusion that we would not have had just the propositional attitudes which we in fact have if certain objects had not existed, a conclusion quite inconsistent with a description theory of thought. It is, of course, open to a description theorist of the second kind to offer a different account of the actual language relation, no longer in terms of propositional attitudes. But until such an account is forthcoming any description theorist who makes a semantic proposal such as that countenanced by Blackburn will seem to have 'ignored the connection between semantics and psychology' (Schiffer, 1978, p. 175).

If the connection between semantics and psychology (between semantics and propositional attitudes) is respected, then serious difficulties arise for description theories of thought. Whatever the details of one's account of this connection one must make room for the idea that in a sincere assertion a speaker expresses a belief, so that the assertion is true or false according as the expressed belief is correct or incorrect. Suppose that someone has had frequent perceptual contact with Whitlam and has thereby built up a dossier, a mixture of information and misinformation, which he labels with the name 'Whitlam'. Suppose that the descriptive material in the dossier fits a certain Johnson far better than it fits Whitlam. And suppose that our man sincerely comes out with 'Whitlam is modest'. What has he asserted, and on what does the truth of his assertion turn? If the relation which is relevant to singular belief ascription is a relation of fit then our man may be reported as believing that Johnson is modest and so, presumably, as asserting that Johnson is modest. The truth of the assertion depends upon whether Johnson is modest. If on the other hand the relation is a causal one then our man may be reported as believing that Whitlam is modest and so, presumably, as asserting that Whitlam is modest. The truth of the assertion depends upon whether Whitlam is modest.

The first answer takes seriously the fact that our man's belief is, according to the description theory, the purely general belief that the object (or perhaps, an object) which is . . . is modest. And it takes seriously the connection between correct belief and true assertion. But as an answer to the question about assertion the first answer is, as Evans says, 'outrageous'. For it has the consequence that

if I was previously innocent of knowledge or belief regarding Whitlam, and Johnson is wrongly introduced to me as Whitlam, then I must speak the truth in uttering 'Whitlam is here' since

107

Johnson satisfies the overwhelming majority of descriptions I would associate with the name and Johnson is here. (Evans, 1973, pp. 194-5; I have altered the example.)

The second answer, on the other hand, is a plausible answer to the question about assertion. Suppose that Whitlam is not modest and that Johnson is modest. Then the assertion is false. But the second answer leaves the description theorist unable to give any account of our man's error in belief which led to this sincere but false assertion. For his belief is the general belief that the object (or perhaps, an object) which is ... is modest, and that belief is correct. Conversely suppose that Whitlam is modest and that Johnson is not modest. Then the assertion is true. But the belief that the object (or an object) which is ... is modest is incorrect. It is certainly the case that our man may believe correctly that someone is modest; so if he makes a sincere true assertion then he has at least one correct belief. But to the extent that this fact is allowed to comfort the description theorist in this case it makes his difficulties in the former case more acute (cf. Blackburn, 1979, p. 35).

The description theorist may, finally, attempt to avoid the difficulties arising from these two possible answers by incorporating the attractive features of the second answer into the first. He may suggest incorporating into the descriptive material which must fit an object (according to the first answer) the predicate 'object which stands in such and such an information yielding causal relation to my "Whitlam" labelled dossier', and he may suggest that fit in respect of this predicate be allowed to outweigh lack of fit in respect of other predicates. But this is a deeply unattractive suggestion, for the conceptual sophistication which it requires of speakers (by requiring mastery of the concept of a certain, rather closely circumscribed, kind of causal relation) is very great. What is more, it is difficult to see how the description theorist can revise the suggestion (to avoid this objection) without either reintroducing the problem that the descriptive material may fit the wrong object or else smuggling into the descriptive material a predicate making use of the notion of a genuinely singular belief.

4   REFERENCE AND PREDICATES

Names refer to objects. The semantic function of names is that of genuine singular reference, and we have some grasp upon that notion at least in the (arguably central) case of genuine singular reference to medium-sized material objects (chairs, cats, or men). Names go together with predicates to form atomic (subject-predicate) sentences. So it is natural to ask whether the semantic function of predicates is anything like genuine singular reference.

To ask this question is not to ask whether predicates are names. It is a familiar point that if predicates were treated as names then one would be left without an account of the difference between a sentence and a list. A predicate is, rather, assigned a semantic property which precisely fits it to go together with a name (or a pair of names) to form a sentence with a meaning and with truth conditions. This latter fact may suggest an easy answer to the original question. For, it may be said, the assignment of a semantic property to the predicate 'is modest' does not involve the assignment to that predicate of an object to which it might stand in a relation analogous to that of genuine singular reference; the predicate 'is modest' is merely true of objects according as those objects are or are not modest. But one must not leap too hastily from the claim that predicates are not names to the claim that predicates are not assigned objects. Certainly a predicate must be assigned a semantic property of a kind different from that assigned to names. Certainly the assignment of such a semantic property need not involve the explicit correlation of an expression and an object. But the assignment to a predicate of a semantic property by which it contributes to the truth conditions of sentences in which it occurs, as for example

$$(\forall \gamma) \, [\ulcorner P_1 \gamma \urcorner \text{ is true} \leftrightarrow Q_1 \, (Ref(\gamma))]$$

can be reformulated as

$$(\forall \gamma) \, [\ulcorner P_1 \gamma \urcorner \text{ is true} \leftrightarrow Ref(\gamma) \in \{x : Q_1 x\}]$$

in which there is explicit correlation of an expression and a set (waiving any difficulties which may arise because of the vagueness of predicates), or as

$$(\forall \gamma) \, [\ulcorner P_1 \gamma \urcorner \text{ is true} \leftrightarrow Ref(\gamma) \text{ exemplifies being } Q_1]$$

in which there is explicit correlation of an expression and a property (or an attribute, or a universal). So the original, natural, question can be asked again. Is the relation of a predicate to its correlated set (its extension) or to its correlated property anything like the relation of genuine singular reference? Let us consider the set and the property in turn.

The relation between the predicate 'is modest' and the set of modest things (call this set 'M') is strikingly unlike the relation of genuine singular reference. First, the truth with respect to counterfactual situations of sentences containing 'is modest' does not turn upon how things are with the set M. If Whitlam is in fact modest then Whitlam is a member of M. But although Whitlam might not have been modest, so that the sentence 'Whitlam is modest' comes out false with respect to some counterfactual situations, Whitlam could not have failed to be a member of M. With respect to counterfactual situations it is sets other than M which are relevant to the truth or falsity of 'Whitlam is modest'. What is more, it is obviously not the case that if two predicates are correlated with the same set then one can be substituted for the other *salva veritate* within intensional operators. In short, the set correlated with a predicate is not tc-salient. Second, the semantic property assigned to the predicate 'is modest' is indifferent to the existence or non-existence of the set M. Suppose (for the purpose of the example) that Nixon is in fact modest. Then, since a set's existence depends upon the existence of its members, if Nixon had not existed then the set M would not have existed. But intuitively the predicate 'is modest' would have made just the contribution to the meanings of sentences which it in fact makes had Nixon not existed. Corresponding to this intuition via the actual language relation is the striking implausibility of the claim that the belief that Whitlam is modest is a belief which it would be impossible to have if Nixon were not to exist. In short, the set correlated with a predicate is not e-salient.

To assign a predicate a semantic property by which it contributes to the meanings of sentences in which it occurs is not to fit that predicate to play a role in the expression of singular beliefs concerning a certain set. To sharpen this point a little we might reflect upon the introduction of a name of a set. If a name of a material object is to be introduced then the surest way is to introduce it via the sort of perceptual contact with the object which will enable a person using the name reliably to identify the object as the same again, that is, will make a person sensitive to the difference between that object and others. This introduction of a name with the semantic function of genuine singular reference stands in contrast to the introduction of an expression which has the syntactic form of a name by some such ruling as 'Let us call whichever object is uniquely F "Jim"'. In this latter case the introduction does not permit the expression of beliefs any less general than those which could be expressed before the introduction. The introduction of what is syntactically a name by the ruling 'Let us call whichever set has as members precisely the modest objects "*M*"' is similar to the second kind of introduction. One could adopt such a ruling without knowing which set had precisely those members. What seems to correspond, in the case of a set, to the perceptual contact which enables one to reidentify a material object is exhaustive knowledge of the membership of the set. Such knowledge would make a person sensitive to the difference between that set and others, and would enable a person to use a name whose relation to the set was that of genuine singular reference. The fact that such knowledge is not required for mastery of the predicate 'is modest' corresponds to the absence of e-salience in respect of the relation between a predicate and its extension.

The relation between the predicate 'is modest' and the property of being modest (modesty) is rather more like the relation of genuine singular reference. First, the truth with respect to counterfactual situations of sentences containing 'is modest' turns upon how things are with the property of being modest. This is so whichever of two possible decisions one takes as to how finely properties are to be discriminated. One possible decision treats 'property' as co-ordinate with 'proposition', so that two predicates are correlated with the same property just in case they are synonymous. The other possible decision treats differences of meaning amongst broadly logically equivalent predicates as corresponding to different ways of thinking about the same property, so that two predicates are correlated with the same property just in case they are broadly logically equivalent. One's actual decision would be answerable to broader theoretical concerns (as perhaps the appeal to properties in scientific explanation). But in either case if two predicates are correlated with the same property then one can be substituted for the other *salva veritate* within intensional operators. In short, the property correlated with a predicate is tc-salient. Second, the semantic property assigned to the predicate 'is modest' is not indifferent to the existence or non-existence of the property of being modest. If there were no such thing as being modest then the predicate 'is modest' would not contribute to the meanings of sentences as it in fact does. Correspondingly, the belief that Whitlam is modest is a belief which it would be impossible to have if there were no such thing as being modest. In short, the property correlated with a predicate is e-salient.

The relation between the predicate 'is modest' and the property of being modest is thus analogous to the relation of genuine singular reference which would hold between a name ('modesty') and that property. To express the point, one naturally reaches for Strawson's (1959, pp. 146-7) terminology. A name and a predicate may *introduce* the same object, namely the same property; the difference between the name and the predicate is not in what is introduced but in the *style of introduction*.

One must acknowledge, however, that the presence of e-salience in respect of the relation between a predicate and a property is simply a product of the fact that we have no grasp on the existence or non-existence of the property of being modest, for example, independent of its being possible or impossible meaningfully to say of things that they are (or are not) modest. (The thinness of this requirement for existence raises a puzzle over what it is that philosophers deny when they deny that properties exist.) What corresponds, in the case of the property of being modest, to the sort of perceptual contact with a material object which makes a person sensitive to the difference between that object and others is just learning what it is for things to be modest. It is this which makes a person sensitive to the difference between that property and others.

Thus, even while one draws an analogy (in the basic case of subject-predicate sentences) between the relation of genuine singular reference to material objects on one hand, and the relation between a predicate and a property on the other, one cannot fail to be impressed by a disanalogy between material objects and the properties which they exemplify. (It is presumably this disanalogy which prompts the claim that properties do not exist.)

> It might be said: . . . we could view [material] particulars as principles of distinction among concepts [properties]. In relation to any given particular at any time, we could sort concepts into those it exemplified at that time and the rest. For an answer to this it is enough to revert to our question of the form: what ultimately differentiates one particular from another, one general concept from another? Concepts are ultimately differentiated just *as* the principles of distinction among particulars that they are. But particulars could not begin to serve as principles of distinction among concepts unless we had some other way of identifying and differentiating them. We . . . ultimately differentiate them . . . by their exclusive occupation of a tract of physical space-time. (Strawson, 1974a, p. 19.)

112

A property collects objects into its extension, and one property is distinguished from another just by being a different way of collecting objects. In the case of sensitivity to the difference between being modest and other properties, there is nothing more to be grasped than the principle of collection (and distinction) by which modest objects are collected and immodest objects excluded. In the case of sensitivity to the difference between one material object and others there is something to be grasped prior to any principle of collection of properties which a material object may (derivatively) furnish. One has to grasp the notion of a certain kind of (contingent) occupant of space and time.

NOTES

In this chapter I am particularly indebted to several conversations with Simon Blackburn and John McDowell. The account of genuine singular reference is essentially that of McDowell (1977) and (1981). McDowell (1978) is a reply to Field (1972). See also Davidson (1977b).

More generally on the topics of this chapter, see Russell (1918, pp. 241-54), Searle (1958), Donnellan (1972), Kripke (1972), and Sainsbury (1979, pp. 57-94). On the subject-predicate distinction, see Strawson (1959, pp. 137-247), (1961), and (1970b). For what is, in effect, the use of 'the*' see, for example, Plantinga (1978).

VI

QUANTIFIERS

1 TRUTH AND SATISFACTION

The languages which we have considered have been syntactically very simple. In each case it has been possible to give a formally straightforward theory of truth conditions and theory of meaning. It is time to consider a quantificational language.

Let L_6 be a language whose atomic sentences are constructed from the one-place predicates 'P_1', ..., 'P_{10}', the two-place predicates 'R_1', ..., 'R_{10}', and the names 'm_1', ..., 'm_{10}'. Further, L_6 contains the truth functional connectives '&', 'v', '→', and '∼'. Finally, L_6 contains the two familiar quantifiers 'V' and 'Ǝ' together with associated variables 'v_1', 'v_2', ... The syntactic rule which governs the quantifiers can be stated as follows. If A is a (possibly complex) sentence in which a name c occurs at least once and in which $\ulcorner v_i \urcorner$ (the ith variable) does not occur, then the result of replacing c at some or all of its occurrences by $\ulcorner v_i \urcorner$ and prefixing the resultant string with $\ulcorner (Vv_i) \urcorner$ or $\ulcorner (Ǝv_i) \urcorner$ is itself a sentence (in which $\ulcorner v_i \urcorner$ occurs as a bound variable). In the complex sentences constructed in accordance with this rule the truth functional connectives have a new syntactic role, for they occur between (or in the case of '∼' in front of) expressions which are not themselves sentences. Thus, along with

$$P_1 m_1 \ \& \ R_1 (m_2, m_3)$$
$$(Vv_1)P_1 v_1 \ \& \ (Ǝv_2)R_1 (m_2, v_2)$$
$$(Vv_1)P_1 v_1 \ \& \ (Vv_1)(Ǝv_2)R_1 (v_1, v_2)$$

we have

114

$$(\forall v_1)(P_1 v_1 \ \& \ R_1(m_2, v_1))$$
$$(\forall v_1)(P_1 v_1 \ \& \ (\exists v_2) R_1(v_2, v_1))$$
$$(\forall v_1)(\exists v_2)(P_1 v_1 \ \& \ R_1(v_2, v_1)).$$

The fact that the connectives have this new role and yet are not ambiguous calls for a degree of sophistication in a semantic theory and, in particular, in a theory of truth conditions. If we are to continue to regard the connectives as fundamentally operators upon sentences then a way has to be found of deriving their contributions to the truth conditions of quantified sentences such as

$$(\forall v_1)(P_1 v_1 \ \& \ R_1(m_2, v_1))$$

in which '&' joins '$P_1 v_1$' and '$R_1(m_2, v_1)$' (which are not sentences and do not have truth conditions), from the familiar axioms which speak only of sentences and truth (see Evans, 1977, p. 471).

A first thought might be this:

'$(\forall v_1)(P_1 v_1 \ \& \ R_1(m_2, v_1))$' is true (in L_6) iff every object (in the domain of quantification) is such that if a name (in L_6) of that object is substituted for 'v_1' in '$P_1 v_1 \ \& \ R_1(m_2, v_1)$' then the result is a sentence which is true (in L_6).

Here the truth conditions of a quantified sentence are specified in terms of the truth conditions of subject-predicate sentences. The connective '&' is certainly regarded as fundamentally an operator upon sentences. But since L_6 contains names of only ten objects and not (we may suppose) of all objects in the domain of quantification, the truth condition specification is incorrect. Objects which are in the domain of quantification but which have no name (in L_6) vacuously meet the condition following 'such that'.

One way around this difficulty is to introduce, as a technical auxiliary, an extended language L^+ containing a name of each object in the domain of quantification of L_6. Thus L^+ is to be a language with two important features. First, its quantifier-free part is an extension of the quantifier-free part of L_6, in the sense that L^+ contains all the predicates, names and connectives of L_6 with the same meanings. Second, L^+ contains a name of each object in the intended domain of quantification of L_6. The idea is then to specify the truth conditions of quantified sentences of L_6 by appealing to L^+. For example,

$$Tr(L_6, \text{'}(\forall v_1) P_1 v_1\text{'}) \leftrightarrow$$
$$(\forall x)(\forall \gamma \in L^+)(Ref(L^+, \gamma) = x \to Tr(L^+, \ulcorner P_1 \ \gamma \urcorner)).$$

('*Tr* $(L_6, \ldots)$' abbreviates '... is true (in L_6)'. The quantifier '$(\forall x)$' is a quantifier in the *ML* whose domain of quantification is exactly that of the *OL* quantifiers. The quantifier '$(\forall \gamma \in L^+)$' ranges over names in L^+. It is made explicit, here and henceforth, that the reference relation holds only relative to a language.) Since the predicate 'P_1' has the same meaning in L^+ as in L_6, and since biconditionals such as

$$Tr\,(L_6, \text{'}P_1 m_1\text{'}) \leftrightarrow Q_1 n_1$$

are assumed to be interpretational, we have

$$(\forall \gamma \in L^+)\,[Tr\,(L^+, \ulcorner P_1\,\gamma \urcorner) \leftrightarrow Q_1\,(Ref(L^+, \gamma))].$$

And since L^+ contains a name of each object we have

$$(\forall x)\,(\exists \gamma \in L^+)\,Ref(L^+, \gamma) = x.$$

Given these it is not difficult to derive

$$Tr\,(L_6, \text{'}(\forall v_1)P_1 v_1\text{'}) \leftrightarrow (\forall x)Q_1 x.$$

However, the matter is complicated by the fact that a sentence of L_6 may contain several quantifiers. Consider, for example,

$$\begin{aligned}Tr\,(L_6, \ulcorner(\forall v_1)(\exists v_2)R_1\,(v_1, v_2)\urcorner) &\leftrightarrow\\ (\forall x)\,(\forall \gamma \in L^+)\,(Ref(L^+, \gamma) = x &\rightarrow\\ Tr\,(L^+, \ulcorner(\exists v_2)\,R_1\,(\gamma, v_2)\urcorner)).\end{aligned}$$

To proceed further we need to be told about the truth (in L^+) conditions of quantified sentences. It is not enough simply to claim that the quantifiers have the same semantic properties in L^+ that they have in L_6, for it is precisely the semantic properties of the quantifiers in L_6 that we are trying to specify.

To deal with this complication we should have the axioms for the quantifiers speak directly of truth in L^+. Indeed, each axiom for a semantic primitive of L_6 can speak directly of truth in L^+ provided that we add an axiom which states that sentences of L_6 are true in L_6 just in case they are true in L^+. Thus consider the theory (call it '$QT\theta$') whose proper axioms are the following:

(*Q1*) $(\forall \sigma \in L_6)\,[Tr\,(L_6, \sigma) \leftrightarrow Tr\,(L^+, \sigma)]$
(*Q2*) $(\forall x)\,(\exists \gamma \in L^+)\,Ref(L^+, \gamma) = x.$

(The quantifier '$(\forall \sigma \in L_6)$' ranges over sentences of L_6.) The justification for (*Q1*) comes in two parts. First, according to the first important feature of L^+, predicates, names and connectives in L_6 have the

116

same meanings in L^+ as in L_6. Second, the semantic properties in L_6 of the quantifiers are being defined in terms of their semantic properties in L^+. Axiom (Q2) simply records the other important feature of L^+.

(Q3.1) $Ref(L^+, 'm_1') = n_1$

and so on up to (Q3.10),

(Q4.1) $(\forall \gamma \in L^+) [Tr(L^+, \ulcorner P_1 \gamma \urcorner) \leftrightarrow Q_1(Ref(L^+, \gamma))]$

and so on up to (Q4.10),

(Q5.1) $(\forall \gamma, \delta \in L^+) [Tr(L^+, \ulcorner R_1(\gamma, \delta) \urcorner) \leftrightarrow$
$S_1(Ref(L^+, \gamma), Ref(L^+, \delta))]$

and so on up to (Q5.10). ('$(\forall \gamma, \delta \in L^+)$' abbreviates '$(\forall \gamma \in L^+)$ $(\forall \delta \in L^+)$'.) These are simply the expected axioms for the subject-predicate part of L_6.

(Q6) $(\forall \sigma \in L^+) [Tr(L^+, \ulcorner \sim \sigma \urcorner) \leftrightarrow \sim Tr(L^+, \sigma)]$.

This is the obvious axiom for '$\sim$'. Axioms (Q7), (Q8) and (Q9) deal similarly with '&', '$\vee$' and '$\rightarrow$'. Finally, we have axioms of a predictable form for the two quantifiers:

(Q10) $(\forall \Phi \in L^+) [Tr(L^+, \ulcorner (\forall v_i) \Phi v_i \urcorner) \leftrightarrow$
$(\forall x)(\forall \gamma \in L^+)(Ref(L^+, \gamma) = x \rightarrow Tr(L^+, \ulcorner \Phi \gamma \urcorner))]$
(Q11) $(\forall \Phi \in L^+) [Tr(L^+, \ulcorner (\exists v_i) \Phi v_i \urcorner) \leftrightarrow$
$(\exists x)(\forall \gamma \in L^+)(Ref(L^+, \gamma) = x \rightarrow Tr(L^+, \ulcorner \Phi \gamma \urcorner))]$.

In these axioms '$(\forall \Phi \in L^+)$' is a quantifier over expressions which result from a sentence (of L^+) containing a name, by removing one or more occurrences of the name and marking the gaps (that is, over complex predicates, in the sense of Dummett, 1973, p. 11). If Φ is such an expression, then $\ulcorner (\forall v_i) \Phi v_i \urcorner$ is the result of putting $\ulcorner v_i \urcorner$ into the marked gaps and prefixing the result by $\ulcorner (\forall v_i) \urcorner$, and if c is a name then $\ulcorner \Phi c \urcorner$ is the result of putting c into the marked gaps.

This theory, together with an obvious canonical proof procedure, is interpretational for L_6, and meets SC. Indeed, if the theory were stated in a ML which contained the OL then that canonical proof procedure would yield homophonic biconditionals.

Although the theory $QT\theta$ is formally slightly complicated, the intuitive semantic picture which it presents is very simple. Consider the sentence 'Everything is modest'. If this sentence is to be true, then the predicate 'is modest' must be *true of* every object in the domain of quantification. Our theory for subject-predicate sentences (Section V.1) suggests an account of 'truth of' in terms of truth. A predicate is true of an object just in case a sentence formed by concatenating a name of that object with the predicate would be a true sentence. Since some objects in the domain of quantification may not have a name in the language in question, we imagine an extended language in which every such object does have a name. In terms of this language we can say what it is for 'is modest' to be true of every object (cf. Dummett, 1973, p. 405). Such an extended language might itself contain infinitely many names and so infinitely many semantic primitives; it might be an unlearnable language. But that fact does not render unlearnable the language originally in question. Appeal to the extended language simply enables us to retain the primacy of sentences and of truth, in a theory of truth conditions. (For the importance of this, see the argument in favour of $QT\theta$ six paragraphs on.)

Two variations on the theme of $QT\theta$ deserve brief mention. First, in the presence of $(Q2)$ and of

$$(\forall \gamma \in L^+) (\exists x) Ref(L^+, \gamma) = x$$

the axioms $(Q10)$ and $(Q11)$ could be replaced by

$$(\forall \Phi \in L^+) [Tr (L^+, \ulcorner (\forall v_i)\Phi v_i \urcorner) \leftrightarrow (\forall \gamma \in L^+) Tr (L^+, \ulcorner \Phi \gamma \urcorner)]$$
$$(\forall \Phi \in L^+) [Tr (L^+, \ulcorner (\exists v_i)\Phi v_i \urcorner) \leftrightarrow (\exists \gamma \in L^+) Tr (L^+, \ulcorner \Phi \gamma \urcorner)].$$

These are certainly neater than $(Q10)$ and $(Q11)$, but the strategy for producing neater axioms does not readily generalize to other quantifiers. Even in a language which, like L^+, contains at least one name of each object, it is not a necessary and sufficient condition for the truth of 'Few things are P_1' that for few names γ, $\ulcorner P_1 \gamma \urcorner$ is true; one object may have many names. Second, it is possible to do without the appeal, in the theory, to a single language which contains a name of each object and so, perhaps, infinitely many names. One can consider instead the family of sublanguages of L^+ each of which extends L_6 by only finitely many new names. In that case an atomic predicate or connective is governed by an axiom which involves quantification ('$(\forall M)$') over that family of languages, as for example

$$(\forall M) (\forall \gamma \in M) [Tr (M, \ulcorner P_1 \gamma \urcorner) \leftrightarrow Q_1 (Ref(M, \gamma))].$$

For names in L_6 we have, for example,

$$Ref (L_6, 'm_1') = n_1$$

and corresponding to (*Q1*) and (*Q2*)

$$(\forall M) (\forall M' \supseteq M) (\forall \gamma \in M) [Ref(M, \gamma) = Ref(M', \gamma)]$$
$$(\forall M) (\forall x) (\exists M' \supseteq M) (\exists \gamma \in M') Ref(M', \gamma) = x.$$

(The quantifier '($\forall M' \supseteq M$)' ranges over languages in the family which contain all the names which are in M.) For the quantifier '$\forall$' we have

$$(\forall M) (\forall \Phi \in M) [Tr(M, \ulcorner(\forall v_i) \Phi v_i \urcorner) \leftrightarrow$$
$$(\forall x) (\forall M' \supseteq M) (\forall \gamma \in M') (Ref(M', \gamma) = x \rightarrow$$
$$Tr(M', \ulcorner \Phi \gamma \urcorner))].$$

There seems to be very little to choose between this second variation and the original theory $QT\theta$. (For theories in this style see e.g. Dummett, 1973, Chapter 2 and Evans, 1977, pp. 471-7.)

Theories in the style of $QT\theta$ are rather different from familiar theories of truth conditions for quantificational languages. In familiar theories the most important syntactic category is not that of sentences but the broader category of formulae. Atomic formulae include atomic sentences and also the results of concatenating variables (rather than names) with predicates. Thus, along with '$P_1 m_1$' and '$R_1(m_1, m_2)$' we have '$P_1 v_1$', '$R_1(v_1, m_2)$', '$R_1(m_1, v_2)$', and '$R_1(v_1, v_2)$'. Complex formulae are built up from atomic formulae using connectives and quantifiers. The introduction of a quantifier results in a bound variable; other variables are free. Sentences are just those formulae which contain no free variables.

Just as the most important syntactic category is that of formulae (rather than sentences), so the most important semantic property employed in familiar theories is that of 'truth of' (rather than truth). Roughly, what a theory of the familiar kind does is to specify under what conditions formulae are true of objects. In fact, since there are formulae containing several free variables, such a theory specifies under what conditions formulae are true of sequences of objects (the position in the sequence corresponding to the subscript on the variable). The basic idea, in the case of quantified formulae, is that '($\forall v_1$) $R_1(v_1, v_2)$', for example, is true of a sequence of objects just in case '$R_1(v_1, v_2)$' is true of every sequence which can be obtained from the original sequence by putting another object into the first place in the sequence (the place corresponding to 'v_1'). A sentence has the property that it is true of all sequences or else of none. A sentence is said to be true (*simpliciter*) just in case it is true of all sequences.

In such a theory there is an axiom corresponding to (*Q2*) of $QT\theta$:

$(S1) \qquad (\forall s)(\forall i)(\forall x)(\exists s')[s'(i) = x \,\&\, s' \overset{i}{\approx} s].$

(Read: for every (infinite) sequence s, every natural number $(1, 2, \ldots)$ i, and every object x there is a sequence s' which has the object x in its ith place and which differs from s at most in what object it has in its ith place.) Corresponding to the reference relation employed in $QT\theta$ is a sequence-relative evaluation function $*$, governed by axioms

$(S2) \qquad (\forall s)(\forall i)[*(s, \ulcorner v_i \urcorner) = s(i)]$

$(S2.1) \qquad (\forall s)[*(s, `m_1\text{'}) = n_1]$

and so on up to $(S2.10)$. (Henceforth, '$s*(\ldots)$' abbreviates '$*(s, \ldots)$'.) Atomic predicates are governed by axioms which specify under what conditions sequences satisfy atomic formulae (where satisfaction is the converse of the 'truth of' relation between formulae and sequences).

$(S3.1) \qquad (\forall s)(\forall t)[s \text{ satisfies } \ulcorner P_1 t \urcorner \leftrightarrow Q_1(s*(t))]$

and so on up to $(S3.10)$. (The quantifier '$(\forall t)$' ranges over names and variables.) The axioms $(S4.1)$–$(S4.10)$ for two-place atomic predicates are similar. For the connective '$\sim$' we have

$(S5) \qquad (\forall s)(\forall \mu)[s \text{ satisfies } \ulcorner \sim \mu \urcorner \leftrightarrow \sim (s \text{ satisfies } \mu)].$

(The quantifier '$(\forall \mu)$' ranges over formulae.) The axioms $(S6)$–$(S8)$ for '&', '∨', and '→' are similar. Finally, we have axioms for the quantifiers

$(S9) \qquad (\forall s)(\forall \Phi)[s \text{ satisfies } \ulcorner (\forall v_i)\Phi v_i \urcorner \leftrightarrow (\forall x)(\forall s' \overset{i}{\approx} s)(s'(i) = x \rightarrow s' \text{ satisfies } \ulcorner \Phi v_i \urcorner)]$

$(S10) \qquad (\forall s)(\forall \Phi)[s \text{ satisfies } \ulcorner (\exists v_i)\Phi v_i \urcorner \leftrightarrow (\exists x)(\forall s' \overset{i}{\approx} s)(s'(i) = x \rightarrow s' \text{ satisfies } \ulcorner \Phi v_i \urcorner)].$

(The quantifier '$(\forall \Phi)$' ranges over expressions which stand to formulae as complex predicates, in Dummett's sense, stand to sentences.) Given the definition of truth (for sentences) as satisfaction by all sequences, it is not difficult to see that for an appropriate choice of canonical proof procedure this theory (call it '$QS\theta$') is just as interpretational as $QT\theta$. Thus, for example, one can prove straightforwardly

$(\forall s)[s \text{ satisfies } `(\forall v_1) R_1(v_1, m_1)\text{'} \leftrightarrow (\forall x)(\forall s' \overset{i}{\approx} s)(s'(1) = x \rightarrow S_1(s'(1), n_1))].$

From that, axiom $(S1)$ yields

$$(\forall s) [s \text{ satisfies } `(\forall v_1)R_1 (v_1, m_1)' \leftrightarrow (\forall x)S_1 (x, n_1)].$$

Given the premise (provided by a theory about sequences) that there is at least one sequence we have

$$(\forall s) (s \text{ satisfies } `(\forall v_1)R_1 (v_1, m_1)') \leftrightarrow (\forall x)S_1 (x, n_1)$$

from which, by the definition of truth in terms of satisfaction we have

$$Tr (L_6, `(\forall v_1)R_1 (v_1, m_1)') \leftrightarrow (\forall x)S_1 (x, n_1).$$

Just as in the case of $QT\theta$, variations on the theme set out here are possible. First, it is possible (and in fact usual) to replace (*S9*) and (*S10*) by the neater axioms

$$(\forall s) (\forall \Phi) [s \text{ satisfies } \ulcorner (\forall v_i) \Phi v_i \urcorner \leftrightarrow$$
$$(\forall s' \overset{i}{\approx} s) (s' \text{ satisfies } \ulcorner \Phi v_i \urcorner)]$$
$$(\forall s) (\forall \Phi) [s \text{ satisfies } \ulcorner (\exists v_i) \Phi v_i \urcorner \leftrightarrow$$
$$(\exists s' \overset{i}{\approx} s) (s' \text{ satisfies } \ulcorner \Phi v_i \urcorner)].$$

This strategy for producing neater axioms can (in a certain sense) be generalized to other quantifiers, principally because for any given sequence s the sequences which differ from s in at most the ith place are in a natural one-to-one correspondence with the objects in the domain of quantification. (We shall return to this point in Section VI.2.) Second, it is possible to do without the appeal to infinite sequences. We can consider instead sequences of all possible finite lengths. It is even possible to do without sequences altogether at the price of regarding 'satisfies' as a *multigrade* predicate (that is a predicate for which there is no fixed number of names which it takes to make a sentence). In particular, 'satisfies' would need to be a predicate which takes any finite number of names of objects, together with one more name (of a formula), to make a sentence (see e.g. Peacocke, 1978, p. 484 and Taylor, forthcoming).

The two theories $QT\theta$ and $QS\theta$ are similar. But there is a difference, and it is not without significance. It is with the sentences of a language that utterance types are correlated (by one component of a theory of force). Utterances of those types are linguistic acts whose contents are specified via the meaning specifications for the correlated sentences. Similarly, in the case of assertions or sayings performed in utterances of indicative types the utterance is TRUE (once and for all) just in case the correlated sentence is true. (We continue to assume that context dependence is absent.) Thus, the concepts of meaning and of truth which are illuminated by the *PAC*s are the concepts of meaning and truth for sentences. One might say that the sentence is the primary semantic unit. '[S]entences are those linguistic expressions by means of which it is possible to *do* something, that is, to *say* something' (Dummett, 1973, p. 195). The significant difference between $QT\theta$ and $QS\theta$ is that $QT\theta$ respects, while $QS\theta$ denies, the semantic primacy of sentences. According to $QS\theta$ the class of sentences is merely a syntactically distinguished subclass of the class of formulae. Sentences and formulae which are not sentences are treated as expressions of the same semantic kind, namely as bearers of satisfaction conditions. 'If sentences are merely a special case of [formulae] ... then, after all, there is nothing unique about sentences: whatever was thought to be special about them should be ascribed, rather, to [formulae] in general' (ibid. p. 196; Dummett is actually speaking about the assimilation of sentences to names, but see also Evans, 1977, p. 476).

The significance of the difference between $QT\theta$ and $QS\theta$ is not diminished by the fact that, in $QS\theta$, truth is defined in such a way as to apply only to sentences. For that is a purely syntactic restriction upon the application of the truth predicate. If truth is satisfaction by all sequences, then every formula has a semantic property which fits it to be the bearer of truth conditions. But for that syntactic restriction, $QS\theta$ would deliver, for example,

$$Tr(L_6, \ 'P_1\nu_1') \leftrightarrow (\forall x)Q_1 x.$$

The idea that, but for a syntactic restriction, all formulae are bearers of truth conditions involves denial of the semantic primacy of sentences just as much as does the idea that sentences, like other formulae, are fundamentally bearers of satisfaction conditions. Thus, we should prefer variations on the theme of $QT\theta$ over variations on the theme of $QS\theta$.

It remains to show how to provide, for a language such as L_6, a theory of meaning standing to $QT\theta$ rather as $M\theta$ (Section II.3) stands to $T\theta$ (Section II.1). For names, atomic predicates and connectives we offer axioms of forms which are, by now, familiar.

$MRef('m_1', n_1)$
$(\forall\gamma)(\forall\nu)[MRef(\gamma, \nu) \rightarrow \ulcorner P_1 \ \gamma\urcorner$ means that $Q_1\nu]$
$(\forall\gamma,\delta)(\forall\nu, w)[(MRef(\gamma, \nu) \& MRef(\delta, w)) \rightarrow$
$\ulcorner R_1(\gamma, \delta)\urcorner$ means that $S_1(\nu, w)]$
$(\forall\sigma)(\forall p)[\sigma$ means that $p \rightarrow \ulcorner{\sim}\sigma\urcorner$ means that ${\sim}p]$

('in L_6' is suppressed throughout). Before stating the axiom for the quantifier '$\forall$' we introduce an abbreviation.

$MCorr\ (\Phi, G)$

abbreviates

$(\forall\gamma)\ (\forall v)\ [MRef\ (\gamma, v) \rightarrow \ulcorner\Phi\gamma\urcorner$ means that $Gv]$.

Then we have for '$\forall$'

$(\forall\Phi)\ (\forall Y)\ [MCorr\ (\Phi, Y) \rightarrow$
$\ulcorner(\forall v_i)\Phi v_i\urcorner$ means that $(\forall x)Yx]$.

(The quantifier '$(\forall\Phi)$' ranges over complex predicates as in $QT\theta$. The quantifier '$(\forall Y)$' is another quantifier similar to '$(\forall p)$' and '$(\forall v)$'. See also Appendix 5.)

This theory of meaning is neither formally nor philosophically very exciting. In the case of quantificational languages the main task for the semantic theorist is to provide structurally adequate interpretational truth theories.

2   BINARY QUANTIFICATION

Suppose that a semantic theorist sets out to construct a theory of meaning or a theory of truth conditions for a fragment of English. Subject-predicate sentences can be dealt with using the resources of Section V.1, and sentences involving the simple quantifier expressions 'everything' and 'something' can be dealt with using the resources of Section VI.1. But that leaves quantified sentences such as

> Every married man is modest
> Some married man is modest

untouched. One common strategy for a semantic theorist is to 'pre-process' these sentences into

> Everything is (if a married man then modest)
> Something is (a married man and modest).

But there are two objections to this strategy. First, in view of *SC*, this strategy ought to seem as unsatisfactory as that of 'preprocessing' sentences involving exclusive disjunction (cf. Section III.4). Second, it is not a generalizable strategy, for consider sentences such as

Most married men are modest.

The 'preprocessing' strategy applied to such sentences beginning with 'most' would involve two steps. First, a 'most' quantifier of the same syntactic kind as '$\mathbf{V}$' and '$\mathbf{\exists}$' would be introduced, so that '$(most\ x)\ Fx$' is true just in case most objects are F. Second, a method would be produced for representing 'Most Fs are G' as

$$(most\ x)\ (Fx * Gx)$$

for some truth functional connective $*$. But it is a well-known fact that this second step is impossible. There is no such connective (see Rescher, 1962). It is intuitively implausible that quantified sentences beginning with 'every' or 'some' should be 'preprocessed', while sentences beginning with 'most' or 'few' should not be. So, since the strategy cannot be applied in the latter cases it should not be applied in the former cases either.

What these two objections suggest is that we should regard sentences such as

> Every married man is modest
> Most married men are modest

and similar sentences beginning with 'all', 'some', 'a', 'few', 'many', and so on, as what they superficially appear to be, namely the results of applying binary (two-place) quantifiers to a pair of predicates. So let us consider a language containing some binary quantifiers. The names, predicates, connectives and variables of L_7 are just those of L_6, but instead of '$\mathbf{V}$' and '$\mathbf{\exists}$' there are four binary quantifiers 'EVERY', 'SOME', 'MOST', and 'FEW'. The syntactic rule which governs these quantifiers is simple. If A and B are (possibly complex) sentences in each of which a name c occurs at least once and in which $\ulcorner v_i \urcorner$ does not occur, and if Q is a quantifier, then

$$(Qv_i)\ (A\,(v_i); B(v_i))$$

is a sentence (where $\ulcorner A(v_i) \urcorner$ and $\ulcorner B(v_i) \urcorner$ are the results of replacing c at some or all of its occurrences in A and in B by $\ulcorner v_i \urcorner$).

It is not difficult to provide a truth theory for L_7 by appealing to an extended language which contains a name of each object in the domain of quantification of L_7. Let us suppose that $L_7{}^+$ is such a language and let us, for convenience, abbreviate '$L_7{}^+$' by 'L^+'. There should be no risk of confusion between this language and the language (which we could have called '$L_6{}^+$') extending L_6.

We only need to concern ourselves with the four axioms for the four new quantifiers. Before stating these we introduce an abbreviation.

$$Sat\,(x,\, \ulcorner\Phi v_i\urcorner)$$

abbreviates

$$(\,\forall\gamma\in L^+)\,(Ref(L^+, \gamma) = x \to Tr\,(L^+, \ulcorner\Phi\gamma\urcorner)).$$

Then we have, for 'EVERY', the axiom

$$(\,\forall\Phi,\,\Psi\in L^+)\,[Tr\,(L^+, \ulcorner(\text{EVERY }v_i)\,(\Phi v_i;\,\Psi v_i)\urcorner) \leftrightarrow$$
$$(\text{EVERY } x)\,(Sat\,(x,\, \ulcorner\Phi\gamma\urcorner);\,Tr\,(L^+, \ulcorner\Psi\gamma\urcorner))]$$

and exactly similar axioms for the other three quantifiers. In each of the four axioms a binary quantifier is used in the *ML*. (To avoid unnecessary complications let us assume that the *ML* contains binary quantifiers but also retains ' $\forall$ ' and ' $\exists$ '.)

In Section VI.1 two variations upon the theme of $QT\theta$ were mentioned. The first variation involved neater axioms for ' $\forall$ ' and ' $\exists$ ', but the strategy for producing neater axioms was not generalizable. Exactly similarly we can produce neater axioms for 'EVERY' and 'SOME' but not for 'MOST' and 'FEW'. For example, the axiom

$$(\,\forall\Phi,\,\Psi\in L^+)\,[Tr\,(L^+, \ulcorner(\text{EVERY }v_i)\,(\Phi v_i;\,\Psi v_i)\urcorner) \leftrightarrow$$
$$(\text{EVERY }\gamma\in L^+)\,(Tr\,(L^+, \ulcorner\Phi\gamma\urcorner;\,Tr\,(L^+, \ulcorner\Psi\gamma\urcorner))]$$

in which a binary quantifier ranging over names in L^+ is used in the *ML* would be acceptable for 'EVERY', but a corresponding axiom would not be acceptable for 'MOST'. The second variation involved replacing the appeal to a single extended language by quantification over a family of languages. This variation can readily be carried over to the case of L_7.

Perhaps not everyone will have been convinced by the argument against the use of the satisfaction theory $QS\theta$. In any case, in order to provide continuity with other literature on the topic of binary quantifiers (e.g. Wiggins, 1980b) we should consider briefly the provision of a satisfaction theory for L_7. Once again, we only have to concern ourselves with the axioms for the binary quantifiers, and to facilitate the statement of the axioms we again introduce an abbreviation.

$$sats\,(s,\, i,\, x,\, \ulcorner\Phi v_i\urcorner)$$

abbreviates

$$(\forall s' \overset{i}{\approx} s) (s'(i) = x \rightarrow s' \text{ satisfies } \ulcorner \Phi v_i \urcorner).$$

Then we have, for 'EVERY', the axiom

$$(\forall s) (\forall \Phi, \Psi) [s \text{ satisfies } \ulcorner(\text{EVERY } v_i) (\Phi v_i; \Psi v_i)\urcorner \leftrightarrow$$
$$(\text{EVERY } x) (sats \ (s, i, x, \ulcorner\Phi v_i\urcorner); sats \ (s, i, x, \ulcorner\Psi v_i\urcorner))],$$

and exactly similar axioms for the other three quantifiers.

It is time to return to the point (mentioned in Section VI.1) that it is usual, in satisfaction theories for '$\forall$' and '$\exists$', to replace

$$(\forall x) (\forall s' \overset{i}{\approx} s) (s'(i) = x \rightarrow s' \text{ satisfies} \ldots)$$

by the neater

$$(\forall s' \overset{i}{\approx} s) (s' \text{ satisfies} \ldots).$$

An exactly similar variation is possible in the case of a satisfaction theory for binary quantifiers. The axiom

$$(\forall s) (\forall \Phi, \Psi) [s \text{ satisfies } \ulcorner(\text{MOST } v_i) (\Phi v_i; \Psi v_i)\urcorner \leftrightarrow$$
$$(\text{MOST } s') (s' \overset{i}{\approx} s \ \& \ s' \text{ satisfies } \ulcorner\Phi v_i\urcorner; s' \text{ satisfies } \ulcorner\Psi v_i\urcorner)]$$

in which a binary quantifier ranging over sequences is used in the *ML* would be acceptable for 'MOST'. This shows that it is an error to suppose that any obstacle is presented to a satisfaction theory which quantifies over sequences by the fact that even if there are only finitely many objects in the domain of quantification (provided there is more than one object) there are uncountably many infinite sequences of such objects. The following claim is certainly correct: 'Sequences being non-denumerably many, we may have trouble making sense of any condition that speaks of "most sequences" fulfilling a condition' (Wiggins, 1980b, pp. 325–6). But the axiom just offered for 'MOST' does not speak of most sequences, but of most sequences which differ from s in at most the ith place and satisfy $\ulcorner\Phi v_i\urcorner$. And there are no more sequences of that kind than there are objects in the domain of quantification. Once 'most' is recognized as a binary quantifier there is no further difficulty presented by the fact that there are uncountably many sequences.

There is a difficulty to be faced (but a different difficulty) if one sets out to give a satisfaction theory for a one-place 'most' quantifier (of the same syntactic kind as '$\forall$'). One might think to offer as an axiom

$$(\forall s) (\forall \Phi) [s \text{ satisfies } \ulcorner(most \ v_i)\Phi v_i\urcorner \leftrightarrow$$
$$(most \ s' \overset{i}{\approx} s) (s' \text{ satisfies } \ulcorner\Phi v_i\urcorner)]$$

in which a one-place 'most' quantifier is used in the *ML*. But if this satisfaction condition specification is to be correct then the expression on the right hand side of the biconditional cannot be regarded as an abbreviation of

$$(most\ s')\ (s' \overset{i}{\approx} s \rightarrow s'\ \text{satisfies}\ \ulcorner \Phi v_i \urcorner)$$

or of

$$(most\ s')\ (s' \overset{i}{\approx} s\ \&\ s'\ \text{satisfies}\ \ulcorner \Phi v_i \urcorner)$$

or of anything else of that general shape. A binary quantifier is needed in the *ML*. In short, if one specifies the satisfaction conditions of *OL* sentences containing a one-place 'most' quantifier by quantifying only over sequences then one must use a binary 'most' quantifier in the *ML*. In contrast, if one quantifies directly over objects then one can use a one-place 'most' quantifier in the *ML* as well, as in the axiom

$$(\forall s)\,(\forall \Phi)\,[s\ \text{satisfies}\ \ulcorner (most\ v_i) \Phi v_i \urcorner \leftrightarrow$$
$$(most\ x)\,(sats\ (s,\ i,\ x,\ \ulcorner \Phi v_i \urcorner))]\,.$$

The points in these last two paragraphs are not of great theoretical or philosophical interest. They are made primarily to remove any confusion which might result from claims such as that made by Platts (1979, p.101): 'What is required is that, in some way, "most" be attached to objects, not sequences, while keeping a definition which relies upon the apparatus of sequences.'

Let us turn again to the imagined project of constructing a semantic theory, in particular a theory of truth conditions, for a fragment of English including quantified sentences. Binary quantifiers allow us to deal with sentences such as

Most philosophers are modest

but one-place quantifiers seemed well suited to deal with sentences such as

Something is modest.

So the semantic theorist has a choice. He may either retain one-place quantifiers as semantic primitives along with their binary counterparts, or else introduce a universal predicate 'Thing' and represent as

(EVERY x) (Thing x; x is modest)

what he previously represented as

(∀x) (x is modest).

Of these two possible courses the second is to be preferred; the first infringes, while the second meets, *SC*. Since it is possible to come to know the meanings of sentences containing 'everything' on the basis of knowledge of the meanings of sentences not containing 'everything' such as

> Every philosopher is modest
> Something is modest
> Some philosopher is modest

the expression 'everything' is not properly regarded as a semantic primitive.

There are still a number of differences between formal languages like L_7 and natural languages like English which a semantic theorist can hardly fail to notice. One such difference is this. In L_7 any expression which can occupy the second place provided by a binary quantifier can also occupy the first place, while in English the first place is invariably occupied either by a common noun or else by a complex phrase built from a common noun together with adjectives in attributive position ('intelligent man', 'modest philosopher', 'tall unmarried person') and relative clauses used restrictively ('man who is unmarried', 'ball which is red', 'person who is loved by no one'). Does this restriction upon English sentences constitute an objection to the semantic theory for L_7, or is the restriction basically a syntactic phenomenon?

Many common nouns are *sortals*, that is, predicates which specify a sort or kind of object. And the distinction between sortals and predicates which are not sortals is a semantic rather than a purely syntactic distinction (see Strawson, 1974a, pp. 103–4). But even if it were the case that the distinction which matters for English is the semantic distinction between sortals and other predicates, it would not follow from that fact alone that semantic theories for languages containing binary quantifiers should mark that distinction. For it is, in general, possible that surface syntactic impoverishment should be the product of a syntactic blocking rule which is sensitive to some semantic property of expressions. Consider an example. Suppose that a semantic theorist sets out to provide a truth theory for a natural language which contains atomic sentences and negation. He offers a theory of the familiar form and then discovers that the negations of sentences about horses are regarded as ungrammatical by speakers of the language. The distinction between sentences which are and sentences which are not about horses is a semantic distinction. But that fact alone does not show that there is something wrong with our theorist's treatment of negation. A person who knows the meanings of some sentences which are about horses and some sentences which are not, and knows the meanings of some sentences which are the negations of sentences which are not about horses, is thereby in a position to know the meanings of some sentences which are the negations of sentences about horses. For the (admittedly semantic) distinction between sentences which are about horses and those which are not is strictly irrelevant to the semantic function of negation. The only semantic property of sentences which is relevant to the semantic function of negation is that sentences are the bearers of truth values.

This is, of course, an extreme example. But it is plausible to maintain that the distinction between sortals and other predicates is similarly irrelevant to the semantic function of binary quantifiers. The only relevant semantic property of the occupants of the gaps provided by binary quantifiers is that they are expressions which take a name (an expression which refers to an object) to make a sentence (a bearer of a truth value). It is not inconsistent to maintain, in this way, that the restriction upon English sentences is, from the point of view of a semantic theorist, basically a syntactic phenomenon and, at the same time, to agree with Strawson (1974a, pp. 104-10) that by appealing to the semantic distinction between sortals and other predicates (and, in particular, by appealing to an analogy between that distinction and the subject-predicate distinction) one can render the restriction upon English sentences unsurprising. And the prospect, in this case, of a semantic underpinning of the syntactic phenomenon marks a significant difference from the more extreme example which we considered.

In fact, the distinction which matters for English sentences is not that between sortals and other predicates. For, first, 'thing', 'object', and 'item' are common nouns and can occupy the first place provided by a binary quantifier, but they do not specify sorts or kinds of object. And, second, for any atomic predicate which is not a sortal one can construct an equivalent complex phrase from the common noun 'thing' together with attributive adjectives and relative clauses. Thus, corresponding to 'is hairy', which is not a sortal and cannot, in English, occupy the first place provided by a binary quantifier, we have 'hairy thing' and 'thing which is hairy' which are not sortals but can, in

English, occupy the first place provided by a binary quantifier. As Strawson shows (ibid.) these facts do not doom the project of rendering unsurprising the restriction upon English sentences. Nor do they show that the difference between common nouns and other predicates is without importance. But they do make it implausible to maintain that the semantic account of binary quantifiers offered in the truth theory for L_7 needs to be, or even could be, substantially altered.

Another striking difference between L_7 and English is this. In a quantified sentence of L_7 such as

$$(\text{MOST } \nu_1)\,(P_1 \nu_1 \,;\, P_2 \nu_1)$$

the expression which literally occupies name position *vis-à-vis* the predicate 'P_2' is a variable. But in a quantified sentence of English such as

Most philosophers are modest

the expression which literally occupies name position *vis-à-vis* the predicate 'is (are) modest' is a quantifier phrase 'most philosophers'. Thus if a semantic theorist working on English wants to use a language similar to L_7 at the level of input to a semantic theory then that semantic theory will have to be accompanied by a syntactic theory. In very simple cases it seems fairly clear what the relevant syntactic rule must do. The sentence

(MOST x) (Philosopher x; x is modest)

at the level of input to a semantic theory becomes, at the surface, a sentence in which a quantifier phrase made up of the quantifier 'most' and the common noun 'philosopher' occupies the vacant name position *vis-à-vis* the predicate 'is modest'. By two similar steps the sentence

(MOST x) (Philosopher x; (SOME y) (Greek y; x admires y))

at the level of input to a semantic theory becomes the surface sentence

Most philosophers admire some Greeks.

For in that surface sentence a quantifier phrase made up of 'most' and 'philosopher' occupies the same vacant name position, *vis-à-vis* the predicate 'admires', as was occupied by the variable 'x' in the sentence at the level of input. And a quantifier phrase made up of 'some' and 'Greek' occupies the same vacant name position, *vis-à-vis* the predicate 'admires', as was occupied by the variable 'y' in the sentence at the

130

level of input. There is no feature of these two steps answering to the fact that 'MOST' (associated with 'x') has wider scope than 'SOME' (associated with 'y'). So, by the same two steps, the same surface sentence will also result from a quite different sentence at the level of input.

$$(\text{SOME } y) (\text{Greek } y; (\text{MOST } x) (\text{Philosopher } x; x \text{ admires } y))$$

So if the surface sentences are to be used in communication a disambiguating rule is needed. Once again, so long as we attend to simple cases, it seems relatively clear what the rule is. In the absence of contrary indications, a surface sentence containing several quantifier expressions is interpreted in such a way that priority in bringing to bear the relevant axioms of a semantic theory corresponds to the left-to-right ordering of quantifier expressions. In short, quantifiers further to the left are interpreted as having wider scope. Thus our surface sentence will be interpreted as corresponding to the first, rather than the second, sentence at the level of input.

If these were the only rules in the syntactic theory then English would suffer from surface syntactic impoverishment with respect to quantified sentences. It would not be impoverishment of the crudest kind, occasioned by a syntactic blocking rule which specifically blocks the occurrence at the surface of certain perfectly comprehensible sentences. Rather, because these rules produce surface sentences which are syntactically much less complicated than sentences at the level of input, they are unable to mark all the needed distinctions. They do not provide for a surface sentence corresponding to each sentence at the level of input which is allowed by the semantic nature of the binary quantifiers.

In fact there are several linguistic devices in English which help to reduce the degree of impoverishment. For example, use of the passive form of a transitive verb allows reversal of left-to-right order. Thus we have

Some Greeks are admired by most philosophers

which is naturally interpreted as corresponding to the second, rather than the first, sentence at the level of input. Another linguistic device, this time only applicable to spoken English, is that of stress. In general it seems that heavy stress on a quantifier results in the sentence being interpreted as though the quantifier is further to the left than it actually is. Further, some quantifiers have a special syntactic form which indicates that the quantifier is to be interpreted as having wide scope. Thus 'every' has the special form 'any', and 'a' or 'some' has the special form 'a certain' or 'certain'.

Much more could be said (and should be said by philosophers and linguists working together) about each of these devices. But none of the devices is fully general. Given all these devices impoverishment would remain. Thus consider the following sentence at the level of input, in which a quantified variable occupies a name position within a relative clause:

$(\text{MOST } x)$ [Philosopher x;
$(\text{SOME } y)$ ((Woman who admires x) y; y is American)].

The surface sentence

Some women who admire most philosophers are
American

is naturally interpreted as corresponding to a quite different sentence at the level of input. The use of the passive 'is admired by' is no help. Stress is certainly no help in written English. And 'most' does not have a special wide-scope form. It is in such cases that natural language users reach for 'such that' or a similar locution. For with the aid of such expressions impoverishment is overcome. We have

Most philosophers are such that some women who
admire them are American

or

Of most philosophers it's true that some women who
admire them are American.

Interesting questions naturally arise. Is there any semantically significant characterization of the point at which 'such that' (or a similar locution) is needed in English? Is the point at which such a locution is needed uniform across different natural languages? But such questions will go unanswered here.

Let us turn from these differences between English and L_7 and compare the four binary quantifiers which we have so far considered with another, namely, 'more'. Consider the following sentences:

Most philosophers are men
There are more philosophers than men.

The expression 'there are more ... than ...' takes two predicates to make a sentence, and it can be assigned a semantic property by an axiom of the same form as that for 'MOST'.

$$(\forall \Phi, \Psi) \, [Tr \, (\ulcorner (MORE \, v_i) \, (\Phi v_i; \Psi v_i) \urcorner) \leftrightarrow$$
$$(MORE \, x) \, (Sat \, (x, \ulcorner \Phi v_i \urcorner); Sat \, (x, \ulcorner \Psi v_i \urcorner))]$$

But there are striking differences between the syntactic behaviour of 'there are more ... than ...' and 'most'. In English both the places provided by 'there are more ... than ...' must be occupied by common nouns or phrases built from common nouns, whereas only the first place provided by 'most' must be so occupied. And the 'there are' form of the 'more' quantifier is reminiscent not so much of the binary 'some' quantifier as of the one-place quantifier 'there are some ...'. What is more, in a satisfaction theory 'MORE' needs an axiom of a slightly different form from that for 'MOST'.

$$(\forall s) \, (\forall \Phi, \Psi) \, [s \text{ satisfies } \ulcorner (MORE \, v_i) \, (\Phi v_i; \Psi v_i) \urcorner \leftrightarrow$$
$$(MORE \, s') \, (s' \overset{i}{\approx} s \, \& \, s' \text{ satisfies } \ulcorner \Phi v_i \urcorner;$$
$$s' \overset{i}{\approx} s \, \& \, s' \text{ satisfies } \ulcorner \Psi v_i \urcorner)]$$

On the right hand side of the biconditional the expression '$s' \overset{i}{\approx} s$' must occur twice (see Humberstone, 1979, p. 176).

These differences, though unimportant in themselves, suggest that there may be a semantic difference between 'most' and 'more' which is worth investigating. This suggestion is correct. To make the difference vivid we should consider first one-place quantifiers. With each one-place quantifier Q we can associate a function f_Q from pairs of cardinalities to truth values (T and F) such that if a is the cardinality of the set of Fs and b is the cardinality of the set of non-Fs then

$$\ulcorner (Qx)Fx \urcorner \text{ is true iff } f_Q \, (<a, b>) = T.$$

Thus, for example, '$(\forall x)Fx$' is true just in case $b = 0$, '$(\exists x)Fx$' is true just in case $a \neq 0$, and (at least in the case where the domain of quantification is finite) '$(most \, x)Fx$' is true just in case a is greater than b. Let us call such functions f_Q 'M-functions' (cf. Mostowski, 1957). One way of generalizing M-functions to the case of binary quantification is to associate with a binary quantifier Q a function f_Q from pairs of pairs of cardinalities to truth values such that if a is the cardinality of the set of Fs, b is the cardinality of the set of non-Fs, c is the cardinality of the set of Gs and d is the cardinality of the set of non-Gs, then

$\ulcorner(Qx)\,(Fx;Gx)\urcorner$ is true iff $f_Q\,(<a,\,b>,<c,\,d>)$ = T.

(For this generalization, see Altham and Tennant, 1975.) But it is clear that 'EVERY', 'SOME', 'MOST', and 'FEW' are binary quantifiers with which no such function can be associated. 'We cannot tell whether most Fs are Gs just by looking at how many Fs, non-Fs, Gs and non-Gs there are. We need to know how the individuals involved are distributed across these sets' (Humberstone, 1979, p. 175). It is equally clear that such a function can be associated with 'MORE', for '(MORE x) (Fx; Gx)' is true just in case a is greater than c.

A different generalization is needed to cover the four binary quantifiers of L_7. With each such binary quantifier Q we can associate a function f_Q from pairs of cardinalities to truth values (indeed the same function as was associated with the corresponding one-place quantifier) such that if a is the cardinality of the set of Fs which are also Gs and b is the cardinality of the set of Fs which are non-Gs then

$\ulcorner(Qx)\,(Fx;Gx)\urcorner$ is true iff $f_Q\,(<a,\,b>)$ = T.

In the case of these quantifiers the cardinality of the set of Fs is not directly relevant. The set of Fs serves only to yield a restriction to a subset of the set of Gs and a subset of the set of non-Gs. It is clear that 'MORE' is not a quantifier with which such a function can be associated.

It is certainly possible to generalize the original notion of an M-function so as to cover the cases of 'MOST' and of 'MORE', and indeed all quantifiers of any number of places (ibid.). But the difference between the two generalizations which we have just considered corresponds to a semantic difference between the binary quantifiers of L_7, on one hand, and 'MORE', on the other. The binary quantifiers of L_7 are *restrictive* binary quantifiers; in each case the first place is restrictive with respect to the second place. The quantifier 'MORE' is a *pure* binary quantifier; neither place is restrictive with respect to the other.

Quantifier expressions in English such as 'most philosophers', 'every man', and so on should be seen as semantically complex expressions which result when the first place of a restrictive binary quantifier is occupied by a restricting common noun. They are *restricted* one-place quantifiers. In the limiting case in which the common noun is 'thing' the restriction is vacuous. But there is another kind of one-place quantifier expression in English, namely 'there are some . . .', 'there are few . . .', and so on. It would be a mistake to treat both the

134

binary quantifier 'some' and the one-place quantifier 'there are some' as semantic primitives. Rather 'there are some' might be seen as resulting when the second place provided by the 'some' quantifier is occupied by a predicate (with the form of a verb) which is as unspecific as the common noun 'thing', namely the predicate 'is' or 'exists'. (See Strawson, 1974a, pp. 114–15 for an interesting suggestion about the occurrence of 'there' in these one-place quantifier expressions.)

The similarity between 'There are some Fs' and 'There are more Fs than Gs' suggests, perhaps, that the binary 'more' quantifier is itself not a semantic primitive, and that we might find a restrictive 'more' quantifier. A first thought would be that the semantically primitive quantifier is the three-place quantifier in 'More Fs are Gs than are Hs'. Of the three places provided by this quantifier the first is restrictive with respect to the second and third. But there is another three-place 'more' quantifier in 'More Fs than Gs are Hs'. Of the three places provided by this quantifier the first and second are both restrictive with respect to the third. And there is a four-place 'more' quantifier in 'More Fs are Gs than Hs are Ks'. Of the four places provided by this quantifier the first and third are restrictive with respect to the second and fourth respectively. Thus we can associate with this four-place quantifier a function f from pairs of pairs of cardinalities to truth values, such that if a is the cardinality of the set of Fs which are Gs, b is the cardinality of the set of Fs which are non-Gs, c is the cardinality of the set of Hs which are Ks, and d is the cardinality of the set of Hs which are non-Ks, then

> 'More Fs are Gs than Hs are Ks' is true iff
> $f(<a, b>, <c, d>) = \text{T}$

For $f(<a, b>, <c, d>) = \text{T}$ just in case a is greater than c.

The natural suggestion is then that at the level of input to a semantic theory for English there should be a single four-place 'more' quantifier 'MORE^4'. According to this suggestion, the surface sentence

> More men than women are philosophers

will be related, by a simple application of a (perhaps complicated) deletion rule in the syntactic theory, to the sentence

> (MORE^4 x) (Man x, x is a philosopher; Woman x, x is a philosopher)

at the level of input. The surface sentence

More men are plumbers than philosophers

will be similarly related to the sentence

(MORE^4 x) (Man x, x is a plumber; Man x, x is a philosopher)

at the level of input. And the surface sentence

There are more cats than dogs

will be related in a slightly more complicated way to

(MORE^4 x) (Cat x, x exists; Dog x, x exists).

It would remain to connect these uses of 'more' with those which seem to have nothing to do with quantification, as in

John is more witty than perceptive

and, indeed, with comparatives in general.

3   PREDICATE QUANTIFICATION

In the quantificational idioms which we have considered (in Sections VI.1 and VI.2), two simple but notable features coincide. First, the bound variables of quantification occupy positions which can be occupied by names, and the axioms stating the semantic properties of the quantifiers speak of sentences in which names (perhaps in an extended language) occupy the position which is occupied in a quantified sentence by a bound variable. In short, the quantification is quantification into name position. Second, the objects some of which are named by names in the original language, and all of which are named by names in the extended language, have the property that the truth of quantified sentences turns upon the difference between one such object and two. Thus, for example, the sentence '($\exists x$) (Gx & Hx)' differs from the sentence '($\exists x$)Gx & ($\exists x$)Hx' precisely in that what is required for the truth of the former sentence is that a single object (of the kind named by occupants of the position here occupied by 'x') should be both G and H. Similarly, the sentence

(SOME x) (Fx; Gx & Hx)

differs from the sentence

$$(\text{SOME } x) (Fx; Gx) \, \& \, (\text{SOME } x) (Fx; Hx)$$

precisely in that what is required for the truth of the former sentence is that a single F object should be both G and H. In short, the quantification is quantification *over* those objects. (For this account of quantification over objects of a certain kind see Evans, 1975.) It does not suffice for a batch of sentences to involve quantification over objects of a certain kind (in the sense just introduced) that the truth of sentences in that batch requires the existence of objects of that kind. No doubt the truth of 'It's raining' requires the existence of raindrops, but a batch of such feature placing sentences does not involve quantification over raindrops so long as mastery of those sentences does not require sensitivity to the occurrence, co-occurrence and non-occurrence of features within the boundaries of single raindrops or to relations between raindrops (see again Evans, 1975).

It is natural to ask whether these two features of the quantificational idioms considered so far are really essential to the semantic nature of quantification. One way to focus upon the question is to consider two apparent counterexamples to the claim that the features are essential, namely quantification into predicate position and substitutional quantification into name position. Quantification into predicate position is an apparent counterexample to the general claim that the features are essential for the very straightforward reason that, since predicates are not names, it is not quantification into name position. Substitutional quantification into name position is an apparent counterexample because it is usually held not to be quantification over objects of the kind named. For, first, a substitutionally quantified sentence may be true in virtue of the truth of an unquantified sentence in which an empty name (an expression with the syntactic form of a name but which is assigned no object as reference) occupies the name position. And, second, it is possible to quantify substitutionally into name positions which do not admit substitution of co-referring names *salva veritate*, thus producing quantified sentences whose truth turns not merely upon the difference between one object of the kind named and two, but also, perhaps, upon the difference between one way of thinking about an object and two. We shall reflect upon these two apparent counterexamples in this section and the next.

The thesis that it is an essential feature of quantification that it be quantification into name position has been maintained by Quine (1970, pp. 66-7):

Consider first some ordinary quantifications: '$(\exists x)(x \text{ walks})$'
.... The open sentence after the quantifier shows 'x' in a
position where a name could stand; a name of a walker, for
instance. ... To put the predicate letter 'F' in a quantifier, then,
is to treat predicate positions suddenly as name positions, and
hence to treat predicates as names of entities of some sort. ...
The logician who grasps this point, and still quantifies 'F', may
say that these entities are attributes. ...

Predicates have attributes as their 'intensions' or meanings...
and they have sets as their extensions; but they are names of
neither. Variables eligible for quantification therefore do not
belong in predicate positions. They belong in name positions.

We are committed (by Section V.4) to agreeing with Quine that predicates are not names of sets or of properties (attributes). But what is
quite unclear is how it is supposed to follow that the position of
predicates is not open to quantification (cf. Boolos, 1975). Perhaps
it would follow if the accessibility of name position to quantification
provided our only grasp upon the concept of a name, and upon the
subject-predicate distinction. But there is much else that can be said
about names and about the subject-predicate distinction, and indeed
that has been said (see Strawson, 1974b, p. 68).

To restrict the number of complications arising, let us consider just
quantification into the position of one-place predicates. The language
L_4 contains ten one-place predicates and ten names. The language L_8
which we shall now consider is an extension of L_4 containing the
connectives '&', 'v', and '$\sim$', and predicate quantifiers together with
associated variables 'F_1', 'F_2', ... The syntactic rule for the quantifiers is exactly analogous to that for the quantifiers into name position
(Section VI.1). If A is a (possibly complex) sentence in which a one-
place atomic predicate C occurs at least once and in which $\ulcorner F_i \urcorner$ does
not occur, then the result of replacing C at some or all of its occurrences
by $\ulcorner F_i \urcorner$ and prefixing the resultant string with $\ulcorner (\forall F_i) \urcorner$ or $\ulcorner (\exists F_i) \urcorner$ is
itself a sentence (in which $\ulcorner F_i \urcorner$ occurs as a bound variable). We might
read the sentence

$$(\exists F_1)((F_1 m_1 \,\&\, F_1 m_2) \,\&\, \sim F_1 m_3)$$

as: There is something which m_1 and m_2 both are but which m_3 is not.
And we might contrast this with: There is something which m_1 and m_2
both are and there is something which m_3 is not.

The task of someone who wants to reject the thesis that it is an essential feature of quantification that it be quantification into name position is to provide a semantic theory for L_8 (in particular, a truth theory) without letting go of the thought that a predicate is not a name. The first thing to notice is that the difference which is crucial for the truth of quantified sentences of L_8 is the difference between one set and two. There are no contexts in this very simple language which are sensitive to the difference between co-extensive properties. What is more, there are no contexts in L_8 which are sensitive to the difference between two sets which differ only in respect of which objects other than objects named in L_8 are members of them. So the quantification in L_8 is over (in the sense recently introduced) subsets of the set of named objects. The domain of quantification is some set of such subsets (perhaps not the set of all such subsets). It will not be surprising, then, that a truth theory for L_8 can be provided by appealing to an extended language $L^+{}_8$ which contains, for each set in the domain of quantification, a one-place atomic predicate with that set as its extension (that is, its extension in the set of named objects). Let us abbreviate '$L^+{}_8$' by 'L^+'.

The theory for L_8 is very similar to $QT\theta$. In order to simplify the presentation of the axioms we introduce an abbreviation.

$$Corr\,(L^+, \Phi, G)$$

abbreviates

$$(\,\forall\gamma \in L_8)\,[Tr\,(L^+, \ulcorner\Phi\,\gamma\urcorner) \leftrightarrow G\,(Ref(L^+,\gamma))]\,.$$

The crucial axioms are

$$(\,\forall\sigma \in L_8)\,[Tr\,(L_8, \sigma) \leftrightarrow Tr\,(L^+, \sigma)]$$

which corresponds to $(Q1)$ in $QT\theta$, the axioms for the quantifiers

$$(\,\forall\Sigma \in L^+)\,[Tr\,(L^+, \ulcorner(\,\forall F_i)\,\Sigma\,(F_i)\urcorner) \leftrightarrow$$
$$(\,\forall X)\,(\,\forall\Phi \in L^+)\,(Corr\,(L^+, \Phi, X) \to Tr\,(L^+, \ulcorner\Sigma(\Phi)\urcorner))]$$
$$(\,\forall\Sigma \in L^+)\,[Tr\,(L^+, \ulcorner(\,\exists F_i)\,\Sigma\,(F_i)\urcorner) \leftrightarrow$$
$$(\,\exists X)\,(\,\forall\Phi \in L^+)\,(Corr\,(L^+, \Phi, X) \to Tr\,(L^+, \ulcorner\Sigma(\Phi)\urcorner))]$$

corresponding to $(Q10)$ and $(Q11)$ of $QT\theta$, and

$$(\,\forall X)\,(\,\exists\Phi \in L^+)\,Corr\,(L^+, \Phi, X)$$

corresponding to $(Q2)$ of $QT\theta$. In these axioms the quantifier '$(\forall\Sigma \in L^+)$' ranges over expressions which result from a sentence (of L^+) containing a one-place atomic predicate by removing one or more occurrences of the predicate and marking the gaps. The quantifier '$(\forall X)$' is a predicate quantifier in the *ML* whose domain of quantification is exactly that of the *OL* quantifiers. The quantifier '$(\forall \Phi \in L^+)$' ranges over one-place atomic predicates of L^+. In the presence of

$$(\forall X)\,(\exists \Phi \in L^+)\ Corr\ (L^+, \Phi, X)$$

and

$$(\forall \Phi \in L^+)\,(\exists X)\ Corr\ (L^+, \Phi, X)$$

the axiom for ' $\forall$ ', for example, can be replaced by

$$(\forall \Sigma \in L^+)\ [Tr\ (L^+, \ulcorner (\forall F_i)\ \Sigma(F_i)\urcorner) \leftrightarrow$$
$$(\forall \Phi \in L^+)\ Tr\ (L^+, \ulcorner \Sigma(\Phi)\urcorner)].$$

This theory, together with an obvious canonical proof procedure, is interpretational for L_8, and meets *SC*. Nothing in the theory suggests that predicates are covertly being regarded as names. On the contrary, the theory is faithful to the idea that a predicate goes together with a name to form a sentence.

The language L_8 is exceedingly simple. If predicate quantifiers are added to a language still not containing intensional or hyperintensional operators but containing quantification into name position (*first-order* quantification), for example the language L_6, and if the domain of the first-order quantification is a set D, then the predicate quantification turns out to be quantification over subsets of D, and the domain of the predicate quantification is some set of subsets of D. If predicate quantifiers are added to a language containing intensional or hyperintensional operators, and if quantification into predicate positions within the scope of such operators is allowed, then in general the difference which is crucial to the truth of quantified sentences is that between one property and two, where properties are discriminated less finely in the case of intensional operators, or more finely in the case of hyperintensional operators. Predicate quantification is quantification over objects, but over which objects depends upon the other resources available in the language.

Whitlam is a politician but might not have been a politician. Thus, there is something that Whitlam is but might not have been. The sentence

$$(\exists X)\,(X(\text{Whitlam})\ \&\ \Diamond \sim X\,(\text{Whitlam}))$$

is true, and what is required for the truth of that sentence is quite different from what is required for the truth of the sentence

$$(\exists X)\, X\,(\text{Whitlam})\ \&\ (\exists X)\, \Diamond \sim X\,(\text{Whitlam}).$$

What is required for the truth of the first sentence is (one naturally says) that there should be a single thing which Whitlam both is and might not have been, that there should be a single property which Whitlam has and might not have had.

It is not being denied that the meaning of a sentence involving predicate quantification over properties may be specified by using a sentence involving first-order quantification into the position of names of properties (and involving 'exemplifies'). It is difficult to find any difference in meaning between 'Whitlam is modest' and 'Whitlam exemplifies modesty', and it is equally difficult to find any difference in meaning between the sentence

$$(\forall X)\, [X\,(\text{Whitlam}) \to \Diamond\, X\,(\text{Fraser})]$$

involving predicate quantification and the sentence

$$(\forall x)\, [\text{Whitlam exemplifies}\, x\ \to\ \Diamond\,(\text{Fraser exemplifies}\, x)]$$

involving first-order quantification into the position of names of properties. But it would require an argument to show that predicate quantification is nothing other than a semantically misleading representation of quantification into the position of names of properties. Such an argument would have to show the following thought to be mistaken (Strawson, 1974a, p. 33; cf. 1974b, p. 78):

> 'Socrates does something' (or 'Socrates is something') is just as good, *and just as direct*, a generalization from 'Socrates swims' (or 'Socrates is brave') as 'Someone swims' (or 'Someone is brave') is. The phrase 'does something' ('is something') replaces specificity with non-specificity just as the phrase 'someone' does.

And no such argument seems to be available.

It is not being denied, either, that natural languages contain quantification into the position of names of properties. Indeed, such forms are commonly used when quantification is restricted. Thus we have

> There is some shape which this ball and this plate exemplify
>
> Belinda exemplifies every virtue
>
> Most attractive properties of Whitlam are also exemplified (exhibited) by Fraser.

But the occurrence of such forms goes no way towards establishing the thesis that it is an essential feature of quantification that it be quantification into name position.

4   SUBSTITUTIONAL QUANTIFICATION

Our reason for considering substitutional quantification is that it constitutes an apparent counterexample to the thesis that it is an essential feature of quantification into name position that it be quantification over objects of the kind named by occupants of that position.

This is not the place for a full account of the formal features of substitutional quantification, but we shall need some terminology. We consider first a *base language* which has the syntactic form of a subject-predicate language but differs semantically in two ways. It is not assumed that each expression which has the syntactic form of a name is assigned an object as its reference, and it is not assumed that atomic sentences admit substitution of co-referring names *salva veritate*. (That is, it is allowed that some contexts for names be *opaque* rather than *transparent*.) The class of expressions of the base language which have the syntactic form of names is called the *substitution class*. The substitutional quantifiers 'A' and 'E' and their associated variables 'v_1', 'v_2', . . . are then introduced. (We use roman, rather than italic, letters to distinguish these variables from those associated with the standard *objectual* first-order quantifiers '$\forall$' and '$\exists$'.) The syntactic formation rule which governs 'A' and 'E' is the same as that which governs '$\forall$' and '$\exists$'. The semantic properties of the substitutional quantifiers are specified in terms of the substitution class. Thus, an existentially quantified sentence is true just in case at least one of its instantiations by a member of the substitution class is true, and a universally quantified sentence is true just in case every such instantiation is true.

It is not here in question that if the truth conditions of sentences of the base language are antecedently fixed then this specification of the semantic properties of the quantifiers serves to fix the truth conditions of all sentences of the quantificational language. To that extent, substitutional quantification is semantically coherent. (For this result in full generality see Kripke, 1976, Section 1.) What is in question is whether substitutional quantification is what it appears to be, namely quantification into name position but not quantification over objects

142

of the kind named, and so whether substitutional quantification con- stitutes a counterexample to a general thesis about the nature of quantification. This question is in part a question about the semantic structure of substitutionally quantified sentences, and to answer we need to consider the prospects for an interpretational truth theory, meeting *SC*, for a substitutionally quantified language.

Someone who wished to defend the general thesis about the nature of quantification need not deny the fact which is not in question. He might argue, rather, that unless substitutional quantification is covertly quantification over objects of the kind named then it is misleadingly represented as quantification into name position. A proper grasp of what is in question will enable us to understand (even if not to agree with) the claim made by Wallace (1972, p. 237) in an influential paper:

> The limits of substitutional quantification . . . are subtle. They
> do not bar someone from saying 'there are men' and meaning
> that some substitution instance of '*x* is a man' is true-in-English.
> Of course not: *someone* might say 'bububu' and mean that.
> But if someone's sentence does mean that, then it has the
> structure, ontology and truth conditions that the sentence
>
>> some substitution instance of '*x* is a man' is
>> true-in-English
>
> has in my language, and not the structure and truth conditions
> the sentence
>
>> there are men
>
> has there.

Before pursuing our question further we must set aside a special case, namely that in which every expression in the base language which has the syntactic form of a name is genuinely a name and so is assigned an object as its reference, and in which every context for names in the base language is transparent rather than opaque. Given such a base language one can certainly introduce quantifiers in such a way that the truth of quantified sentences is indifferent to the state of anonymous objects. But the resulting quantification into name position is also quantification over objects of the kind named. All that is achieved is that the domain of quantification is restricted to those objects which have names in the base language. Our question cannot be answered by attending to cases in which the base language has these two features. For in such cases 'there is indeed little difference between a substitutional quantifier and a referential [objectual] quantifier ranging over the set of denotata' (Kripke, 1976, p. 351). We must, rather, consider cases in which the base language contains either empty names or opaque contexts for names.

Since we aim to construct interpretational truth theories we shall expect to use in the *ML* sentences which themselves involve substitutional quantification to state the truth conditions of quantified *OL* sentences. And since the truth of a substitutionally quantified sentence is sensitive precisely to instantiations by members of the substitution class we shall need to ensure that the substitution class for substitutional quantification in the *ML* is the same as that for substitutional quantification in the *OL*. In fact, let us assume that the *OL* is part of the *ML*, and let us aim at homophony in our truth theories.

The form of homophonic truth theories for substitutionally quantified languages has been dealt with rigorously by Kripke (1976, Section 5). The main idea is very simple. Names and empty names are governed by axioms employing a new semantic notion which we may call *pseudo-reference* (*PRef*). Thus, if 'James' is a name then the theory will contain an axiom

$PRef$ ('James', James)

(in which the language parameter is suppressed), and if 'Alpha' is an empty name then the theory will contain an axiom

$PRef$ ('Alpha', Alpha).

An atomic predicate 'is modest' is governed by an axiom in the statement of which substitutional quantification is used in the *ML*

$(\forall \gamma) (Ax) [PRef (\gamma, x) \rightarrow (Tr (\gamma \cap$ 'is modest')
$\leftrightarrow x$ is modest)].

Since it is not assumed that the *PRef* axioms admit even substitution of synonymous names *salva veritate*, axioms of the same form as this one for 'is modest' can be used for expressions which have the syntactic form of atomic predicates but which create opaque contexts for names. The substitutional quantifier 'E', for example, is governed by an axiom in the statement of which objectual quantification over expressions is used in the *ML*:

$(\forall \Phi) [Tr (\ulcorner (Ev_i) \Phi v_i \urcorner) \leftrightarrow (\exists \gamma) Tr (\ulcorner \Phi \gamma \urcorner)].$

And objectual quantification over expressions is related to substitutional

144

quantification in the *ML* by a pair of axioms:

$$(\forall \gamma)\,(Ex)\; PRef\,(\gamma, x)$$
$$(Ax)\,(\exists \gamma)\; PRef\,(\gamma, x).$$

From such axioms homophonic biconditionals are straightforwardly forthcoming. Let us then examine such a truth theory a little more closely first, in the case in which the base language contains empty names, and second, in the case in which the base language contains opaque contexts for names.

Consider the sentence '$(Ev_1)\; v_1$ is modest'. Unless the syntactic form of this sentence is highly misleading it has as a semantic constituent the predicate 'is modest'. So the canonical derivation of a truth condition specifying biconditional should employ the axiom for that predicate. This fact serves to focus our attention upon that axiom, which appears to offer a uniform account of atomic sentences of two kinds: atomic sentences containing names and atomic sentences containing empty names. As semantic theorists with some grasp upon subject-predicate sentences containing (non-empty) names we may well doubt that any such uniform account is genuinely possible, and in particular we may doubt that there is any such notion as pseudo-reference which includes the reference relation between names and objects as a special case. In short, so far from providing an answer to our question about quantification this case simply raises a host of problems of its own.

To say this is not to deny that one might simply award the sentence 'Alpha is modest' truth conditions (and so a truth value) by fiat, nor that one might introduce a context C for predicates such that $\ulcorner C(\text{is modest})\urcorner$ is true just in case for some name γ, $\gamma \cap$ 'is modest' is true. Of course one can do those things. But this fact highlights the difference between what is not, and what is, here in question. It does not help towards an answer to our question that C can be introduced as an abbreviation of the context

for some name γ, $\gamma \cap$ ' . . . ' is true.

Let us henceforth leave empty names out of consideration.

The case in which the base language contains opaque contexts for names includes two subcases corresponding to two kinds of opacity. On one hand, an expression with the syntactic form of an atomic predicate may take a name to yield a sentence in which that name occurs as a semantic constituent, creating a context which, though opaque, does admit substitution of synonymous names *salva veritate*. This is the kind of opacity produced by hyperintensional operators. The syntactic form of the name is strictly irrelevant to the meaning of the resulting sentence; all that is relevant is the meaning of the name (as stated in an *MRef* axiom). It is because the presence, in the language, of hyperintensional sentence operators would block the construction of a truth theory meeting *SC* that we here imagine the same kind of opacity to be introduced by an expression with the syntactic form of an atomic predicate. (It is a further question whether any such expressions of natural language introduce this kind of opacity.) On the other hand, an expression with the syntactic form of an atomic predicate may take a name to yield a sentence in which that name does not occur as a semantic constituent (but is merely mentioned) creating a context which does not admit substitution of synonymous names (but only of equiform names) *salva veritate*. This is the kind of opacity produced by quotation. The meaning of the name is strictly irrelevant to the meaning of the resulting sentence; all that is relevant is the syntactic form of the name. (These two subcases are not exhaustive. The expression

> . . . is so-called because of his height

takes a name to make a sentence in which the name occurs as a semantic constituent but also creates a context which does not admit substitution of synonymous names *salva veritate*.)

It is a relatively straightforward matter to provide a truth theory (of the Kripkean form) for a substitutionally quantified language whose base language involves opacity of just the first kind. Thus suppose that L_9 is a substitutionally quantified language whose base language contains the ten one-place predicates 'P_1', . . ., 'P_{10}' and ten names 'm_1', . . ., 'm_{10}', together with ten *quasi-predicates* X_1, . . ., X_{10} which introduce opacity of the first kind. Because of this opacity axioms for the names must specify more than simply a reference for each name. But because the opacity is of the first kind no new notion of pseudo-reference is needed; the familiar *MRef* will serve. Thus for a name 'm_1' we have

$$MRef(L_9, 'm_1', m_1)$$

for a predicate 'P_1' we have

$$(\forall \gamma \in L_9)(Ax)[MRef(L_9, \gamma, x) \rightarrow (Tr(L_9, \ulcorner P_1 \gamma \urcorner) \leftrightarrow P_1 x)]$$

146

and for a quasi-predicate 'X_1' we have

$$(\forall \gamma \in L_9)(\text{Ax}) [MRef(L_9, \gamma, x) \rightarrow (Tr(L_9, \ulcorner X_1 \gamma \urcorner) \leftrightarrow X_1 x)].$$

Truth functional connectives are governed by axioms of the familiar form. For 'E' we have

$$(\forall \Phi \in L_9) [Tr(L_9, \ulcorner (\text{Ev}_i) \Phi v_i \urcorner) \leftrightarrow (\exists \gamma \in L_9) \, Tr(L_9, \ulcorner \Phi \gamma \urcorner)].$$

There is a similar axiom for 'A', and we need

$$(\forall \gamma \in L_9)(\text{Ex}) \, MRef(L_9, \gamma, x)$$

and

$$(\text{Ax})(\exists \gamma \in L_9) \, MRef(L_9, \gamma, x).$$

The provision of such a truth theory does not reveal any particular quantificational idiom of natural language as substitutional quantification. It simply establishes the possibility of a quantificational idiom which has the syntactic form of quantification into name position, whose syntactic form is not misleading as to its semantic nature, and which is not quantification over objects of the kind named. And that possibility is enough to refute the thesis presently under consideration about the essential features of quantification. The quantification in L_9 is not quantification over objects of the kind named because the truth of '$(\text{Ev}_1)X_1 v_1$', for example, does not turn upon there being a (named) object with a certain property (associated with 'X_1'). The difference which is crucial for the truth of quantified sentences of L_9 is not that between one (named) object and two, nor that between one name and two (for there are no sentences whose truth is sensitive to the difference between one name and two with the same meaning). Rather, this quantification is quantification over meanings of names in L_9. If we were to accept that the meaning of a name is determined by an object referred to and a (relatively unspecific) way of thinking about that object, then we might say that the quantification is over ordered pairs of objects and ways of thinking, where the domain of relevant pairs is restricted in some way to those associated with names in L_9. If the quasi-predicate 'X_1' has the meaning of

Harry believes that . . . is modest

then we might specify the meaning of '$(\text{Ev}_1)X_1 v_1$' as that there is an object (named in L_9) and a way of thinking about that object (expressed by a name in L_9) such that Harry believes, concerning that object,

147

thought about in that way, that it is modest. (The restrictions are in parentheses since the restriction of the domain to the correct class of ordered pairs might be achieved in some way other than by explicit appeal to the notion of a name in L_9.)

We saw (in Section VI.3) that it is not an essential feature of quantification that it should be quantification into name position. We have now seen, by considering a substitutionally quantified language whose base language involves opacity of just the first kind (the kind that would by introduced by hyperintensional sentence operators), that it is not an essential feature of quantification into name position that it should be quantification over objects of the kind named. (For a substitutionally quantified language whose base language involves opacity of the second kind, that is, of the kind introduced by quotation, see Appendix 6.)

NOTES

The possibility of employing a theory in the style of $QT\theta$ rather than a theory in the style of $QS\theta$ was pointed out to me by Gareth Evans, and my reasons for preferring $QT\theta$ over $QS\theta$ are just those which he gave. See Evans (1977). He called theories of the first kind 'Fregean', on the basis of Dummett (1973, Chapter 2). Theories of the second kind he called, of course, 'Tarskian'. See Tarski (1956), and for a standard textbook treatment see eg. Mendelson (1964, Chapter 2).

On binary quantification see also Wallace (1965). On substitutional quantification see also Dunn and Belnap (1968), Wallace (1971), Camp (1975), and Wallace (1975b).

VII

DESCRIPTIONS

1 DESCRIPTIONS AND QUANTIFIERS

In English, and doubtless in other natural languages, definite descriptions have (almost) the same privileges of occurrence as proper names. What is more, (singular) definite descriptions and proper names both introduce individual objects which a sentence may be said to be about (in a highly pretheoretic sense of 'about'). So, someone might suggest, definite descriptions and proper names are semantically akin; expressions of both kinds are singular terms. (See Appendix 7.)

This suggestion is unconvincing. For two very clear reasons a semantic theorist should not rush to assign to definite descriptions the semantic property of genuine singular reference to objects. The first reason is that it is not only definite descriptions which have (almost) the same privileges of occurrence as names. What holds for 'the elephant' holds equally for 'some elephant(s)', 'every elephant', 'most elephants', and 'few elephants'. Indeed, it is impossible not to be impressed by the similarity of syntactic function between 'the' and expressions which are clearly binary quantifiers. The second reason is that, in the pretheoretic sense of 'about', quantifier phrases also introduce objects which a sentence may be said to be about. The sentence 'All elephants are playful' is, in that sense, about all elephants. Nor would it be wise for someone to take a stand on the fact that a (singular) definite description introduces a single object. It is too easy to ignore the fact that there are plural definite descriptions for which this is not the case.

The suggestion is unconvincing because it is based upon quite superficial similarities between definite descriptions and names. Given

149

a firm grasp upon the semantic difference between names on the one hand, and quantifier phrases on the other, it is easy to see that, at least in some of their uses, definite descriptions belong semantically with quantifier phrases. Let us recall the two main features (or batches of features) of the reference relation between names and objects. The object which is assigned to a name as its reference is tc-salient and e-salient (Section V.2). And let us consider, as a typical example of a quantifier phrase, the expression 'all philosophers'. Suppose that $X, Y, \ldots, Z$ are all the philosophers there are. Then the semantic property assigned to the phrase 'all philosophers' is indifferent to the existence or non-existence of $X, Y, \ldots, Z$. The meanings of sentences containing that quantifier phrase are existence independent (rather than existence dependent) with respect to those objects. Similarly, the beliefs expressed by sentences containing that quantifier phrase are existence independent. They are not singular beliefs concerning $X, Y, \ldots, Z$, since a man may well believe that all philosophers are modest, say, even though he has been totally causally isolated from $X, Y, \ldots, Z$. Those objects are not e-salient, and clearly no other objects are e-salient either. What is more, the truth of sentences containing 'all philosophers' does not depend (with respect to actual and counterfactual situations) upon how things are with $X, Y, \ldots, Z$. Those objects do not 'enter the truth conditions' of sentences containing that phrase. The sentence 'All philosophers are modest' could be true, for example, even though none of $X, Y, \ldots, Z$ was modest. Those objects are not tc-salient, and clearly no other objects are tc-salient either. Thus, in general, one cannot assign to a quantifier phrase objects which are tc-salient and e-salient. In this semantic respect quantifier phrases are sharply different from names.

Let us distinguish one kind of use of definite descriptions. A speaker may come out with the sentence

> The tallest philosopher is over seven feet tall

to make a sincere assertion even though there is no person concerning whom the speaker believes that he is the tallest philosopher. The speaker may simply believe, on purely general grounds, that there is some philosopher who is taller than the rest, and that whoever is tallest is over seven feet tall. The speaker might equally well have come out with the sentence

> The tallest philosopher, whoever that is, is over seven
> feet tall

to indicate his lack of singular beliefs. Let us call such uses '*whatever-that-is uses*'. In at least these uses definite descriptions are semantically akin to quantifier phrases. Thus suppose that, in fact, X is the tallest philosopher. The sentence 'The tallest philosopher is over seven feet tall' would mean just what it in fact means even if X were not to exist. Similarly, the belief that the tallest philosopher is over seven feet tall is a belief which it would be possible to have even if X were not to exist. The object X is not e-salient, and clearly no other object is e-salient either. What is more, the truth of sentences containing 'the tallest philosopher' in whatever-that-is uses does not depend (with respect to actual and counterfactual situations) upon how things are with X. That object does not 'enter the truth conditions' of sentences containing that definite description in that kind of use. The sentence 'The tallest philosopher is over seven feet tall' could be true, for example, even though X was not over seven feet tall. The object X is not tc-salient, and clearly no other object is tc-salient either.

In whatever-that-is uses, definite descriptions are semantically akin to quantifiers, and it is quite plausible that in such uses a definite description 'the F' is logically equivalent to the complex expression

$$(\exists x) [Fx \;\&\; (\forall y)(Fy \to y = x) \;\&\; \ldots x]$$

so that a sentence 'The F is G' containing a definite description in such a use is equivalent to

$$(\exists x) [Fx \;\&\; (\forall y)(Fy \to y = x) \;\&\; Gx].$$

Let us call this equivalence the *Russellian equivalence* (cf. Russell, 1905, p. 44). One can consistently accept the Russellian equivalence but reject the suggestion that each surface sentence containing a definite description in a whatever-that-is use should be 'preprocessed' into a sentence, at the level of input to a semantic theory, which does not contain a definite description but is (according to the Russellian equivalence) logically equivalent to the surface sentence. And one should reject that further suggestion, for it clearly infringes *SC*. (Rejection of that suggestion is not *ipso facto* criticism of Russell, for it is arguable that Russell's proposal for eliminating definite descriptions answered to a project quite different from that of constructing structurally adequate semantic theories for natural languages. See Sainsbury, 1979, pp. 154–60.)

It is a straightforward matter to add one more binary quantifier 'THE' to the language L_7, and to add one more axiom to the truth theory for that language. If, as we supposed (Section VI.2), the *ML* contains the binary quantifiers of the *OL* together with the one-place quantifiers '$\forall$' and '$\exists$' then the Russellian equivalence, in the form

$$(\text{THE } x)\,(Fx;\,Gx) \leftrightarrow (\exists x)\,[Fx \,\&\, (\forall y)\,(Fy \to y = x) \,\&\, Gx]$$

will be a theorem schema of the logic of the *ML*. The quantifier 'THE', like the quantifiers of L_7, is a restrictive binary quantifier. For we can associate with 'THE' a function f from pairs of cardinalities to truth values such that if a is the cardinality of the set of Fs which are Gs and b is the cardinality of the set of Fs which are non-Gs then

$$\text{'}(\text{THE } x)\,(Fx;\,Gx)\text{' is true iff } f(<a,\,b>) = \text{T},$$

namely the function f such that $f(<a,\,b>) = \text{T}$ just in case $a = 1$ and $b = 0$.

2   SPEAKER'S REFERENCE

Sentences containing definite descriptions in their whatever-that-is uses can be represented with the help of the binary quantifier 'THE'. The question which confronts the semantic theorist is whether the semantic account which he offers for whatever-that-is uses also covers other uses of definite descriptions. For there are certainly uses which are quite unlike whatever-that-is uses. Consider the following extended passage from Mitchell, *An Introduction to Logic* (1962, pp. 84-5):

> Definite descriptions, occurring as the subjects of sentences, have at least two distinct functions, which may be illustrated by two sets of examples:
>
> 1. 'The Prime Minister presides at Cabinet meetings'
>   'The Sovereign of Great Britain is the head of the Commonwealth'
>   'The man who wrote this unsigned letter had a bad pen'
> 2. 'The Prime Minister has invited me to lunch'
>   'The Queen made a tour of the Commonwealth'
>   'The author of *Waverley* limped'
>
> It is not difficult to see that the grammatical subjects of the sentences quoted in List 1 are not used — as proper names, for example, are used — to refer uniquely. For 'The Prime Minister' and 'The Sovereign' we can substitute, without change of

meaning, 'Whoever is Prime Minister' and 'Whoever is Sovereign'
. . . With the sentences in List 2 the case is different. The subject-
phrases serve to identify individuals, and what is predicated in
each case is predicated of the individuals so identified.

On the one hand, a speaker may know or believe that there is a unique
Prime Minister and know or believe that the office of Prime Minister
involves presiding over Cabinet meetings, without knowing or believing
concerning any particular object that it is Prime Minister or that it
presides at Cabinet meetings. If such a speaker comes out with the
first sentence on List 1 to make an assertion then he does not express
a singular belief and his audience can know perfectly well what he has
asserted without, for example, coming to believe concerning some
particular object that it presides at Cabinet meetings or is believed by
the speaker to preside at Cabinet meetings. This is a whatever-that-is
use of the definite description, and the sentence as used on such an
occasion would be represented at the level of input to a semantic
theory as containing the binary quantifier 'THE'. On the other hand,
a speaker may know concerning a particular object that it is Prime
Minister and may want to put his audience in a position to know
concerning that object that it has invited the speaker to lunch. Such
a speaker may come out with the first sentence on list 2 precisely in
order to communicate, or 'get across', to his audience the information
concerning that object that it has invited him to lunch. This is not a
whatever-that-is use of the definite description. The question for the
semantic theorist is whether the difference in uses corresponds to a
semantic difference in the definite description as used on the two
occasions, whether, that is, the definite article 'the' is ambiguous.

In order to characterize the second kind of use more precisely,
let us introduce a notion closely related to that of s-meaning (cf.
Section I.2). A speaker S *s-means concerning an object* z that it is
thus and so, by his utterance (token) x directed at audience A, just
in case

(1) S intends concerning z that x will produce in A an (activated)
      belief concerning it (z) that it is thus and so;
(2) for some feature F of x, S intends that A should recognize
      S's primary intention in part by recognizing x to have
      feature F; in particular, for some feature G of x, S intends
      that A should recognize concerning z that S's primary
      intention concerns it in part by recognizing x to have feature G;

(3) *S* intends that *A*'s recognition of *S*'s primary intention should be part of *A*'s reason for believing concerning *z* that it is thus and so;

(4) *S* does not intend that *A* should be deceived about *S*'s intentions.

What is characteristic of the second kind of use is that the speaker s-means concerning, for example, the object *z* which is in fact the Prime Minister that it has invited him to lunch. In this case the relevant feature (*G*) of the utterance might be that it contains a definite description such that it is common knowledge between speaker and audience that each believes the description to apply literally to the object *z*. But other cases are possible. It is certainly possible for a speaker to s-mean concerning *z* that it is modest by an utterance of 'The tallest philosopher is modest' even though *z* is not, and is not believed by speaker and audience to be, the tallest philosopher. The relevant feature of the utterance might be, for example, that it contains a description which patently does not apply literally to *z* (an ironic or 'scare quoted' use of a description). Let us say that when a speaker s-means concerning *z* that it is thus and so there is *speaker's reference* to *z*.

In his influential paper, 'Reference and definite descriptions' (1966), Donnellan offered labels for roughly these two kinds of use of definite descriptions. He called the whatever-that-is uses '*attributive*' and the uses in which there is speaker's reference to a particular object '*referential*' (Donnellan, 1966, p. 285):

> A speaker who uses a definite description attributively in an assertion states something about whoever or whatever is the so-and-so. A speaker who uses a definite description referentially in an assertion, on the other hand, uses the description to enable his audience to pick out whom or what he is talking about and states something about that person or thing.

Having labelled two kinds of use, Donnellan went on to argue that a Russellian theory, even if appropriate for attributive uses, would not cover referential uses. (He seemed, in short, to be arguing for an ambiguity in 'the', although at one point he explicitly denied that definite descriptions are ambiguous: ibid. p. 297).

Before we consider further the prospects for a Russellian theory, it is important to clarify what is, in fact, a very wide variety of uses of definite descriptions. For the variety may be obscured by the use of just two labels. The first thing to notice is that Donnellan's positive accounts of attributive and referential uses are, in a certain sense, incommensurable. His positive account of attributive uses is in terms of the speaker's reason or grounds for his assertion: 'Suppose first that we come upon poor Smith foully murdered. From the brutal manner of the killing and the fact that Smith was the most lovable person in the world, we might exclaim, "Smith's murderer is insane"' (ibid. p. 288). But his positive account of referential uses is in terms of the speaker's intentions in making his utterance (ibid.):

> The contrast with such a use of the sentence is one of those
> situations in which we expect and intend our audience to realize
> whom we have in mind when we speak of Smith's murderer and,
> most importantly, to know that it is this person about whom we
> are going to say something.

What this incommensurability suggests is that the classification of uses as attributive or referential is neither exhaustive nor exclusive, and the suggestion is correct. The classification is not exhaustive since it is possible that a speaker's grounds for an assertion that the F is G may be furnished by his beliefs concerning some particular object that it is uniquely F and that it is G, even though the speaker has no intentions that his audience should come to believe concerning that object that it is G. The classification is not exclusive since it may be common knowledge between a speaker and his audience that each believes concerning, say, z that it is uniquely F, and the speaker may trade upon this common knowledge in order to s-mean concerning z that it is G, even though his beliefs concerning z did not furnish the grounds for his assertion. (Donnellan in fact points out that beliefs concerning a particular object may accompany what is, by his positive account, an attributive use but fails to note that common knowledge of shared beliefs concerning a particular object may provide a situation ripe for an attributive use accompanied by speaker's reference.)

A distinction which yields a classification which is neither exhaustive nor exclusive is not a good starting point for an argument that definite descriptions are ambiguous. A better starting point for such an argument would be the distinction between referential and non-referential uses. In a later paper, 'Speaker reference, descriptions and anaphora', Donnellan (1978, p. 50) proposes that the term 'attributive' should be applied to precisely non-referential uses, and gives an example which surely would not have been classified as attributive on the basis of his earlier positive account:

Suppose . . . that my grounds for my statement [that the strongest
man in the world can lift at least 450 pounds] are that I believe
of Vladimir that he is the strongest and believe that *he* can lift
450 pounds. Still, those are my *grounds*, if I do not expect
nor intend that my audience shall recognize that I want to
talk about Vladimir and to become informed [*sic*] about *his*
strength, we have no reason to say that I referred to Vladimir.
What I have been describing, of course, is a case of what I
would call an attributive use of a definite description.

Clarity will be served if we do not use 'attributive' interchangeably
with 'non-referential', but rather reserve the former term for uses
which are classified as attributive on the basis of Donnellan's earlier
positive account. Armed with that terminological convention we can
specify more accurately the relation between whatever-that-is uses
and attributive uses. Whatever-that-is uses are non-referential. So,
since attributive uses may be referential, it is not necessary that all
attributive uses are whatever-that-is uses. Conversely, since a speaker
who lacks relevant singular beliefs may make an assertion without
having any grounds at all (he may simply guess), it is not necessary
that all whatever-that-is uses are attributive uses. The relation seems,
rather, to be this. If a speaker lacks relevant singular beliefs and yet
has grounds for his assertion then those grounds will be such as to
render his whatever-that-is use also an attributive use.

The boundary between attributive and non-attributive uses is itself
not sharp. For it is possible that a speaker might have mixed grounds
for his assertion. Thus suppose that a speaker comes upon poor Smith
who has been murdered moderately foully. Suppose that the speaker
is moderately, but not overwhelmingly, inclined to believe that whoever murdered Smith was insane. Suppose further that the speaker
comes to believe on independent grounds that Jones murdered Smith,
and has always been moderately, but not overwhelmingly, inclined to
believe that Jones is insane. On the basis of all his evidence the speaker
might conclude that Smith's murderer, that is Jones, is certainly insane,
and on those grounds assert that Smith's murderer is insane. It is simply
unclear whether this use of the definite description 'Smith's murderer'
is attributive or not (see Kripke, 1977, note 28).

If we are to clarify the wide variety of uses of definite descriptions
then there is a second thing to notice, namely the range of uses which
are neither whatever-that-is uses nor referential uses. Suppose, for

example, that X lives with a woman Y and that X knows (and so believes) concerning Y both that she is the woman he lives with and that she was born in Alice Springs. And suppose that, on the basis of what he knows about Y, X says to a colleague Z,

The woman I live with was born in Alice Springs.

Suppose that X does not believe that Z has any belief concerning any particular woman that she is the woman X lives with, but that Z in fact knows that X lives with Y. This is a non-referential use. We might vary the example by supposing that X knows all along that Z knows that X lives with Y and intends that Z should learn that Y was born in Alice Springs, but that X also intends that Z should not realize that X knows that Z knows that X lives with Y, and so should not realize that X intends that Z should learn that Y was born in Alice Springs. This also is a non-referential use. And it is possible to construct further examples, ever more remote from whatever-that-is uses, yet still falling short of referential uses.

These non-referential uses are clearly also not attributive. (They demonstrate how far the referential/attributive distinction falls short of providing an exhaustive classification.) The grounds for X's assertion are furnished, not by some such general consideration as that it must be the case that whoever he lives with was born in Alice Springs, but by his beliefs concerning Y. Let us say that in such cases of non-attributive use the speaker *talks about* the object beliefs concerning which prompted his assertion. (This piece of terminology is borrowed from Evans, 1977, p. 516. The use of 'talks about' as a term of art is not intended to answer to any pretheoretic use of that expression.)

With the wide variety of uses of definite descriptions thus (partially) clarified, we can consider the prospects for a Russellian theory in the face of the phenomenon of speaker's reference. Let us say that a *Russellian theorist* is one who proposes to represent sentences containing definite descriptions in their referential uses with the help of the binary quantifier 'THE'. On the other hand, an *ambiguity theorist* is one who proposes to represent sentences containing definite descriptions in their referential uses as semantically quite different from sentences containing definite descriptions in their non-referential uses. In particular, such a theorist proposes that in their referential uses definite descriptions should be assigned the semantic property of genuine singular reference, so that sentences containing definite descriptions in such uses should (relative to those occasions of use) be assigned strict and literal meanings which are existence dependent. Indeed, what a sentence literally means (relative to such an occasion of use) should be just what the speaker s-means in his act of speaker's reference.

To the extent that the ambiguity theorist's case rests upon the mere existence of referential uses it is extraordinarily weak. Let us consider just two related weaknesses. First, both the ambiguity theorist and the Russellian theorist have to offer an account of the fact that when X says

The woman I live with was born in Alice Springs

with no speaker's reference, Z may come to believe concerning Y that she was born in Alice Springs. Since X's use of the definite description is non-referential, both theorists will agree that the sentence, as used on that occasion, can be represented as

(THE x) ((Woman with whom I live)x;
x was born in Alice Springs).

And presumably both theorists will say that Z comes to his belief concerning Y on the basis jointly of his knowing what X literally asserted or said, and of his non-semantic belief that X lives with Y uniquely. This account can be naturally extended to cover cases in which there is speaker's reference, and the Russellian theorist so extends it. The ambiguity theorist, by contrast, treats cases in which there is speaker's reference in a radically different way. The only principle which would clearly justify such a difference in treatment is the principle that it is not possible that a speaker should assert or say (and so s-mean or ws-mean) one thing and in addition s-mean something else. But this principle has unacceptable consequences in a host of cases. Irony provides one example. A burglar who comes out with the words 'Some police are coming' and s-means that it is time to leave provides another (see Kripke, 1977, p. 262).

The second weakness of the ambiguity theorist's case is that if the existence of referential uses of definite descriptions suffices to show that definite descriptions are ambiguous then surely the occurrence of speaker's reference in some uses of quantifier phrases such as 'a philosopher', 'every philosopher in this room', 'at least three philosophers', and so on, reveals those phrases as ambiguous as well. Consider an example. Suppose that X and Z are at a party and that it is common knowledge between them that there are five philosophers in the room, of whom a certain two are paragons of virtue. Suppose that it is also common knowledge between them that both U and V are in trouble with the law, and that the legal standing of the fifth philosopher, W, has been a matter of some speculation. Then X may very well come out with the words 'Most philosophers in this room are in trouble with the law' and s-mean concerning W that he is in trouble with the law. Yet the idea that the phrase 'Most philosophers in this room' is ambiguous as between a quantifier phrase and a genuine singular referring expression is a *reductio ad absurdum* of the ambiguity theorist's position. (For a number of other arguments against the ambiguity theorist see Kripke, 1977. Donnellan, 1978, offers on behalf of the ambiguity theorist an argument which turns upon the use of pronouns in discourse after a referential use of a definite description. This argument requires separate consideration and will be discussed briefly in Section VII.5.)

It is a feature of some of Donnellan's examples of referential uses of definite descriptions that the description does not literally apply to the object to which there is speaker's reference. The possibility of such cases may seem to constitute a difficulty for the Russellian theorist. For suppose that a speaker uses the definite description 'Smith's murderer' with speaker's reference to Jones in his utterance of 'Smith's murderer is insane'. Suppose that Jones did not murder Smith but is insane, and that the person who did murder Smith is quite unknown to the speaker but is, as it happens, not insane. Then has not the speaker said (at least in a pretheoretic sense of 'said') something true about Jones, namely that he is insane? Yet the Russellian theorist judges the truth or falsity of the utterance according as there is or is not a person who both uniquely murdered Smith and is insane, and consequently judges that the speaker spoke falsely.

Such an example may seem to constitute a difficulty for the Russellian theorist. But, in fact, what it reveals is a strength rather than a weakness in his position. The Russellian theorist can acknowledge both that the speaker strictly and literally said something false and that the speaker communicated or 'got across' something concerning Jones which was true. And he can point out that in ordinary usage 'says' covers more than 'strictly and literally says'. The ambiguity theorist who represents the expression 'Smith's murderer', as used on this occasion, as a genuine singular referring expression, referring to Jones, must claim that all that was said (in however broad or narrow a sense of 'said') was true. By his account, the speaker comes out with 'Smith's murderer is insane' believing falsely that Jones murdered Smith, Smith's actual murderer is not insane, and yet the speaker says nothing false. It is this position, rather than the Russellian theorist's position, which is counterintuitive.

It should, in any case, be clear that building into examples the feature that the definite description used does not literally apply to the object to which there is speaker's reference cannot advance the argument once it is agreed that the existence of speaker's reference in cases in which the definite description does literally apply to the object does not endanger the Russellian theorist's position. For either the speaker believes that the definite description literally applies to the object or else he does not. If the speaker does believe that the definite description literally applies to the object, then the Russellian theorist can give an account which naturally extends the account which both theorists would give of cases in which there is no speaker's reference but the speaker intends his audience to come by a belief concerning a particular object to which, the speaker believes (falsely), the definite description literally applies. If the speaker does not believe that the definite description literally applies to the object, then his use of the definite description is an ironic or 'scare quoted' use. And we precisely expect a gap between what is said and what is s-meant in such uses.

3   UNDERSPECIFICATION AND ANAPHORA

It is a striking feature of our use of definite descriptions in English that we readily tolerate the use of a definite description even in circumstances in which it is quite clear that there is no object to which the description uniquely applies. Thus, someone who visits a farmhouse and reports at breakfast that the rooster crowed at 5 a.m. is not taken to be claiming that there is just one rooster in the universe. This fact may seem to threaten the Russellian equivalence

$$(\text{THE } x)(Fx; Gx) \leftrightarrow (\exists x)\,[Fx \;\&\; (\forall y)(Fy \rightarrow y=x) \;\&\; Gx]$$

and so to present a difficulty for the Russellian theorist.

The breakfast table report is, in fact, an instance of a more general, and relatively well understood, phenomenon, namely contextual limitation of the domain of quantification. Thus, in the context provided by breakfast time on a farm it might very naturally be assumed, during ✶ a particular stretch of conversation, that the domain of quantification is limited to objects on the farm. In that context, and under that assumption, the speaker will be taken to be committing himself to No. there being just one rooster on the farm. If there is more than one rooster on the farm then someone might correct the speaker in the words, 'Not the rooster, but a rooster; there are several'. As this response would itself make clear, contextual limitation of the domain of quantification affects the interpretation which is put upon all quantified sentences and not just sentences containing definite descriptions. Thus, a householder who is explaining to a friend the details of ownership of the various items in his house may say, 'Every piece of furniture is mine but the cat belongs to the neighbours'. Just as he is not taken to be claiming that there is just one cat in the universe, so also he is not taken to be claiming that every piece of furniture in the universe is his.

There are two courses which a semantic theorist might take in response to these features of language use. On the one hand he might insist that the strict and literal meaning of quantifier expressions involves no limitation of the domain beyond that provided by the common noun or noun phrase which is explicitly used. On this account, contextual limitation of the domain of quantification would be relevant to what is s-meant (or ws-meant) rather than to what is strictly and literally asserted (or said). On the other hand the semantic theorist might incorporate context dependence into the strict and literal meaning of the quantifiers. On this account, contextual limitation of the domain of quantification would be relevant to what is strictly and literally asserted (or said). Whichever course the semantic theorist opts for, he can hold to the Russellian equivalence. So the features of language use which we have considered do not present a difficulty for the Russellian theorist (see Sainsbury, 1979, pp. 113–16).

However, it is not the case that appeal to contextual limitation of the domain of quantification can account for all uses of definite descriptions in circumstances in which it is quite clear that there is no object to which the description uniquely applies. Consider the following pair of sentences:

I met a linguist. The linguist was educated in California.

The use of the definite description 'the linguist' obviously does not commit the speaker to there being just one linguist in the universe. Rather, the second sentence in the pair is naturally interpreted as equivalent to

The linguist whom I met was educated in California.

But this is not just a matter of contextual limitation of the domain of quantification. For it is a very striking fact that while in the pair

> I met some linguists. The linguists were educated in
> California

the second sentence is naturally interpreted as equivalent to

> The linguists whom I met were educated in California

it is not the case that in the pair

> I met some linguists. Most linguists were educated in
> California

the second sentence is naturally interpreted as equivalent to

> Most linguists whom I met were educated in California.

Here we are confronting a phenomenon which is tied to the use of the definite article as against other quantifiers. (One can hardly fail to be struck by the difference between the last pair of sentences and the following pair:

> I met some linguists. Most of the linguists were educated
> in California.

This time the second sentence is naturally interpreted as equivalent to

> Most linguists whom I met were educated in California.)

It was examples like these which prompted Vendler (1967, p. 46) to put forward the following hypothesis: '[T]he definite article in front of a noun is always and infallibly the sign of a restrictive adjunct, present or recoverable, attached to the noun'. Without evaluating this hypothesis in full generality we can agree that definite descriptions which do not, as they stand, apply uniquely to any object (even taking into account contextual limitation of the domain of quantification) are often used, and are interpreted as though they contained further descriptive material (in the form of a restrictive relative clause). Vendler (1967, pp. 45–6) himself gave a particularly clear example:

Consider the following sequence:
I saw a man. The man wore a hat.
Obviously, the man *I saw* wore a hat. *The*, here, indicates a

162

deleted but recoverable restrictive adjunct based upon a previous occurrence of the same noun in an identifying context.

It is interesting to notice that in the pair of sentences

> I saw a man. The man who slipped on a banana skin wore a hat

the second sentence, in which the common noun 'man' is followed by a restrictive relative clause, is not naturally interpreted as equivalent to

> The man whom I saw (and) who slipped on a banana skin wore a hat.

But in the pair of sentences

> I saw a man. The man, who slipped on a banana skin, wore a hat

the second sentence, in which the relative clause is not restrictive, is naturally interpreted as equivalent to

> The man whom I saw, who slipped on a banana skin, wore a hat.

It seems that the absence of a restrictive relative clause in the definite description serves, in such cases, as an indicator that further descriptive material, to be recovered in some (regular) way from the introductory sentence, must be added to the definite description.

There are then several courses which, at least at first glance, may appear open to a semantic theorist. First, he might take Vendler's hypothesis to heart. He might both represent the surface sentence 'The man wore a hat' as it occurs in the given linguistic context, by the sentence

$$(\text{THE } x) ((\text{Man whom I saw})x; x \text{ wore a hat})$$

at the level of input to a semantic theory, and go on to insist that at the level of input every definite description must contain a restrictive adjunct. But, in fact, this is not a course which is open to a semantic theorist. For it is simply not possible to give a general semantic account of common nouns and restrictive relative clauses, and of the way in which such expressions occur in quantified sentences, and to give an account of definite descriptions which contain restrictive relative clauses, without *ipso facto* giving an account of definite descriptions which contain no restrictive adjunct. The fact that this is not possible

163

simply corresponds to the fact that someone who knows the meanings of such quantified sentences as

> Some linguists whom I met are American
> Some linguists are American
> Most linguists whom I met are American
> Most linguists are American

and who knows the meaning of the sentence

> The linguist whom I met is American

is thereby in a position to know the meaning of the sentence

> The linguist is American.

Thus a semantic theorist is bound to allow, at the level of input to a semantic theory, definite descriptions which contain common nouns (or, in fact, other predicates) standing alone, along with those which contain complex noun phrases.

A second course, which may appear rather more attractive, is this. A semantic theorist may insist that, even in the linguistic context set up in Vendler's example, the strict and literal meaning of 'The man wore a hat' is such that the utterance is literally false provided that there is more than one man in the universe. Because of the introductory sentence 'I met a man' the speaker may succeed in communicating or 'getting across' that the man whom he met wore a hat. But that is not a matter of what is strictly and literally asserted or said. This course may appear attractive (in part because it allows the semantic theorist simply to ignore the phenomena in question) and there is no conclusive argument against following it. But two points deserve consideration. One point is that the features of the use of definite descriptions with which we are concerned are conventional features of their use, and features which cannot be explained in terms of general conventions of conversational practice (since they are specific to the definite article). And conventional features of the use of a particular expression in acts of s-meaning and so on have a *prima facie* claim upon the attention of a semantic theorist. The second point is that there are features of the use of pronouns which, intuitively, are closely related to these features of the use of definite descriptions (see Section VII.4). In the pair of sentences

> I saw a man. He wore a hat

the second sentence is naturally interpreted as equivalent to

The man whom I saw wore a hat.

And it is simply not open to a semantic theorist to ignore these features of the use of pronouns, since there is no alternative account which he can offer of the strict and literal meaning of 'He wore a hat' as it occurs in the given linguistic context (except, wildly implausibly, that it means that the unique male object in the universe wore a hat). What these two points together suggest is that a semantic theorist should allow that, in certain linguistic contexts, a sentence containing a definite description without a restrictive relative clause may have the strict and literal meaning of a related sentence containing a definite description with a restrictive relative clause. And to allow that is not, of course, to depart from a Russellian theory.

There is thus a third course which a semantic theorist might take. At the level of input to a semantic theory there will be sentences containing definite descriptions without restrictive relative clauses (and without other restrictive adjuncts such as attributive adjectives) and sentences containing definite descriptions with restrictive relative clauses. These sentences will, in particular, contain the binary quantifier 'THE'. In certain linguistic contexts, surface sentences containing definite descriptions without restrictive relative clauses will be represented at the level of input to a semantic theory as sentences containing definite descriptions with restrictive relative clauses. Exactly how the impact of linguistic context upon representation at the level of input is to be registered will depend, in part, upon the accompanying syntactic theory. There are at least two broad strategies. Upon one strategy a syntactic rule is incorporated into the syntactic theory which simply allows a restrictive relative clause to be deleted provided that it stands in a certain (syntactically characterized) relation to material in the preceding sentence which constitutes the linguistic context. Upon the other strategy there is no such rule in the syntactic theory. Rather, the impact of the linguistic context in these cases is accounted for by a fully general theory of context dependence.

The use, by actual speakers of English, of definite descriptions which do not, as they stand, apply uniquely to any object (even taking into account contextual limitation of the domain of quantification) certainly introduces complications. But it does not constitute an objection against the Russellian theorist. In particular, it does not provide any support for a suggestion that definite descriptions should sometimes be treated as genuine singular referring expressions.

4 PRONOUNS AND ANAPHORA

The *anaphoric* use of pronouns has already been mentioned. In the pair of sentences

> Mary owns a dog. It is lazy

the second sentence is naturally interpreted as equivalent to

> The dog which Mary owns is lazy.

Similarly, in the pair of sentences

> Mary owns some dogs. They are lazy

the second sentence is naturally interpreted as equivalent to

> The dogs which Mary owns are lazy.

The occurrence of two separate sentences is not an essential feature of the example. The sentence

> Mary owns some dogs and they are lazy

is naturally interpreted as equivalent to

> Mary owns some dogs and the dogs which Mary owns
> are lazy

and so is naturally judged to be false if some dogs which Mary owns are not lazy. For 'the definite article marks the speaker's intention to exhaust the range determined by the restrictive clause' (Vendler, 1967, p. 51). Similarly, the sentence

> John owns some sheep and Harry vaccinates them

is naturally interpreted as equivalent to

> John owns some sheep and Harry vaccinates the sheep
> that John owns

and so is naturally judged to be false if there are some sheep which John owns but which Harry does not vaccinate. (This example is borrowed from Evans, 1977, p. 492. This whole section simply states some of the main points of that paper.) For this reason, the sentence cannot be represented at the level of input to a semantic theory as

> (SOME x) (Sheep x; John owns x & Harry vaccinates x).

For, even if 'SOME' is interpreted as plural, the truth of that last sentence is consistent with there being some sheep which John owns but which Harry does not vaccinate. The pronoun 'them' in its anaphoric use does not, then, correspond to a bound variable at the level of input to a semantic theory.

Let us recall that the sentence

$$(\text{MOST } x) \text{ (Philosopher } x; x \text{ is modest)}$$

at the level of input becomes, at the surface, a sentence in which a quantifier phrase made up of the quantifier 'most' and the common noun 'philosopher' occupies the vacant name position *vis-à-vis* the predicate 'is modest'. In a similar way, sentences of the form

$$(Qx) \text{ (Philosopher } x; x \text{ frowns when } x \text{ is thinking)}$$

at the level of input become, at the surface, sentences in which a quantifier phrase containing the common noun 'philosopher' occupies the vacant name position *vis-à-vis* the predicate 'frowns' and a pronoun 'he' or 'they' occupies the vacant name position *vis-à-vis* the predicate 'is thinking'. Thus, in the surface sentences

> Every philosopher frowns when he is thinking
> Some philosopher frowns when he is thinking
> Some philosophers frown when they are thinking
> Most philosophers frown when they are thinking
> Few philosophers frown when they are thinking

and in the sentences

> No philosopher frowns when he is thinking
> Exactly three philosophers frown when they are thinking

the pronouns 'he' and 'they' correspond to bound variables at the level of input.

We might expect that sentences of the form

$$(Qx) \text{ (Philosopher } x; \text{ if } x \text{ frowns then } x \text{ is thinking)}$$

would be similarly related to surface sentences. But consider the surface sentences

> If every philosopher frowns then he is thinking
> If some philosopher frowns then he is thinking
> If some philosophers frown then they are thinking

> If most philosophers frown then they are thinking
> If few philosophers frown then they are thinking
> If no philosopher frowns then he is thinking
> If exactly three philosophers frown then they are thinking.

The first of these sentences is only dubiously intelligible; the pronoun 'he' has to be heard as referring to some (perhaps demonstrated) object. The syntactically similar sentence

> If every philosopher frowns then they are thinking

is more intelligible but it does not correspond to

> (EVERY x) (Philosopher x; if x frowns then x is thinking)

for the surface sentence is naturally interpreted as equivalent to

> If every philosopher frowns then the philosophers who
> frown are thinking.

Similarly, the second and third sentences on the list are naturally interpreted as equivalent to

> If some philosopher frowns then the philosopher who
> frowns is thinking
> If some philosophers frown then the philosophers who
> frown are thinking.

The fourth sentence admits of two readings, on only one of which the pronoun corresponds to a bound variable. The fifth sentence admits of only one reading, and on that reading the pronoun does not correspond to a bound variable. The sixth sentence, like the first, is only dubiously intelligible. It is, in fact, bizarre in just the way that

> If no philosopher frowns then the philosopher who
> frowns is thinking

is bizarre. Finally, the seventh sentence admits of only one reading and on that reading the pronoun does not correspond to a bound variable.

The surface sentences which we listed do not correspond to the sentences at the level of input from which we began. In particular, the pronouns in those surface sentences do not correspond to bound variables at the level of input. This is not to say, of course, that no surface sentences correspond to those sentences at the level of input. On the contrary, surface sentences such as

Every philosopher is such that if he frowns then he is
thinking

Exactly three philosophers are such that if they frown
then they are thinking

precisely so correspond. In particular, the pronouns in those surface
sentences do correspond to bound variables at the level of input.

There is a pattern in these facts. In order to state what the pattern
is we have to make use of a rather technical syntactic relation between
expressions, in particular between occurrences of names and so derivatively between name positions. One expression in a sentence is said to
govern another just in case the least complex syntactic constituent of
the sentence which, according to the syntactic theory, has the first
expression as a syntactic constituent and has some other syntactic
constituent as well, also has the second expression as a syntactic constituent (either an immediate or a mediate constituent). For example,
in the sentence

John frowns when Bert is thinking

the expression 'John' governs the expression 'Bert'. For the adverbial
phrase beginning with 'when', and of which 'Bert' is a syntactic constituent, attaches syntactically to the verb 'frowns'. Thus, the least
complex syntactic constituent of the sentence which has 'John' as a
syntactic constituent and has some other syntactic constituent as well
is the whole sentence which, of course, has 'Bert' as a (mediate) syntactic constituent. In the sentence

John owns Larry and Harry vaccinates Flo

the expression 'Larry' does not govern the expression 'Flo'. For 'and'
syntactically conjoins two sentences in one of which 'Larry' is a syntactic constituent, and in the other of which 'Flo' is a syntactic constituent.
So it is not the case that the least complex syntactic constituent of the
whole sentence which has 'Larry' as a syntactic constituent and has
some other syntactic constituent as well also has 'Flo' as a syntactic
constituent. Rather similarly, in the sentence

If John frowns then Bert is thinking

the expression 'John' does not govern the expression 'Bert'. The governing relation is not symmetric. If one expression governs another then
the first is sometimes said to *C-command* the second, and the second is

said to be *in construction with* the first (see e.g. Wasow, 1979, p. 203).
In

> x frowns when x is thinking

the first name position governs the second, while in

> John owns x and Harry vaccinates x

and in

> if x frowns then x is thinking

the first name position does not govern the second. So the pattern in our examples seems to be this. A surface sentence in which a quantifier phrase occupies one name position and a pronoun (agreeing in number and gender) occupies a later name position is naturally interpreted as though the pronoun corresponds to a bound variable (associated with the quantifier phrase) just in case the first name position governs the second. If the first name position does not govern the second then, at least in the cases in which the quantifier phrase begins with 'a' or 'some', the sentence is naturally interpreted as equivalent to one in which a definite description replaces the pronoun. It is an important feature of 'such that' that in, for example,

> Every philosopher is such that if he frowns then he is
> thinking

the name position occupied by 'every philosopher' governs both the positions occupied by the pronoun 'he'. (See Evans, 1977, pp.495-7; also Appendix 8.)

A sentence which contains an anaphoric pronoun is naturally interpreted as equivalent to a sentence in which the pronoun is replaced by a definite description systematically related to other material in that sentence or a preceding sentence. Let us try to make this a little more precise. Let us consider just sentences containing one quantifier phrase and an anaphoric pronoun, such as

> Mary owns a dog and it is lazy

and pairs of sentences in which the first contains one quantifier phrase and the second contains an anaphoric pronoun, such as

> Mary owns a dog. It is lazy.

And let us say that the *antecedent sentence* is the smallest sentence which contains all the expressions which the quantifier phrase governs (which are in construction with the quantifier phrase). Thus in each case the antecedent sentence is

Mary owns a dog.

This sentence is represented at the level of input as

(SOME x) (Dog x; Mary owns x).

And the definite description which can replace the anaphoric pronoun is 'the dog which Mary owns'. This same definite description or its plural could replace the anaphoric pronoun if the antecedent sentence was any of the following:

Mary owns every dog.
Mary owns most dogs.
Mary owns few dogs.
Mary owns exactly three dogs.
Mary owns no dog.

(This last case will not arise, of course, if the occurrence of anaphroic pronouns after antecedent sentences containing 'no' is blocked by the syntactic theory.) In this very simple case the pattern seems clear enough. If the antecedent sentence is represented at the level of input as

(Qx) (Fx; Gx)

then an anaphoric pronoun can be replaced by a definite description 'the F which is G' or 'the Fs which are Gs'.

Complications are introduced into this simple picture of a definite description replacing the anaphoric pronoun by the fact that surface sentences containing definite descriptions are often ambiguous. Thus, the surface sentence

The President of the USA used to be a Democrat

is ambiguous as between

PAST [(THE x) ((President of the USA) x; x is a Democrat)]

and

(THE x) ((President of the USA) x; PAST[x is a Democrat]).

The surface sentence

The animal which John bought might have been a donkey

is ambiguous as between

> ◊ [(THE *x*) ((Animal which John bought) *x*;
> *x* is a donkey)]

and

> (THE *x*) ((Animal which John bought) *x*;
> ◊ [*x* is a donkey]).

And the surface sentence

> John believes that the murderer of Smith is Spanish

is ambiguous as between, on one hand, a sentence which results by the application of a hyperintensional sentence operator to the sentence 'The murderer of Smith is Spanish', and, on the other hand,

> John believes concerning the murderer of Smith that
> he is Spanish.

Someone who holds that anaphoric pronouns simply go proxy for definite descriptions must uncover an ambiguity in corresponding sentences containing anaphoric pronouns.

Let us first consider some examples with the 'believes' operator. Evans has pointed out that the sentence

> A man murdered Smith, but John does not believe
> that he murdered Smith

'attributes to John merely a non-contradictory belief *of* [concerning] the murderer that he is not the murderer' (Evans, 1977, p. 519). And it is true that this is by far the more natural interpretation of that sentence. But consider the following sentence:

> A man murdered Smith, and the police believe that he
> used a knife.

This sentence is not naturally interpreted as attributing to the police a belief concerning the murderer that he used a knife, but simply a belief that whoever murdered Smith used a knife. These two sentences are each relatively unambiguous, but they are unambiguous in opposite ways. And the second sentence of the pair

> A man came into the room. I believe he was over six
> feet tall

172

is ambiguous. So there is nothing in these examples to threaten the view that anaphoric pronouns simply go proxy for definite descriptions.

Let us then consider some examples with temporal and modal operators. Evans (1977, p. 519) gives the following example with the past tense operator:

> Boston has a Mayor and he used to be a Democrat

is unambiguous, while its prolix version is ambiguous

> Boston has a Mayor and the Mayor of Boston used to
> be a Democrat.

It is certainly true that one reading of the sentence containing the anaphoric pronoun is strongly preferred, and more strongly preferred than the corresponding reading of the sentence containing the definite description. But that fact is not enough to show that anaphoric pronouns do not go proxy for definite descriptions. For it might be, for example, that it is more difficult in the case of pronouns than it is in the case of explicit quantifier phrases to use stress (or anything else) to override the indication of relative scope which is provided by the syntactic form of the sentence. What would count decisively in favour of the view that anaphoric pronouns do not simply go proxy for definite descriptions would be agreement amongst speakers that in the pair

> The USA has a President. It used to be the case that
> he was a Democrat

the second sentence can only be interpreted in such a way that its truth requires that the man who is now President of the USA used to be a Democrat. But, in fact, speakers vary in their intuitions about such examples. Similarly, at least some speakers hear the second sentence of the pair

> John bought his children an animal. It might have
> been the case that it was a donkey

as ambiguous, and in particular as having one reading upon which all that is required for its truth is that John might have bought his children a donkey (uniquely). So let us, at least provisionally, accept that anaphoric pronouns go proxy for definite descriptions. (The alternative view, which Evans prefers, is that anaphoric pronouns have their reference *fixed* by definite descriptions. This does not have the, obviously unwanted, consequence that anaphoric pronouns are genuine singular referring expressions. The net effect, rather, is to ensure that the object, if any, to which the definite description now, in fact, applies is tc-salient. Thus, on this view, the second sentence of the last pair requires for its truth that the animal which John in fact bought for his children is an animal which might have been a donkey. A similar net effect could be achieved by use of 'the*' — cf. Section V.3. For the notion of a reference fixing description, see Kripke, 1972, p. 274. See also Section IX.3.)

To say that anaphoric pronouns behave semantically like definite descriptions (or like expressions whose reference is fixed by description) is not, of course, to say how anaphoric pronouns will be treated in a syntactic theory. As in the case of definite descriptions without restrictive relative clauses, there are at least two possible strategies. Upon one strategy a pronominalization rule is incorporated into the syntactic theory which allows a definite description to be replaced by a pronoun provided that the description stands in a certain (syntactically characterized) relation to material in the antecedent sentence. Upon the other strategy there is no such pronominalization rule in the syntactic theory. Rather, the impact of the antecedent sentence upon the anaphoric pronoun is accounted for by a fully general theory of context dependence. (The first strategy is discussed by Cooper, 1979, pp. 82-5. For an instance of the second strategy, see Hausser, 1979.)

This is certainly not the place to assess these two (or any other) strategies. But two putative objections to the first strategy can be considered very briefly. The first is a semantic objection. Consider the sentence

Every man who owns a donkey beats it.

The first strategy will result in this sentence being treated as equivalent to

Every man who owns a donkey (at least one donkey)
beats the (unique) donkey which he owns.

This sentence is false if some man who owns at least one donkey owns more than one, whereas the original sentence is not naturally interpreted as excluding that possibility. The second strategy might avoid this difficulty by allowing more flexibility in the replacement of pronoun by definite description (see Cooper, 1979, p. 84). There are at least two replies which might be made to this objection. One is that the quantifier expression 'a' is ambiguous as between 'at least one' and 'exactly one', and that in the original sentence 'a' is naturally interpreted in the second way. The other, perhaps preferable, reply is this. The presence of the singular pronoun 'it' in the original sentence is the result of an agreement rule, since 'a donkey' is syntactically singular. To the extent that 'a donkey' is naturally interpreted as equivalent to 'at least one donkey' it would be semantically less misleading if 'it' were replaced by 'it/them' (a pronoun which is neutral as to number).

The second objection is syntactic. The definite description which is replaced by a pronoun (according to the first strategy) does not itself occur in the antecedent sentence. So the pronoun is not strictly a *pronoun of laziness*, in the way that 'it' is a pronoun of laziness going proxy for 'his paycheck' in

> The man who gave his paycheck to his wife was wiser
> than the man who gave it to his mistress.

Indeed, Cooper (1979, p. 83) claims

> [T]here is no way that I am aware of to encode the relationship
> that 'the donkey that he owns' bears to 'man who owns a
> donkey' into the structural description of a transformation,
> given the usual theory of transformations.

There is no swift reply to this objection. But it is interesting to note that for the purposes of semantic theory the relationship between 'the donkey that he owns' and 'man who owns a donkey' is not strictly relevant. For it is only necessary to recover a definite description after the axiom stating the semantic property of 'EVERY' has been brought to bear. The truth conditions of

> Every man who owns a donkey beats it

are specified in terms of the truth conditions of sentences of the form

> (Man who owns a donkey) γ

and sentences of the form

> γ beats it.

The axiom which states the semantic property of relative pronouns will result in the truth conditions of the former sentences being specified in terms of the truth conditions of sentences of the forms

> Man γ

and

γ owns a donkey.

Once attention is turned from the single quantified sentence to triples of sentences

Man γ; γ owns a donkey; γ beats it

the problem of recovering a definite description is much less difficult. If the second sentence of the triple is taken as the antecedent sentence, then clearly 'it' is to be replaced by 'the donkey which γ owns'. And once this replacement is made, the derivation of a truth condition specification can proceed (see Evans, 1977, pp. 524–5). To note all this is not to answer the second, syntactic, objection to the first strategy. But it suggests that something like that strategy might be workable. Both strategies need to be considered further. But they will not be considered further here. (For an argument against the second strategy, see Evans, 1980, pp. 348–53.)

5   PRONOUNS AND SPEAKER'S REFERENCE

We have so far discovered nothing in the wide variety of uses of definite descriptions and anaphoric pronouns which would threaten the general position of the Russellian theorist. We must now consider the use of pronouns a little further, both because it is important that a semantic theorist should have a realistic view of the use of pronouns in natural language and because we shall thereby be in a position to examine briefly (as promised in Section VII.2) an argument offered by Donnellan (1978) in support of the view that uses of definite descriptions and pronouns which involve speaker's reference present a difficulty for the Russellian theorist.

One feature of the use of anaphoric pronouns which we have so far ignored is this. An anaphoric pronoun is sometimes used when the definite description to which it is intuitively equivalent does not (even taking into account contextual limitation of the domain of quantification) apply uniquely to any object. Thus consider the pair of sentences

A man came to the office today. He tried to sell me
an encyclopedia

(Donnellan, 1978, p. 57). '[T]he speaker is surely not committed to the idea, nor does he intend to suggest, that only one man came to the office that day' (ibid. p. 60). Yet, on the account of anaphoric pronouns which we have offered, the second sentence of the pair is equivalent to

> The man who came to the office today tried to sell me
> an encyclopedia

and so is false if more than one man came to the office on the day in question.

We have already introduced the expression 'talks about' in respect of certain non-attributive uses of definite descriptions. A speaker may talk about a particular object in his use of other quantifier phrases too. Thus we are to imagine that the speaker's grounds for asserting, in the present example, that a man came to the office today are furnished by his belief concerning some particular man that he came to the office today. The singular belief prompts the speaker's assertion, and he is talking about that particular man. He has that man *in mind*. The fact that the speaker has a particular man in mind is of clear relevance to the audience, even though the audience may not believe concerning any particular man that it is he that the speaker is talking about. 'The speaker having some person or persons in mind to talk about can provide the needed definiteness' (Donnellan, 1978, p. 61).

It is not altogether clear exactly what use the semantic theorist should make of the fact that the speaker is talking about a particular man. Clearly there are several possibilities, and the choice amongst these possibilities is not indifferent to choices which may have been made earlier in the semantic and syntactic account of anaphoric pronouns. Here are just three possibilities.

(1) The second sentence of the pair is literally false. But this is tolerated by an audience who believes that the speaker could answer the question 'He? Who?' and, by using a definite description containing more descriptive or demonstrative material, say something true (provided that the man the speaker has in mind did try to sell him an encyclopedia).

(2) The truth conditions of the second sentence are simply indeterminate until the speaker has answered the question 'He? Who?', after which the anaphoric pronoun is treated as going proxy for, or having its reference fixed by, a definite

177

description recovered from that answer (cf. Evans, 1977, pp. 516–17).

(3) The second sentence of the pair is literally true, because the anaphoric pronoun goes proxy for, or has its reference fixed by, the definite description 'the object which the speaker has in mind'.

It is not necessary, for the restricted purposes of this section, that we make a choice between these possibilities.

Let us consider another example in which the speaker has a particular object in mind (Evans, 1977, p. 517):

> *A*: A man jumped out of the crowd and fell in front
> of the horses.
> *B*: He didn't jump, he was pushed.

Speaker *B* is surely not committed to the idea that a man both jumped out of the crowd and did not jump out of the crowd. Yet, if the sentence uttered by *A* is the antecedent sentence and the pronoun 'he' in *B*'s sentence is an anaphoric pronoun, then, on the account which was offered in Section VII.4, *B*'s sentence is equivalent to

> The man who jumped out of the crowd and fell in
> front of the horses did not jump but was pushed

and so is false under any circumstances.

Once again, the fact that *A* has a particular object in mind is of clear relevance to *B*. It would be natural to say that *B*'s remark is correct provided that the person about whom *A* was talking did not jump but was pushed. And once again there are several things that a semantic theorist might say about such cases. For example, he might say (cf. (1)) that *B*'s sentence is literally false, but that *B* means (s-means or ws-means) something true because in the description for which 'he' goes proxy the phrase 'jumped out of the crowd' is used ironically. Speaker *B* could have achieved the same net effect by saying

> The man who 'jumped out of the crowd' and fell in
> front of the horses did not jump but was pushed.

We do not have to choose between the various things that a semantic theorist might say, in order to recognize that we have in these examples uses of anaphoric pronouns concerning which we make intuitive judgments of correctness which are not explained merely by appealing to the account of anaphoric pronouns offered in the last section. Let us call these uses *non-literal anaphoric uses*. The most vivid kind of non-literal anaphoric use occurs when, as in this second example, one speaker uses a pronoun in correcting another speaker's use of the antecedent sentence.

It is clearly not a necessary condition for a vivid non-literal use that the first speaker's utterance should be accompanied by speaker's reference to a particular object. It is not even a necessary condition that the first speaker should be talking about a particular object. For consider the following example. Suppose that *A* comes upon Smith's body and, lacking relevant singular beliefs, says

A madman has murdered Smith.

Speaker *B* might reply

He was no madman; Smith had done him wrong

and *B*'s remark would intuitively be correct, provided that the person who brought about Smith's death was not mad and had been wronged by Smith. In this case the evidence which furnished the grounds for *A*'s assertion provides a causal route to a particular man even though *A* has no singular beliefs concerning that man. So someone might suggest that we should generalize the concept of talking about an object. But, in fact, not even a causal route to a particular object is required for a vivid non-literal use of a pronoun. For consider the following example. Suppose that *A* has a reputation for making predictions about criminal activity, by employing certain mathematical functions and a telephone directory, and that *A* says

A tall blond man murdered Smith at 4 p.m.

Speaker *B*, who also claims powers of prediction and doubts *A*'s accuracy in matters of detail, might reply

He was tall but he wasn't blond

and *B*'s remark would intuitively be correct provided that a tall, non-blond man uniquely murdered Smith at 4 p.m.

Let us turn to the use of pronouns following uses of definite descriptions. A pronoun which follows a sentence

The *F* is *G*

179

might be regarded as an anaphoric pronoun going proxy for the definite description 'The *F* which is *G*' or as a pronoun of laziness going proxy for 'The *F*'. But whichever account is offered, something more needs to be said to explain our intuitive judgments of correctness concerning the following exchange (in which *A*'s utterance is accompanied by speaker's reference).

> *A*: The Australian philosopher we met yesterday has
> just got his doctorate.
> *B*: He isn't Australian, because he was born in England.

This is an example of a non-literal use of a pronoun following a referential use of a definite description.

Donnellan (1978, p. 55) attaches considerable importance to such examples.

> The [referential/non-referential] distinction . . . will have
> semantic importance because it will mark the dichotomy between
> occurrences of definite descriptions that can initiate strings of
> pronouns whose reference depends upon the speaker's reference
> and those that do not.

This remark suggests two things. One is that a semantic theorist is bound to treat non-literal uses of pronouns in such a way that our intuitive judgments of correctness and incorrectness accord with judgments of strict and literal truth and falsity. It suggests, wrongly, that there is no possibility corresponding to (1) above. The other thing which the remark suggests, also wrongly, is that non-referential uses of definite descriptions cannot be followed by non-literal uses of pronouns. Suppose that *A* has *X* in mind and says

> The Australian philosopher I met yesterday has just
> got his doctorate

without realizing that *B* knows that he met *X*. Then it is still perfectly possible for *B* to correct *A*'s use of the definite description by saying

> He isn't really Australian; he just sounds like it.

So no particular significance attaches to the referential/non-referential distinction as a result of non-literal uses of pronouns.

In fact, it is not difficult to produce examples of non-literal uses of pronouns following uses of definite descriptions in which the speaker has no particular object in mind, and even uses where the evidence which furnishes the speaker's grounds does not provide a causal route to any particular object. First, suppose that Brown, Jones, and now Smith have been found dead and apparently murdered, and that it is common knowledge between A and B that each believes that a single person murdered all three, although neither has any view as to who the culprit is. Suppose further that A hears that another person has been found dead in similar circumstances while B learns that Smith died, after all, of natural causes. Then A might say

> Smith's murderer has been at it again

and B might reply

> He didn't murder Smith; Smith died of a heart attack.

In this case A has no particular person in mind, although the evidence which furnished his grounds did provide, we may suppose, a causal route to a particular person. But consider the following example. Suppose that A, on the basis of his general beliefs about crime and about the alphabetical distribution of victims, comes to believe that Smith has been murdered, and on the basis of his general beliefs about genetics comes to believe that the culprit is tall and blond. Suppose that A decides to make a pronouncement and says

> Smith's murderer is tall and blond.

Suppose that, in reality, a tall, blond man did go to Smith's house intending to kill Smith and indeed did put a bullet through Smith, but that Smith was already dead from a heart attack. Then B, knowing these facts, might reply (intuitively correctly)

> You are almost right. He was tall and blond but he
> didn't really murder Smith.

In this case A's evidence, such as it was, cannot be said to provide a causal route to the man who put a bullet through Smith.

Finally, let us consider Donnellan's main argument against the Russellian theorist. The argument runs as follows. A speaker who has a particular object z in mind may come out with a pair of sentences

> An F is G. It is H

or with the single sentence

> The F which is G is H

accompanied by speaker's reference to z. Which of these two things he does depends upon his beliefs about the audience's ability to recognize which object he has in mind. Anaphoric pronouns sometimes have non-literal uses. So the truth of the second sentence of the pair may turn upon how things are with z even though z is not uniquely F and G. A difference in the speaker's expectations about the audience's recognition does not call for a difference in truth conditions between

> It is H

in the given context and

> The F which is G is H

accompanied by speaker's reference to z. Therefore the truth of the latter sentence may turn upon how things are with z even though z is not uniquely F and G. But this is incompatible with the Russellian theory.

This is certainly an ingenious argument. But it is an argument which seems to be flawed at a number of points. It is enough to mention four flaws to which the Russellian theorist might direct attention.

(1) The argument requires the premise that, in the given context, 'It is H' is literally true provided that z is H. But, as we saw, this is only one of several possibilities open to the semantic theorist.

(2) If the required premise is granted, then there is a reason to expect a difference in truth conditions between the sentence containing the anaphoric pronoun and the sentence containing the definite description. For it is an essential feature of the way anaphoric pronouns work that such a pronoun follows an antecedent sentence the utterance of which provides a context which determines the semantic properties of the pronoun as used on that occasion. There is no similar essential feature of the semantic function of definite descriptions with restrictive relative clauses.

(3) The best examples of non-literal anaphoric uses of pronouns are provided by one speaker's use of a pronoun in correcting another speaker's use (or his own appreciably earlier use) of the antecedent sentence. But Donnellan's argument requires us to consider cases in which a single speaker comes out with the antecedent sentence and immediately uses the anaphoric

182

pronoun. This severely restricts the range of possible incompatibilities with the Russellian theory.

(4) The argument would prove too much. For a speaker who has z in mind may come out with

The F which is G is H

accompanied by speaker's reference to z, or he may come out with that same sentence, making it manifest that he has an object in mind, but without speaker's reference to z. Which of these two things the speaker does depends upon his expectations about the audience's recognition. But a difference in such expectations does not, according to the argument, call for a difference in truth conditions. Thus, if the Russellian theory is incorrect for some referential uses of definite descriptions then it is also incorrect for some non-referential uses. So Donnellan's argument would, at best, show that the distinction which is semantically important is not the referential/non-referential distinction.

It seems reasonable to conclude that, although the various uses of definite descriptions and pronouns each have their own semantic interest, none presents an insuperable difficulty for the Russellian theorist.

NOTES

On definite descriptions in general, see Russell (1905), and Strawson (1950) and (1964b). Much recent interest can be traced back to Donnellan (1966). See also Donnellan (1968).

The view that many uses of pronouns correspond to bound variables is associated primarily with Geach. See, for example, Geach (1963), (1964), (1968), and (1969). Evans (1977) focuses upon issues raised by Geach. Evans (1980), on the other hand, is addressed more directly to linguists. On anaphoric pronouns, see also the five papers in Part I of Heny and Schnelle (1979).

PART THREE

NECESSITY AND ACTUALITY

VIII

NECESSITY

1   NECESSITY AND SENTENCES

There are very many semantically important features of natural languages of which we have so far provided no account. One such feature is the occurrence of modal adverbs such as 'necessarily' and 'possibly' and the corresponding phrases 'it is necessary that' and 'it is possible that'. Thus consider the following sentences:

> Necessarily there are precisely seven planets.
> It is necessary that $2 + 2 = 4$.
> If water is H_2O then necessarily water is H_2O.
> It is possible that some whales should have been fish.

There are three things to be noticed immediately. First, at least in these examples, the modal adverbs and phrases take a sentence to make a sentence; they seem to belong in the syntactic category S/S. Second, the non-modal sentence which is within the scope of the modal adverb or phrase is a semantic constituent of the resulting modal sentence; it is used and not mentioned. Third, the sentences are naturally interpreted in such a way that the modal adverb 'necessarily' and the phrase 'it is necessary that' express broadly logical necessity rather than, on the one hand, narrowly logical necessity which attaches only to truths of logic and perhaps of mathematics or, on the other hand, mere causal or natural necessity which attaches even to such truths as that men do not swim across the Atlantic or leap over tall buildings. Similarly, 'possibly' and 'it is possible that' express broadly logical possibility (see Plantinga, 1974, pp. 1–9). The first two facts could be summarized by saying that the modal adverbs and phrases, at least as they occur in these examples, are sentence operators. The third fact could be summarized by saying that the modal adverbs and phrases, at least as they occur in these examples, correspond semantically to the intensional sentence operators '□' and '◇' (cf. Sections II.4 and V.2). Thus a semantic theorist who is interested in natural languages has a reason to investigate the semantic nature of those modal operators.

Let us then consider a very simple modal language. Recall that the language L_1 has just three atomic sentences s_1, s_2, and s_3, and the connectives '&' 'v', and '~'. The modal language L_{10} extends L_1 by the addition of '□' and '◇'. It is an absolutely straightforward matter to provide a theory of meaning for L_{10}. For we already know how to provide a theory of meaning for L_1 (the theory $M\theta$ of Section II.4), and for a language (L_2) which extends L_1 by the addition of the hyperintensional sentence operator 'John believes that' (cf. Section II.5). The axioms for '□' and '◇' in a theory of meaning for L_{10} are of exactly the same form as those for '~' and for 'John believes that'. Thus for '□' we have

$$(\forall \sigma)(Ap)\,[(\sigma \text{ means (in } L_{10}) \text{ that p})\to$$
$$({}^{\ulcorner}\Box\sigma{}^{\urcorner} \text{ means (in } L_{10}) \text{ that } \Box \text{p})].$$

(In earlier sections the quantifier '(Ap)' was written '$(\forall p)$'. See again the last paragraph of Appendix 6.) But the fact that the axiom for '□' in a theory of meaning has the same form as the axiom for '~' and the axiom for 'John believes that' must not be allowed to obscure important semantic differences. For '□' is an intensional sentence operator, unlike '~' which is extensional and unlike 'John believes that' which is hyperintensional.

These semantic differences become clear when we try to construct theories of truth for languages containing the three operators. For a theory which yields only material truth condition specifications (of the form

$$Tr(s) \leftrightarrow p$$

where '↔' is the material biconditional in the ML) does not state enough about, say, the sentence s_1 to yield any consequences at all for the material truth conditions of either ${}^{\ulcorner}\Box s_1{}^{\urcorner}$ or ${}^{\ulcorner}$John believes that $s_1{}^{\urcorner}$. Intensional and hyperintensional operators thus resist treatment in a theory which yields only material truth condition specifications (cf. Section II.5, and in particular the discussion of rules of proof at the end of that section). Hyperintensional operators also resist treatment in a theory which yields strict truth condition specifications (of the form

$$\Box \, [Tr(s) \leftrightarrow p]$$

where '$\leftrightarrow$' is the material biconditional in the *ML* and '$\Box$' is a modal operator in the *ML* expressing broadly logical necessity). For such a theory does not state enough about, say, the sentence s_1 to yield any consequences at all for the material or strict truth conditions of ⌜John believes that s_1⌝. But, as we shall now see in some detail, the intensional operators '$\Box$' and '$\Diamond$' can be treated as sentence operators in a theory which yields strict truth condition specifications (see also Peacocke, 1978, pp. 476–7).

Before we give the axioms of a truth theory for L_{10} we must specify the background logic of the *ML* in which the theory is cast. In particular, we must specify the modal component of that background logic. First, as a kind of preliminary, we have the axiom schema

$$\Diamond \alpha \leftrightarrow {\sim}\Box{\sim}\alpha$$

relating the two modal operators. Then we have the following rule of proof, called 'Necessitation' (*Nec*):

$$\frac{\vdash \alpha}{\vdash \Box \alpha}$$

(Here '$\vdash$' is read as 'there is a proof from the logic alone of . . .'.) And we have the axiom schema

$$\Box \, (\alpha \to \beta) \to (\Box \alpha \to \Box \beta).$$

This schema and the rule *Nec* could, in the presence of the non-modal component of the logic (classical propositional calculus, say), be replaced by the extended rule of necessitation

$$\frac{\alpha_1, \ldots, \alpha_n \vdash \beta}{\Box \alpha_1, \ldots, \Box \alpha_n \vdash \Box \beta}$$

(where '$\vdash$' is read as 'yield by the logic alone'). In either case the resulting system is the very weak modal logic K. The slightly stronger system T is the result of adding to K the following axiom schema (the T axiom):

$$\Box \alpha \to \alpha.$$

189

Clearly, the axioms and rules of the system T are faithful to the intended meanings of '$\Box$' and '$\Diamond$'. The system $S4$ is the result of adding to T the following axiom schema (the $S4$ axiom):

$$\Box\alpha \rightarrow \Box\Box\alpha.$$

Arguably, this too is faithful to the intended meaning of '$\Box$'. Finally, the system $S5$ is the result of adding to $S4$ the following axiom schema (the *Brouwerian* axiom):

$$\alpha \rightarrow \Box\Diamond\alpha.$$

The system $S5$ can also be obtained by adding to T the following axiom schema (the $S5$ axiom):

$$\Diamond\alpha \rightarrow \Box\Diamond\alpha.$$

This schema seems to be no less faithful to the intended meaning of '$\Diamond$' than the $S4$ axiom is to the intended meaning of '$\Box$'. (Cf. Hughes and Cresswell, 1972, pp. 22–60).

We can now give the axioms of a truth theory for L_{10} cast in a ML whose background logic has as its modal component the system $S5$. The axioms for the atomic sentences s_1, s_2, and s_3 must, obviously, specify the strict truth conditions of those sentences. So we have

$(NT1a)$ $\Box$ $[Tr(L_{10}, s_1) \leftrightarrow$ snow is white]

for s_1, and similar axioms $(NT1b)$ and $(NT1c)$ for s_2 and s_3. (It is worth repeating here that there is no objection to be made against $(NT1a)$ by claiming that s_1 might have meant something different. See Peacocke, 1978, pp. 477–8.) We have

$(NT2)$ $\Box$ $(\forall\sigma)(\forall\tau)$ $[Tr(L_{10}, \ulcorner\sigma \,\&\, \tau\urcorner) \leftrightarrow$
$(Tr(L_{10}, \sigma) \,\&\, Tr(L_{10}, \tau))]$

for '&', and similar axioms $(NT3)$ and $(NT4)$ for 'v' and '~'. (We should not allow our use of corner quotes in abbreviating what would otherwise be written out using the concatenation functor '$\cap$' to obscure the fact that the truth of these axioms depends upon the following property of that functor. Whatever the value of that functor applied to a pair of expressions in fact is, it is not possible that the value of that functor applied to those expressions should have been anything other than what it in fact is. See Peacocke, 1978, note 8.) From these axioms we can prove, for example,

$$\Box \, [Tr(L_{10}, \ulcorner\sim s_1\urcorner) \leftrightarrow \sim (\text{snow is white})] \,.$$

190

For we know from our consideration of the truth theory $T\theta$ for L_1 that from the unmodalized versions of *(NT1a)* and *(NT4)* we can prove, by (non-modal) logic alone, the biconditional

$$Tr(L_{10}, \ulcorner \sim s_1 \urcorner) \leftrightarrow \sim (\text{snow is white}).$$

So, given the extended rule of necessitation, we can prove the strict truth condition specification for $\ulcorner \sim s_1 \urcorner$ from the modalized axioms *(NT1a)* and *(NT4)*. The axioms for '$\Box$' and '$\Diamond$' have the same form as that for '$\sim$'. Thus for '$\Box$' we have

$$(NT5) \quad \Box (\forall \sigma) [Tr(L_{10}, \ulcorner \Box \sigma \urcorner) \leftrightarrow \Box Tr(L_{10}, \sigma)].$$

But the use of *(NT5)* in the derivations of strict truth condition specifications is slightly different from that of *(NT4)*. Thus consider the sentence $\ulcorner \Box s_1 \urcorner$. It is not the case that from the unmodalized versions of *(NT1a)* and *(NT5)* we can prove the material truth condition specification

$$Tr(L_{10}, \ulcorner \Box s_1 \urcorner) \leftrightarrow \Box (\text{snow is white}).$$

For, since '$\Box$' is intensional, a material truth condition specification for s_1 (provided by the unmodalized version of *(NT1a)*) has no consequences for the material truth conditions of $\ulcorner \Box s_1 \urcorner$. In order to derive even a material truth condition specification for $\ulcorner \Box s_1 \urcorner$ we have to make use of a strict truth condition specification for s_1 (provided by the modalized axiom *(NT1a)*). From *(NT1a)* we have

$$\Box Tr(L_{10}, s_1) \leftrightarrow \Box (\text{snow is white})$$

and this, together with the unmodalized version of *(NT5)*, yields (by propositional calculus alone)

$$Tr(L_{10}, \ulcorner \Box s_1 \urcorner) \leftrightarrow \Box (\text{snow is white}).$$

Thus, in order to apply the extended rule of necessitation and so to derive a strict truth condition specification for $\ulcorner \Box s_1 \urcorner$, we need the modalized axiom *(NT5)* and the following doubly modalized biconditional

$$\Box\Box [Tr(L_{10}, s_1) \leftrightarrow \text{snow is white}].$$

This last follows from *(NT1a)* by the *S4* axiom.

The formal difference between the derivations of strict truth condition specifications for $\ulcorner \sim s_1 \urcorner$ and for $\ulcorner \Box s_1 \urcorner$ corresponds to the deep semantic difference between the extensional operator '$\sim$' and the intensional operator '$\Box$'. Certainly the sentence s_1 contributes to the strict truth conditions of both $\ulcorner \sim s_1 \urcorner$ and $\ulcorner \Box s_1 \urcorner$ by its own strict truth conditions; '$\sim$' and '$\Box$' are alike in not being hyperintensional. But the fact that s_1 contributes to the strict truth conditions of $\ulcorner \sim s_1 \urcorner$ by its own strict truth conditions is related very simply (by the extended rule of necessitation) to the fact that s_1 contributes to the material truth conditions of $\ulcorner \sim s_1 \urcorner$ by its own material truth conditions. In contrast, the fact that s_1 contributes to the strict truth conditions of $\ulcorner \Box s_1 \urcorner$ by its own strict truth conditions is related rather differently (by the *S4* axiom and the extended rule of necessitation) to the fact that s_1 contributes even to the material truth conditions of $\ulcorner \Box s_1 \urcorner$ by its own strict truth conditions.

Let us call this truth theory '$NT\theta$'. The derivations of strict truth condition specifications for $\ulcorner \sim s_1 \urcorner$ and $\ulcorner \Box s_1 \urcorner$ are enough to indicate a canonical proof procedure which yields, for each sentence of L_{10}, a canonical theorem of the form

$$\Box \, [Tr(L_{10}, s) \leftrightarrow p].$$

We shall say that a theory of strict truth conditions for a language L, together with a canonical proof procedure, is interpretational just in case replacing

$$\Box \, [Tr(L, \ldots) \leftrightarrow \text{———}]$$

by

$$\ldots \text{means (in } L) \text{ that } \text{———}$$

in the canonical theorems yields correct meaning (in L) specifications. Then, given that $T\theta$ is interpretational for L_1, it follows that $NT\theta$ (together with the indicated canonical proof procedure) is interpretational for L_{10}. What is more, $NT\theta$ meets *SC*. In particular, the canonical derivation of a strict truth condition specification for a modal sentence $\ulcorner \Box \sigma \urcorner$ employs resources already sufficient for the canonical derivation of a strict truth condition specification for the contained sentence σ. This answers to the fact that someone who knows what a modal sentence $\ulcorner \Box \sigma \urcorner$ means is thereby in a position to know what the contained sentence σ means. We noticed at the beginning of this section that it is a feature of modal sentences of English that the sentence which is within the scope of a modal adverb or phrase is a semantic constituent of the resulting modal sentence. So, to that extent a theory in the style of $NT\theta$ would be appropriate for a fragment of English containing modal adverbs and phrases.

A truth theory in the style of $NT\theta$ would not be appropriate for a fragment of English containing the modal adverb 'necessarily' if the following claim about that adverb were strictly correct (Quine, 1960, p. 196):

> 'necessarily' amounts to 'is analytic' plus an antecedent pair of quotation marks. For example, the sentence
>
> (1) Necessarily 9 > 4
>
> is explained thus
>
> (2) '9 > 4' is analytic.

The primary reason is not that the use of the predicate of sentences 'is analytic' renders the necessity too narrow, and certainly narrower than broadly logical necessity. The inappropriateness which is our present concern would remain if 'is analytic' were replaced by some other predicate of sentences such as 'is a necessarily true sentence'. The crucial point is that if the modal adverb really amounted to a predicate of sentences plus an antecedent pair of quotation marks then someone could know the meaning of a modal sentence without being in a position to know the meaning of the contained sentence, for the contained sentence would be mentioned but not used. So if the claim in the passage from Quine were strictly correct, if modality were really metalinguistic, then a theory in the style of $NT\theta$ would infringe *SC*. Of course, no concession to the idea that modality is metalinguistic is made by the presence in a truth theory of the biconditional

$$(\forall \sigma) \, [Tr(L_{10}, \ulcorner \Box\sigma \urcorner) \leftrightarrow \Box Tr(L_{10}, \sigma)] \, .$$

That biconditional no more shows that modal sentences are metalinguistic than the biconditional

$$(\forall \sigma) \, [Tr(L_{10}, \ulcorner \sim\sigma \urcorner) \leftrightarrow \sim Tr(L_{10}, \sigma)]$$

shows that negative sentences are metalinguistic.

2 POSSIBLE WORLDS

It is common, natural, and heuristically useful to say that a modal sentence $\ulcorner \Box\sigma \urcorner$ is true just in case σ is true with respect to every possible (actual or counterfactual) situation, or every possible state of affairs, or every possible world, and similarly that $\ulcorner \Diamond \sigma \urcorner$ is true just in case σ is true with respect to some possible situation, possible state of affairs, or possible world. Yet in the truth theory $NT\theta$ for the modal language L_{10} no explicit use is made of the concept of a possible world. We must examine that concept a little more closely, and enquire after its proper role in semantic theorizing about modal sentences.

Let us begin with some reflections concerning the relation between model theory and truth theory, for such reflections may seem to provide an argument in favour of the explicit employment of the apparatus of possible worlds in a truth theory for a modal language. The central concept of model theory is truth-in-a-model or truth-upon-an-interpretation, and the business of model theory is to characterize validity. An argument from $\alpha_1, \ldots, \alpha_n$ to β is said to be valid just in case β is true in every model in which all of $\alpha_1, \ldots, \alpha_n$ are true. Derivatively, a sentence is said to be valid just in case it is true in every model. Consider the quantificational language L_6. A model appropriate for L_6 comprises a set of objects (the domain of the model) together with an appropriate assignment of an extension for each atomic predicate and a reference for each name in L_6. Most standard treatments of model theory for quantificational languages make use of a model-relative satisfaction relation between sequences of members of the domain and formulae of the language. Truth-in-a-model is then defined in terms of satisfaction-in-a-model. A model theory for L_6 will deliver such theorems as

$$(\forall I)\ [Tr_I\ ('P_1 m_1') \leftrightarrow Ref_I\ ('m_1') \in Ext_I\ ('P_1')]$$
$$(\forall I)\ [Tr_I\ ('\forall v_1) P_1 v_1') \leftrightarrow$$
$$(\forall x \in Domain\ (I))\ (x \in Ext_I\ ('P_1'))]$$

(where the quantifier '$(\forall I)$' ranges over models appropriate for L_6, and the language parameter is suppressed). One needs two things in order to proceed from such a model theory to a truth theory (in this case, perhaps, a satisfaction theory) for L_6. One is a specification of an intended model or interpretation I^*, that is a specification of an intended domain of quantification, an intended extension for each atomic predicate and an intended reference for each name. The other is the biconditional

$$(\forall \sigma)\ [Tr\ (\sigma) \leftrightarrow Tr_{I^*}\ (\sigma)]$$

(truth is just truth upon the intended interpretation, or truth in the intended model). The model I^* is not merely a pure set theoretic

194

structure which is isomorphic to the model whose domain comprises the objects to which speakers of the language refer and over which they quantify. Rather, I^* itself has those objects in its domain.

Consider now the modal language L_{10}. A model appropriate for L_{10} is a triple $<W, w^*, V>$ where W is a set, w^* is a particular designated member of W, and V assigns to each ordered pair of a member of W and an atomic sentence of L_{10} a truth value. The function V is extended (in a way which does not vary from model to model) to a function V^+ which assigns to each ordered pair of a member of W and any sentence of L_{10} a truth value. If $V^+ (w, \sigma) = T$ then σ is said to be true with respect to w (in that model). If $V^+ (w^*, \sigma) = T$ then σ is said to be true in the model $<W, w^*, V>$. The members of W are often spoken of as possible worlds, but for the purposes of model theory the metaphysical nature of the members of W does not matter; they can be assumed to be set theoretic objects. The relation between model theory and truth theory in the case of L_6 may lead one to expect that a truth theory for L_{10} should be obtained from the model theory just indicated by the specification of an intended set of possible worlds (not just set theoretic objects but 'real' possible worlds), an intended designated world (the actual world), and an intended evaluation function (assigning sentences truth values with respect to possible worlds). Thus one may be led to expect that a truth theory for L_{10} should make explicit use of the apparatus of possible worlds.

To the extent that these reflections provide an argument in favour of a possible worlds truth theory the argument is unsuccessful. It is certainly correct that if the concept of validity is to have any interest then it must be a consequence of the validity of an argument from α_1, . . ., α_n to β that if α_1, . . ., α_n are all true (*simpliciter*) then β is true, and it must be a consequence of the validity of a sentence that that sentence is true. It is also correct that it is sufficient to establish this proper relation between validity and truth that truth should be equated with truth in an intended model, and so sufficient that truth theory and model theory should be related as they are in the case of L_6. This is sufficient, but it is not necessary. For it is sufficient to establish the proper relation between validity and truth that there should simply be some model appropriate for the language in question such that all and only the sentences of the language which are in fact true are true in that model. In the case of the modal language L_{10}, in particular, it is sufficient that there should be some pure set theoretic model such that all and only the sentences of L_{10} which are in fact true are true in that model. Acceptance of the existence of such a model does not require any sympathy at all for the idea of possible worlds. Still less does it require explicit employment in a truth theory for L_{10} of the possible worlds apparatus. (Cf. Plantinga, 1974, pp. 126-8. This account of the relation between validity and truth raises questions about the idea that model theory explains the validity of arguments; cf. Evans, 1976.)

For all that has been said so far, it is open to a semantic theorist to provide, for a modal language, either a possible worlds truth theory or a truth theory in the style of $NT\theta$. In fact, however, there seem to be reasons for preferring a theory in the style of $NT\theta$ (an operator theory). There are two ways in which a semantic theorist might provide a possible worlds truth theory. On the one hand he might 'preprocess' the sentences of L_{10}, say, so that at the level of input the sentence $\ulcorner \Box s_1 \urcorner$ is represented as

$$(\forall w)\,(World\,(w) \to s_1{}'(w))$$

or perhaps as

$$(EVERY\ w)\,(World\,(w);\,s_1{}'(w)).$$

According to this first strategy the language at the level of input would be a quantificational language with a one-place atomic predicate '*World*' and a one-place atomic predicate (true of possible worlds) corresponding to each atomic sentence of L_{10}. The quantificational language would contain no operators which are other than extensional, and the truth theory would take the familiar shape of theories of material truth conditions for quantificational languages. On the other hand, the semantic theorist might apply a truth theory to L_{10} directly, and make use of the apparatus of possible worlds only in stating in the *ML* the truth conditions of *OL* sentences. In particular, the truth predicate would be explicitly relativized to possible worlds, and the theory would deliver such theorems as the following:

$$(\forall w)\,[Tr\,(w,\,s_1) \leftrightarrow \text{snow is white in } w]$$
$$(\forall w)\,(\forall\sigma)\,[Tr\,(w,\,\ulcorner\Box\sigma\urcorner) \leftrightarrow (\forall w')\,Tr\,(w',\sigma)].$$

Against the first strategy there is a *prima facie* objection that in such a truth theory the resources used in the canonical derivations of biconditionals for sentences at the level of input which correspond to sentences of L_{10} are already sufficient for the derivation of biconditionals for sentences such as

$(\forall w)$ *World* (w)

$(\forall w) ((\textit{World}\ (w)\ \vee \sim s_1{}'(w))\ \&\ s_2{}'(w))$

which do not correspond to any sentence of L_{10}. (Cf. Wallace, 1972, p. 243. This objection also applies if binary quantification is used.) The theorist who adopts this first strategy seems bound to hold that L_{10} is an impoverished language, and this is inconsistent with the claim already made for $NT\theta$ that it both meets SC and delivers truth condition specifications for precisely the sentences of L_{10}. It is possible to alter the first strategy so as to meet this *prima facie* objection, for one can do away with the predicate '*World*' and assume that the domain of quantification is already restricted to possible worlds. In that case the 'preprocessed' form of $\ulcorner \Box s_1 \urcorner$ would be simply $\ulcorner (\forall w)s_1{}'(w) \urcorner$. But once the first strategy is altered in this way the best that can be said for it is that the 'preprocessing' is quite trivial: one writes '$s_1{}'(w)$' instead of 's_1' and '$(\forall w)$' instead of '$\Box$'. And the worst that can be said for it is that it seems to involve a denial that the expressions s_1, s_2, and s_3 of L_{10} are really sentences (cf. Section VIII.3). The first strategy is not, then, particularly attractive.

The main difference between the theory which results upon the second strategy and the operator theory $NT\theta$ is that the former is cast in a *ML* which contains no operators which are other than extensional while the latter is cast in a *ML* which itself contains intensional operators. In the former case the background logic of the *ML* is standard first-order logic; in the latter case the background logic of the *ML* is modal logic. A crucial feature of the second strategy is that in the axioms for atomic sentences we find *ML* predicates of one more place than might have been expected. In the expression 'snow is white in w' we have not the one-place predicate 'white' but a two-place predicate 'white'' true of pairs of material objects and possible worlds. Similarly, if one constructed a truth theory for a modal language extending L_4, then one would on this second strategy have as a theorem

$$(\forall w)\ [Tr(w, \text{`}P_1 m_1\text{'}) \leftrightarrow Q_1{}'\ (n_1, w)].$$

On the right hand side of this biconditional we have not the one-place predicate 'Q_1' but a two-place predicate '$Q_1{}'$'. The typographical similarity between the new two-place predicates and the familiar one-place predicates must not be allowed to obscure the fact that some account must be given of the meanings of *ML* sentences containing the new expressions. The only available account seems to be along the following lines. If γ is a name of an object x and δ is a name of a possible world w then $\ulcorner$White$'(\gamma, \delta)\urcorner$ is true just in case x would be white if w were to obtain ($\ulcorner Q_1{}'(\gamma, \delta)\urcorner$ is true just in case x would be Q_1 if w were to obtain). But this account at least suggests that it would be preferable to do without the new two-place predicates, and instead regard $\ulcorner$White$(\gamma)\urcorner$ as a sentence and $\ulcorner$in $\delta\urcorner$ as an intensional sentence operator (equivalent to $\ulcorner$if δ were to obtain then . . .$\urcorner$). And this last has the added advantage that it avoids the denial (implicit in the second strategy) that *ML* expressions such as 'snow is white' and '$Q_1 n_1$' are really sentences. But, of course, this advantageous alteration to the second strategy destroys the main difference between the resulting theory and the operator theory $NT\theta$. For once that alteration is made the expression '$(\forall w)$ (. . . (in w))' is revealed as an intensional sentence operator. Thus a semantic theorist who both cares about semantic structure and values such grasp as he may have upon the notion of a sentence will do well to adopt an operator theory in the style of $NT\theta$.

For a semantic theorist who adopts an operator theory there remains the question whether it is really even legitimate to speak of possible worlds and to say that certain sentences are true with respect to certain possible worlds. On the one hand, David Lewis (1973, pp. 84, 85) has written, 'I believe that there are possible worlds other than the one we happen to inhabit' and 'Our actual world is only one world among others'. On the other hand, many philosophers have rejected such realism about possible worlds. Colin McGinn (1981), for example, has urged, in short, that 'there *are* no possible worlds in objective reality'.

Possible worlds terminology is undoubtedly heuristically useful. If we are to continue to use it, even in informal exposition, then we must at least reflect briefly upon the nature of our commitment to possible worlds. The continued use of the heuristically useful terminology is consistent with two intuitively plausible claims. One is that possible worlds are abstract objects rather than, as on Lewis's view, objects of the same kind as 'I and all my surroundings'. The other is that the notion of a possible world is conceptually posterior to the notions of necessity and possibility expressed by '$\Box$' and '$\Diamond$'. (These two claims might be attributed to Stalnaker, 1976 and Kripke, 1972, respectively.) So let us briefly attempt to mark out a position embodying these two claims and intermediate between the position of Lewis, on the one hand, and the position of those for whom McGinn speaks, on the other.

Consider the following celebrated passage from Lewis (1973, p. 84):

> I believe, and so do you, that things could have been different
> in countless ways. But what does this mean? Ordinary language
> permits the paraphrase: there are many ways things could have
> been besides the way they actually are. On the face of it, this
> sentence is an existential quantification. It says that there exist
> many entities of a certain description, to wit 'ways things could
> have been'. I believe that things could have been different in
> countless ways; I believe permissible paraphrases of what I believe;
> taking the paraphrase at its face value, I therefore believe in the
> existence of entities that might be called 'ways things could have
> been'. I prefer to call them 'possible worlds'.

Clearly this passage does not provide any support for the idea that possible worlds are objects of the same sort as 'I and all my surroundings'. Rather, the passage supports the idea that possible worlds (ways things could have been) are akin to properties rather than to material objects. Stalnaker (1976, p. 68) has argued precisely this, against Lewis: '*The way things are* is a property or state of the world, not the world itself ... *the way the world is* could exist even if a world that is that way did not.'

It is not enough to say that a possible world is a way things could have been. No doubt things could have been different in such a way that Fraser would have been an opera singer. But there would be wide agreement amongst those who make use of the concept of a possible world that one does not fully specify a possible world merely by saying that with respect to it, Fraser is an opera singer (Plantinga, 1974, pp. 44–5):

> A possible world, then, is a possible state of affairs – one that is
> possible in the broadly logical sense. But not every possible state
> of affairs is a possible world. To claim that honour, a state of
> affairs must be *maximal* or *complete*. . . . [A] state of affairs S
> is *complete* or *maximal* if for every state of affairs S', S includes
> S' or S precludes S'.

In fact, there are two slightly different ways in which the idea that a possible world is a maximal or complete state of affairs may be developed. On the one hand, we may consider states of affairs which are maximal relative to a given language, where a state of affairs is maximal relative to L just in case, with respect to that state of affairs, each sentence of L is determinately either true or false. On the other hand, we may consider states of affairs which are maximal relative to all possible languages, that is, which are such that, with respect to that state of affairs, every sentence of every language (including languages which no one uses or even could use) is determinately either true or false. The relation between the two concepts of maximality is analogous to the relation between regions and points of space. Fully determinate states are like points. States which are maximal relative to a language L are like regions whose points cannot be distinguished by sentences of L. Regions are divisible: a language can be extended so as to make finer discriminations. And points are the (perhaps idealized) limits of this process of division.

There are doubts that can be raised about the coherence of the notion of a fully determinate counterfactual state of affairs (see Appendix 9). In any case, let us opt for regions rather than points. Then a possible world can be specified by a set of sentences of the language in question. Some philosophers might, indeed, prefer to identify possible worlds with sets of sentences (or with sets of propositions expressed by (context independent) sentences). But nothing actually requires this. It is open to us to agree with Lewis (1973, p. 85; and, in effect, with Stalnaker, 1976, p. 70) that 'Possible worlds are what they are, and not some other thing'.

To say that a possible world is a possible state of affairs (actual or counterfactual situation) which is maximal relative to a certain language, and to say no more, may be to suggest that the concept of a possible world can provide a reductive explanation of the concepts of broadly logical necessity and possibility. But, in reality, the direction of explanation is quite the reverse. The question which cries out for an answer is 'Which states of affairs are possible?' A set of sentences cannot be used to specify a possible world unless it is genuinely possible that those sentences should all be true together (that is, unless the sentences are *compossible*). This requirement clearly rules out the occurrence in a single set of a sentence together with its own negation, and it rules out the occurrence of such pairs as

Someone is an oculist. No one is an eye doctor.

But questions remain. It is not obvious, for example, whether the requirement rules out the occurrence of the English sentence 'Whitlam is an alligator', for it is not obvious whether it is possible that Whitlam should have been an alligator. Certainly we can say that it is possible that Whitlam should have been an alligator just in case 'Whitlam is an alligator' is true with respect to some possible world (just in case in some possible world Whitlam is an alligator). But this is a constraint upon the concept of a possible world. (Someone who did not recognize it as a constraint would not have grasped the concept of a possible world.) It is not an explanation (or even the beginning of an explanation) of the concept of broadly logical possibility.

The intermediate position which we have been attempting to mark out embodies the claim that the notion of a possible world is conceptually posterior to the notion of broadly logical possibility. But it does not commit us to abstinence from modal theorizing (cf. Lewis, 1973, p. 85). Someone could adopt this intermediate position and go on to relate the question whether it is possible that Whitlam should have been an alligator (and so, derivatively, the question whether there is a possible world in which Whitlam is an alligator) to more general philosophical questions about the relation between an object and its origin. He could proceed to draw an analogy between the causal continuity from origin to object and the causal continuity of an object persisting through time. He could discover or invent ties between continuity, identity, and sortal predicates. Such a philosopher, whether his reasoning yielded essentialist or anti-essentialist conclusions, would be engaged in modal theorizing. Nor does the intermediate position involve the claim that possible worlds exist only as a product of our thought, that possible worlds are creatures of our imagination (Lewis, 1973, p. 88), or that questions as to what possible worlds there are can be settled by stipulation (cf. McGinn, 1981).

Finally, we should clarify the use of the expression 'the actual world'. One amongst the possible worlds is actual, or obtains. This possible world is the actual world. It is an abstract object just like all the other possible worlds. The actual world (in this sense) is not to be identified with Lewis and all his surroundings. Its actuality consists in the fact that just those sentences are true with respect to it which are, in fact, true.

3   MODALITY AND TENSE

As the development of the discipline of tense logic parallel to that of modal logic indicates, there are many formal similarities between temporal adverbs and modal adverbs. These formal similarities and the underlying conceptual differences are worth pursuing, and can profitably be pursued before we become involved with quantified modal languages. In order to uncover the conceptual differences we need to bring together some reflections concerning sentences, context dependence, and sentence operators.

Let us begin by recalling Dummett's (1973, p. 195) remark about sentences (cf. Section VI.1): '[S]entences are those linguistic expressions by means of which it is possible to *do* something, that is, to *say* something.' And let us add (cf. Section II.2) that when a speaker makes an utterance and thereby says something, or asserts something, his utterance is evaluable for TRUTH. (TRUTH is the primary dimension of assessment for utterances.) Typically the speaker expresses a belief about the way the world is; if the world is, in fact, that way then his utterance is TRUE and his belief is correct. What is more, evaluation of an utterance for TRUTH is a once-for-all matter; TRUTH is not temporally relative. Concerning such evaluation Gareth Evans (forthcoming b, Section I) wrote the following:

> One who utters the sentence-type 'It is raining' rules out dry
> weather only at the time of utterance; he does not rule out later
> dryness, and hence there can be no argument from the later state
> of the weather to a reappraisal of his utterance. Utterances have
> to be evaluated according to what they rule out, and so different
> utterances of the same tensed sentence made at different times
> may have to be evaluated (once and for all) differently.

(It does not, of course, follow that the TRUTH of an utterance is, in general, anything other than a contingent matter.) Putting these points together we have the idea that an indicative sentence is an expression utterances of which are evaluable for (non-relative) TRUTH.

This idea about sentences does not have the consequence that every sentence can be assigned a condition for the application of a non-relative truth predicate. On the contrary, a sentence might have semantic properties which yield a non-relative truth condition only when a context of utterance is fixed. Let us say that such a sentence is context dependent. While context dependence is absent the connection between the TRUTH of utterances and the truth of sentences is very simple, for the truth predicate applicable to sentences is just as non-relative as the TRUTH predicate applicable to utterances. Once context dependence enters, however, a semantic theorist may need to employ a context-relative truth predicate in his theory. It is then a constraint upon the concept of context-relative truth of sentences that an utterance of a sentence in a context is TRUE just in case the sentence is true relative to that context.

In these reflections concerning sentences and context dependence we are simply following Frege (1918, p. 37):

> But are there not thoughts which are true today but false in six
> months time? The thought, for example, that the tree there is
> covered with green leaves, will surely be false in six months time.
> No, for it is not the same thought at all. The words 'this tree is
> covered with green leaves' are not sufficient by themselves for
> the utterance, the time of utterance is involved as well. Without
> the time-indication this gives we have no complete thought,
> *i.e.* no thought at all. Only a sentence supplemented by a time-
> indication and complete in every respect expresses a thought. But
> this, if it is true, is true not only today or tomorrow but timelessly.

But we need, in addition, some reflections concerning sentence operators. So long as context dependence is absent we can say, simply
enough, that a sentence operator O takes a sentence s to yield a sentence $\ulcorner Os \urcorner$ whose meaning depends systematically upon the meaning
of s. And, if O is an extensional or intensional sentence operator, we
can add that the strict condition for the (non-relative) truth of $\ulcorner Os \urcorner$
depends systematically upon that for the (non-relative) truth of s.
Once context dependence enters, however, we must be more careful.
(In particular we must be more careful in our use of the expression
'meaning'.) For a context dependent sentence can be assigned two
quite different kinds of semantic property. It can be assigned a semantic property just as it stands, and it can be assigned a semantic property
relative to a given context. Kaplan (1977, Section VI) has suggested
some useful terminology to mark the distinction. A sentence has a
character just as it stands, and it has a *content* relative to a given
context. It is the character which 'determines the content in varying
contexts'; so the character might be thought of as a function from
contexts to contents. Relative to a given context, it is the content
of a sentence which determines (in effect by rule (T) of Section II.1)
a non-relative truth condition. Thus Kaplan's notion of a content
corresponds to Frege's notion of a complete thought, and to the
traditional notion of a proposition. And the notion of a character
corresponds, perhaps, to the pretheoretic notion of the meaning of
a context dependent sentence.

Having thus distinguished the two kinds of semantic property which can be assigned to a context dependent sentence, we can continue our reflections concerning sentence operators. In the case of a context independent sentence we need consider only a content. (The character can be thought of as a constant function taking all contexts to that same content.) So if we have an account of the application of a sentence operator O to context independent sentences then we have an account of the way in which the meaning (content) of $\ulcorner Os \urcorner$ depends systematically upon the meaning (content) of s, and we can associate with O a function f_O from contents to contents. This account yields immediately and naturally an account of the application of O to context dependent sentences. The content of $\ulcorner Os \urcorner$ relative to a given context is simply the value of the function f_O applied to the content of s relative to that same context. Thus, for example, if O is an extensional or intensional operator then the account of the way in which, if s is context independent, the non-relative truth condition of $\ulcorner Os \urcorner$ depends systematically upon that of s provides immediately an account of the way in which, if s is context dependent, the non-relative truth condition of $\ulcorner Os \urcorner$ in a given context depends systematically upon that of s in that same context. Let us explicitly reserve the expression 'sentence operator' for an operator O with the property that the content of $\ulcorner Os \urcorner$ relative to a given context depends systematically upon the content of s relative to that same context. In contrast, a *context shifting operator* is an operator O with the property that the content of $\ulcorner Os \urcorner$ relative to a given context depends systematically upon the content of s relative to other contexts. It is not easy to provide examples of context shifting operators from natural languages, since it is far from clear that such operators occur in natural languages. But the following passage from David Lewis (1980, p. 84–5) provides a theoretically possible example:

> To be sure, we could speak a language in which 'As for you, I am hungry.' is true iff 'I am hungry.' is true when the role of speaker is shifted from me to you – in other words, iff you are hungry.
> We could – but we don't.

Armed now with these reflections concerning sentences, context dependence, and sentence operators, we can compare languages containing modal and temporal adverbs. Let us consider first modal languages. There can be significant use of modal adverbs without any involvement with context dependence. The atomic sentences of L_{10}, for example, can be assigned non-relative truth conditions just as they stand. And if we consider a context dependent sentence such as 'I am hungry now' then it is very clear that the non-relative truth condition of

□ (I am hungry now)

in a given context can be fully accounted for in terms of the semantic properties of '□' and the non-relative truth condition of 'I am hungry now' in that same context. The modal operators are sentence operators, as recently defined.

Let us consider second a language with significant use of temporal adverbs, and let us focus upon the temporal adverbs which are formally analogous to '□' and '◊', namely, 'always' and 'sometimes'. In order to maintain a strict parallel with the modal case one would need to hold that in the temporally modified sentences

Always (Whitlam is angry)
Sometimes (Fraser is hot)

the expressions 'Whitlam is angry' and 'Fraser is hot' themselves occur as sentences, and the expressions 'Always' and 'Sometimes' are sentence operators, as recently defined. It is certainly the case that an utterance of 'Whitlam is angry', for example, in a certain temporal context, that is, at a certain time, is TRUE just in case Whitlam is angry at that time. So the expression 'Whitlam is angry' is (at least when it stands alone) a (context dependent) sentence. But if one then represents

Always (Whitlam is angry)

as the result of the application of the operator 'Always' to that context dependent sentence then one must acknowledge that 'Always' is not a sentence operator, as recently defined, but a context shifting operator. (The truth of the temporally modified sentence, relative to a given context, depends upon the truth of the contained sentence relative to (all) other contexts.) And to acknowledge that is to acknowledge a conceptual difference between the modal and the temporal cases. (The last two paragraphs state the main points of Evans, forthcoming b, Section III.)

Someone may try to restore an analogy by pointing out that just as 'Whitlam is angry' is a sentence which is true relative to various temporal contexts and 'Always (Whitlam is angry)' is a sentence which is true just in case the contained sentence is true relative to every temporal context, so the atomic sentence s_1 (of L_{10}), for example, is true relative to various actual and counterfactual situations and $\ulcorner \Box s_1 \urcorner$ is a sentence which is true just in case s_1 is true relative to every actual and counterfactual situation. But pointing this out is not enough. For, according to this first account of the temporally modified sentences, 'always' is a context shifting operator. So, in order to restore an analogy between the modal and the temporal cases, one would have to show that the relativity of the truth of a sentence to actual and counterfactual situations is a kind of context dependence. But that relativity is not a kind of context dependence; the sentences (of L_{10}) to which the modal operators are attached can be assigned contents just as they stand. Kaplan (1977) introduced the notion of content as corresponding to the pretheoretic notion of *what is said*. If we were to regard the relativity of truth to situations as a kind of context dependence, then we should have to say (absurdly) that one cannot know what has been said in an utterance of s_1 unless one knows everything that is the case (that is, unless one knows which possible world is actual). And we should have to say that if the world had been different in any respect then something different would have been said (that is, the very same utterance would have expressed a different complete thought). There is thus no way to restore an analogy between the modal and the temporal cases if temporal adverbs are treated as context shifting operators.

It is not obligatory that the temporal adverbs 'always' and 'sometimes' should be treated as context shifting operators. Nor is it obviously desirable. For so treating those adverbs seems to make more difficult a semantic account of sentences in which context dependent expressions like 'a moment ago' occur within the scope of those adverbs. Consider, for example, the sentence 'Sometime, everyone who coughed a moment ago will sneeze'. If 'sometime' is treated as a context shifting operator then that sentence is true relative to a given temporal context t just in case, for some temporal context t' the sentence 'Everyone who coughed a moment ago sneezes' is true relative to t'. The expression 'a moment ago' is context dependent, so the truth of the latter sentence relative to the temporal context t' requires that everyone who coughed just before t' should sneeze at t'. But it is neither necessary nor sufficient for the truth of the temporally modified sentence relative to the temporal context t, that there should be a time t' such that everyone who coughed just before t' sneezes at t'. What is necessary and sufficient for the truth of that sentence relative to t is that there should be a time t' such that everyone who coughed just before t sneezes at t'.

Treating those temporal adverbs as context shifting operators is a consequence of treating the expression 'Whitlam is angry' as a sentence even as it occurs in 'Always (Whitlam is angry)'. An alternative strategy is possible, and apparently preferable. One can hold that an expression such as 'Whitlam is angry' is, strictly speaking, ambiguous. As it stands alone, it is a context dependent sentence, but as it occurs within the scope of the temporal adverbs it is not a sentence at all; rather, it is similar to a predicate of times.

Let us consider, by way of analogy, the following two examples. First, suppose that a language contains a range of one-place atomic predicates 'P_1', ..., 'P_{10}', together with the quantifiers '$\forall$' and '$\exists$' (and associated variables). And suppose that it is a convention in the use of the language that an utterance of an atomic predicate standing alone is TRUE just in case the predicate is true of Tiny Tim. Thus a speaker who comes out with 'P_1' says that Tiny Tim is Q_1, while a speaker who comes out with '$(\forall v_1)P_1 v_1$' says that everything is Q_1. In this case the expression 'P_1', as it occurs in the surface language, is ambiguous as between a sentence and a predicate. At the level of input to a semantic theory this ambiguity would be removed. The surface sentence 'P_1' would be represented as 'P_1(Tiny Tim)'. Second, suppose that the same predicates and quantifiers are used, but that there is a rather different convention governing the use of atomic predicates standing alone. An utterance of an atomic predicate standing alone is TRUE just in case the predicate is true of the person making the utterance. A speaker who comes out with 'P_1' says that he himself is Q_1, while a speaker who comes out with '$(\forall v_1)P_1 v_1$' says that everything is Q_1. In this case also it would be natural to say that the expression 'P_1', as it occurs in the surface language, is ambiguous as between a (context dependent) sentence and a predicate. At the level of input to a semantic theory this ambiguity would be removed. The surface sentence 'P_1' would be represented as 'P_1(I)' (where 'I' is the first person singular pronoun, a context dependent genuine singular referring expression). In a semantic theory the truth predicate and the reference functor would be relativized to contexts. This relativity would be idle in the axioms for atomic predicates and for the quantifiers, but would be crucial in the derivation of a truth condition specification for 'P_1(I)'. We should expect some such theorem as the following:

$$(\forall c)\,[Tr(c, `P_1(\text{I})\text{'}) \leftrightarrow Q_1(sp(c))]$$

(where, for any context c, $sp(c)$ is the speaker in c).

The alternative (and apparently preferable) strategy for treating temporal adverbs is analogous to the strategy indicated in this second example. Let us say that expressions such as 'Whitlam is angry' are *t-predicates*. (Evans, forthcoming b, calls them *situation expressions*.) The temporal adverbs take a t-predicate to make a sentence. It is a convention in the use of the language that an utterance of a t-predicate standing alone is TRUE just in case the t-predicate is true of the time at which the utterance is made. Thus (on this alternative strategy) the expression 'Whitlam is angry', as it occurs in the surface language, is ambiguous as between a (context dependent) sentence and a t-predicate. At the level of input to a semantic theory this ambiguity would be removed. The surface sentence 'Whitlam is angry' would be represented as

Now (Whitlam is angry)

(where 'Now' is a context dependent operator which takes a t-predicate to make a sentence). A semantic theory could be set up analogous to the satisfaction theory $QS\theta$ or analogous to the truth theory $QT\theta$ (cf. Section VI.1). In the latter case we would introduce, as a technical auxiliary, an extended language containing, for each time which is relevant to the truth of temporally modified sentences, an operator which takes a t-predicate to make a sentence which is true just in case the t-predicate is true of that time. In either case the truth (or satisfaction) predicate would be relativized to contexts. This relativity would be idle in the axioms for t-predicates and for the temporal adverbs 'always' and 'sometimes', but would be crucial in the derivation of a truth condition specification for 'Now (Whitlam is angry)'. We should expect some such theorem as the following

$(\forall c) [Tr(c, \text{'Now (Whitlam is angry)'}) \leftrightarrow$
$(\text{At } t(c)) (\text{Whitlam is angry})]$

(where, for any context c, $t(c)$ is the time of c). (The last four paragraphs state the main points of Evans, forthcoming b, Section II; cf. Lewis, 1980, Section 8.)

This alternative strategy, like the earlier strategy (treating temporal adverbs as context shifting operators), reveals a conceptual difference between the modal and the temporal cases. For there is no reason to maintain that the expression s_1 as it occurs in $\ulcorner \Box s_1 \urcorner$, for example, is anything other than a sentence which can be used, standing alone, to make a TRUTH evaluable utterance.

Someone might reply that the condition for the TRUTH of an utterance of s_1 standing alone is the result of a convention governing the use of that expression which is quite analogous to the conventions governing the use of 'P_1' (in the two examples) and the convention governing the use of t-predicates. For, such a person might say, if expressions were so used that an utterance of s_1 standing alone was TRUE just in case snow would be white if such and such were the case, then s_1 would be ambiguous. As it stood alone it would have a semantic property different from that by which it contributes to the meaning of $\ulcorner \Box s_1 \urcorner$, for example. At the level of input to a semantic theory this ambiguity would be removed. The surface sentence s_1 would be represented as $\ulcorner Os_1 \urcorner$, for some operator O. And, such a person might continue, as expressions are in fact used, an utterance of s_1 standing alone is TRUE just in case snow is white as things actually are (or, in the actual world). In general an utterance of a sentence standing alone is TRUE just in case the sentence is true with respect to the actual world, while a sentence contributes to the meanings of modal sentences containing it by a semantic property which determines the condition for its truth with respect to other possible worlds. So, as expressions are in fact used, sentences are ambiguous. Consequently, the modal case and the temporal case are analogous.

This reply is unsuccessful. It is certainly correct that an utterance is TRUE just in case the sentence uttered is true with respect to the actual world. But this is not a consequence of any additional semantic property which sentences have when they stand alone, and which has to be specified by employing an antecedently available concept of the actual world. It is, rather, a consequence of the connection between TRUTH of utterances and truth of sentences, and the way the concept of actuality is introduced via the antecedently available concept of truth. An utterance is TRUE just in case the sentence uttered is true. The actual world is that possible world with respect to which those sentences are true which are, in fact, true.

4   NECESSITY, QUANTIFICATION, AND EXISTENCE

We have so far considered the addition of modal operators to a very simple language. Now we must consider a quantified modal language. So let L_{11} extend the quantificational language L_6 (with '$\mathbf{V}$' and '$\mathbf{\exists}$') by the addition of '$\Box$' and '$\Diamond$' (with the same syntactic properties as '~'). In order to reduce complexities to a minimum while retaining the main features of a quantified modal language, let us at first ignore the fact that with respect to some counterfactual situations some of the objects which in fact exist may not exist, and other objects may exist. That is, let us ignore the fact that the domain of quantification varies from possible world to possible world. (And let us ignore the fact that ultimately we need to consider the modal extension of L_7, the language with binary quantifiers, instead of L_6.)

The main features of such a quantified modal language are these. The modal operators are sentence operators. They are not extensional but intensional operators. And (what is a consequence of this) sentences containing the modal operators admit substitution of co-referring genuine singular referring expressions (in particular, co-referring names) *salva veritate* (cf. Section V.2). Thus quantification into name positions which are within the scope of the modal operators is standard objectual quantification, that is, it is quantification over objects of the kind named (cf. Section VI.4). The sentence

$$(\exists v_1) \, \Box P_1 v_1$$

for example, is true just in case there is some object in the domain of quantification which is necessarily Q_1, that is, is Q_1 in every possible world. (Recall that we are ignoring the fact that some objects fail to exist in some possible worlds.) Similarly, the sentence

$$(\forall v_1) \, (P_1 v_1 \rightarrow \Box P_1 v_1)$$

is true just in case every object in the domain of quantification which is Q_1 is necessarily Q_1.

There is an argument (the *Frege argument*) which may seem to threaten the semantic coherence of a language with these features. It purports to show that any sentence operator O which admits substitution of broadly logical equivalents *salva veritate*, and also admits substitution of co-referring singular terms *salva veritate*, is after all extensional. One version of the argument is as follows (cf. Quine, 1960, pp. 148–9). Suppose that s and s' are two sentences alike in truth value, and that the symbol 'δ' is introduced with the property that for any sentence σ, $\ulcorner \delta \sigma = 1 \urcorner$ is true if σ is true and $\ulcorner \delta \sigma = 0 \urcorner$ is true if σ is false. Then consider the following sequence of sentences.

(1) $O(s)$
(2) $O(\delta s = 1)$

(3) $O(\delta s' = 1)$
(4) $O(s')$

The steps from (1) to (2) and from (3) to (4) are simply the results of substitution of broadly logical equivalents, for we can agree on the truth of

$$\Box(s \leftrightarrow (\delta s = 1))$$

and

$$\Box(s' \leftrightarrow (\delta s' = 1)).$$

So (2) has the same truth value as (1) and (3) has the same truth value as (4). The step from (2) to (3) is the result of substituting $\ulcorner \delta s' \urcorner$ for $\ulcorner \delta s \urcorner$, and since s and s' have the same truth value this, according to the argument, is a case of substitution of co-referring singular terms. So (3) has the same truth value as (2). Thus (4) has the same truth value as (1) provided only that s and s' are alike in truth value, and so O is extensional.

This argument turns upon the claim that $\ulcorner \delta s \urcorner$ and $\ulcorner \delta s' \urcorner$ are singular terms. We can admit that this is so, upon a suitably generous construal of the expression 'singular term'. But $\ulcorner \delta s \urcorner$ and $\ulcorner \delta s' \urcorner$ are not genuine singular referring expressions, and the fact that they are not is crucial to the claim that, for example, s and $\ulcorner \delta s = 1 \urcorner$ are broadly logically equivalent. They are, in fact, definite descriptions. Quine (1960, p. 148) introduced 'δ' this way: 'Let us write "δp" . . . as short for the description: the number x such that $((x = 1)$ and $p)$ or $((x = 0)$ and not $p)$.' So (2) and (3) in the Frege argument should properly be written out as

(2′) $O((\text{THE } x)(((x = 1) \,\&\, s) \vee ((x = 0) \,\&\, \sim s); x = 1))$
(3′) $O((\text{THE } x)(((x = 1) \,\&\, s') \vee ((x = 0) \,\&\, \sim s'); x = 1))$

or, if the binary quantifier 'THE' is not present in the language, as expressions obtained from these by the Russellian equivalence. The step from (2′) to (3′) is the result of substitution of co-extensive predicates in the first gap provided by the binary quantifier 'THE'. (The predicates are co-extensive since each is true of just the number 1, if s and s' are both true, and just the number 0, if s and s' are both false.) So what is correct about the Frege argument is this. Any sentence operator which admits substitution of broadly logical equivalents *salva veritate*, and also admits substitution of co-extensive predicates *salva veritate*, is extensional. But this poses no threat to the semantic coherence of a quantified modal language, such as L_{11}, with the features set out two paragraphs back.

With any apparent threat from the Frege argument now removed we can provide a truth theory for L_{11}. Indeed, it is quite straightforward to construct a theory related to $QT\theta$ (the truth theory for L_6) as $NT\theta$ is related to $T\theta$ (the truth theory for the language L_1 of which L_{10} is the modal extension). There is no need to go through all the details but one feature of the theory deserves comment. Consider a sentence in which a name occurs within the scope of a modal operator, say '$\Box P_1 m_1$'. At some point in the derivation of a truth condition specifying biconditional for that sentence we shall need to proceed from

$$\Box Q_1\,(Ref(L^+,\,`m_1\textrm{'}))$$

to

$$\Box Q_1 n_1.$$

('L^+' abbreviates 'L_{11}^+'; L_{11}^+ contains a name of each object in the domain of quantification.) But the *ML* expression

$$Ref(L^+,\,`m_1\textrm{'})$$

is like a definite description

the reference of 'm_1' in L^+

and so the step in question may seem to be of rather the same kind as the step from (2) to (3) in the Frege argument, and so to be inadmissible given that '$\Box$' is not extensional. But there is an important difference between the cases. It is a contingent fact that the definite descriptions $\ulcorner\delta s\urcorner$ and $\ulcorner\delta s'\urcorner$ in the Frege argument apply to the same number. But it is a non-contingent fact that the reference of 'm_1' in L_{11}, and so in L^+, is n_1. The step in the derivation of a biconditional for '$\Box P_1 m_1$' will be warranted by a modalized axiom

$$\Box\,[Ref(L^+,\,`m_1\textrm{'}) = n_1]$$

(corresponding to axiom $(Q3{:}1)$ of $QT\theta$). Essentially the same point can be made regarding the derivation of a biconditional for a quantified sentence such as '$(\exists v_1)\,P_1 v_1$'. If this sentence is true then there is an object x and a name, say γ_0, of x such that $\ulcorner\Box P_1 \gamma_0\urcorner$ is true (in L^+). At some point in the derivation we shall need to proceed from

$$\Box Q_1\,(Ref(L^+,\,\gamma_0))$$

to

$$\Box Q_1 x.$$

This step will be warranted by the hypothesis

$$\Box [Ref(L^+, \gamma_0) = x]$$

and ultimately by an axiom

$$\Box (\forall x)(\exists \gamma \in L^+) \Box [Ref(L^+, \gamma) = x]$$

(corresponding to axiom ($Q2$) of $QT\theta$). The second occurrence of '$\Box$' in this axiom is not eliminable.

Let us now recall that, in reality, the domain of quantification does vary from world to world. There are, in particular, many objects which exist and which might not have existed. This fact gives rise to questions about the exact interpretation of the operators '$\Box$' and '$\Diamond$'. Various interpretations are semantically coherent, and it is unclear which best fits the facts of natural language use. Suppose, for example, that the object n_1, named by 'm_1', exists merely contingently, and consider the sentence '$\Box P_1 m_1$'. Upon one possible interpretation of '$\Box$', a *weak* interpretation, that sentence is true provided that n_1 is Q_1 in every possible world in which n_1 exists at all. Upon another possible interpretation, a *strong* interpretation, that sentence is not true unless n_1 exists and is Q_1 in every possible world. Upon the weak interpretation the sentence may perhaps be true (depending on what property being Q_1 is); upon the strong interpretation the sentence is certainly false (since in some possible worlds n_1 does not exist).

We shall focus briefly upon the weak interpretation, for it answers well to at least one feature of the use of modal adverbs in English. When someone comes out with such a sentence as

Whitlam is necessarily human

to make a claim (whether it be true or false) about Whitlam's essential nature, that speaker does not take himself to be committed to denying that Whitlam's parents might never have met, or that they might have remained childless. In short, he does not take himself to be committed to denying that Whitlam might never have existed. (What he denies is that Whitlam might have existed without being human.) So if the modal sentence of English is to be represented, at the level of input to a semantic theory, as the result of applying a sentence operator '$\Box$' to 'Whitlam is human' then that sentence operator must be given a weak interpretation. We have, so far, specified the weak interpretation of '□' only in the case in which the contained sentence is atomic. Let us now specify that for any sentence σ (atomic or complex), the only possible worlds which are relevant to the truth of $\ulcorner\Box\sigma\urcorner$ are those in which all the objects named in σ exist. (The modal sentence is true just in case, in every possible world in which they all exist, those objects are thus and so.) And let us say that, on this interpretation, '□' expresses *weak necessity* (cf. Kripke, 1971, p. 137). (As a result of the relation between '□' and '◊', a sentence $\ulcorner\Diamond\sigma\urcorner$ is true just in case there is a world in which all the objects named in σ exist and are thus and so.)

When we come to provide a truth theory for a quantified modal language in which '□' expresses weak necessity, care is required at two points. One concerns the background logic of the *ML*. The other concerns the interpretation of modal sentences of the *ML* in which truth is predicated of *OL* sentences. First, we have by (non-modal) logic alone

$$Q_1 n_1 \rightarrow (\exists x) Q_1 x$$

and so we have, by *Nec*,

$$\Box(Q_1 n_1 \rightarrow (\exists x) Q_1 x).$$

But this yields, by an instance of the schema

$$\Box(\alpha \rightarrow \beta) \rightarrow (\Box\alpha \rightarrow \Box\beta)$$

the conditional

$$\Box Q_1 n_1 \rightarrow \Box(\exists x) Q_1 x.$$

And this conditional is not, in general, true. For n_1 might be Q_1 in every possible world in which n_1 exists and yet there might be possible worlds in which n_1 does not exist and in which nothing else is Q_1 (see Wiggins, 1976, p. 302). The same conditional can, of course, be derived via the extended rule of necessitation. So if '□' is to express weak necessity then the axioms and rules of *S5* must be subject to a restriction. In instances of the schema

$$\Box(\alpha \rightarrow \beta) \rightarrow (\Box\alpha \rightarrow \Box\beta)$$

we require that all the names (and free variables) which occur in α occur also in β. Correspondingly, in the extended rule of necessitation

214

$$\frac{\alpha_1, \ldots, \alpha_n \vdash \beta}{\Box\alpha_1, \ldots, \Box\alpha_n \vdash \Box\beta}$$

we require that all the names (and free variables) which occur in α_1, $\ldots$, α_n occur also in β. For what is problematic is not the modalized conditional

$$\Box(Q_1 n_1 \rightarrow (\exists x) Q_1 x).$$

This sentence is true, for in every possible world in which n_1 exists, if n_1 is Q_1 then something is Q_1. What is problematic is the move from this sentence to a conditional with modalized antecedent and modalized consequent, where the set of possible worlds relevant to the truth of the antecedent does not include all the worlds which are relevant to the truth of the consequent.

The second point at which care is needed is this. The objects to which names in L_{11} refer exist (we suppose) merely contingently. But languages have their semantic properties non-contingently. So (it is natural to suppose) the language L_{11} itself exists merely contingently; that language would not exist if some of the objects named in L_{11} were not to exist. But in that case consider the *ML* sentence

$$\Box Tr(L_{11}, \text{'}P_1 m_1\text{'}).$$

If '$\Box$' expresses weak necessity then, it seems, all that is required for the truth of this *ML* sentence is that the *OL* sentence '$P_1 m_1$' should be true with respect to every possible world in which L_{11} exists, that is, with respect to every possible world in which all the objects named in L_{11} exist. This is much less than is required for the truth (in L_{11}) of the *OL* sentence '$\Box P_1 m_1$'. The sentence '$P_1 m_1$' might be true with respect to every possible world in which all the objects named in L_{11} exist, and yet '$\Box P_1 m_1$' might be false. So the biconditional

$$Tr(L_{11}, \text{'}\Box P_1 m_1\text{'}) \leftrightarrow \Box Tr(L_{11}, \text{'}P_1 m_1\text{'})$$

(which one would expect to be a theorem of a truth theory for L_{11}) is not in general true. If, on the other hand, we were to maintain that languages exist non-contingently then, it seems, more would be required for the truth of the *ML* sentence

$$\Box Tr(L_{11}, \text{'}P_1 m_1\text{'})$$

than is required for the truth of '$\Box P_1 m_1$' and so, again, the biconditional would not in general be true. There are at least two ways of meeting this difficulty. One way is to maintain that L_{11} exists contingently and that, since '$\square$' expresses weak necessity, the biconditional is not in general true, and to replace that biconditional by one in which a language is mentioned on the right hand side whose contingency of existence exactly matches that of the objects named in the sentence 'P_1m_1'. The sublanguage of L_{11} which omits all names save 'm_1' is such a language. This first way involves complicating the axiom for '$\square$' in the truth theory, although the complication is relatively superficial. The other way is to maintain that '$\square$' expresses weak necessity when it is applied to *OL* sentences or to *ML* sentences in which *OL* expressions are not mentioned, and that the interpretation of modal sentences in which truth (in L_{11} or in L^+) is predicated of *OL* sentences should be constrained by the requirement that such biconditionals as

$$Tr(L_{11}, `\square P_1 m_1`) \leftrightarrow \square\, Tr(L_{11}, `P_1 m_1`)$$

be true. The possible worlds which are relevant to the truth of the *ML* sentence on the right hand side of this biconditional are, according to this second way, just those which are relevant to the truth of '$\square P_1 m_1$' (Peacocke, 1978, pp. 490–1):

> [T]he truth values of semantical predicates in various possible worlds with respect to various objects must be allowed to fall where they may according to our best insights into the truth of *OL* sentences and constraints on the concepts of truth and satisfaction.

There is no need for us to choose between these ways here.

The weak interpretation presents no insuperable obstacle to the semantic theorist, and it answers well to one feature of the use of modal adverbs in English. But it has its disadvantages. For if '$\square$' expresses weak necessity then there is no way in which one can use '$\square$' to represent the (false) sentence

> Whitlam exists necessarily.

Suppose that 'P_{10}' is an existence predicate. Then the sentence '$P_{10}m_1$', for example, is trivially true since, in every possible world in which n_1 exists, n_1 exists (cf. Wiggins, 1976, p. 301 and Hazen, 1976, p. 30). It may well be the case that the sentence

> Whitlam necessarily exists

can be heard (or even is naturally heard) as trivially true. In that case, that sentence (at least on that reading) can be represented using '$\Box$'. But it is indubitable that the sentences

Whitlam exists necessarily

and

Necessarily Whitlam exists

are naturally heard in such a way that they are false. (Their truth requires that Whitlam share with God and numbers the property of non-contingent existence.)

A first thought might be that these false sentences should be represented using a predicate of necessary existence, and without using a modal sentence operator at all. This thought may have its merits, but it leaves quite untouched some closely related false sentences such as

Necessarily, if Whitlam exists then Fraser exists.

So a second thought might be to make use of a strong interpretation of '$\Box$'. It will not help, of course, to interpret '$\Box$' in such a way that for any sentence σ (atomic or complex), the truth of $\ulcorner \Box \sigma \urcorner$ requires *inter alia* that in every possible world all the objects named in σ exist. Rather we specify, first, that an atomic sentence is false (and its negation true) with respect to those possible worlds in which some of the objects named in the sentence do not exist, and, second, that for any sentence σ, the modal sentence $\ulcorner \Box \sigma \urcorner$ is true just in case σ is true with respect to every possible world. This has the consequence that if σ is atomic then the truth of $\ulcorner \Box \sigma \urcorner$ requires *inter alia* that in every possible world all the objects named in σ exist. (It is a strong interpretation.) But if σ is the negation of an atomic sentence then the truth of $\ulcorner \Box \sigma \urcorner$ on this strong interpretation requires nothing more than the truth of that sentence on the weak interpretation of '$\Box$'. What is important for present purposes is that if σ_1 and σ_2 are both atomic then the truth of $\ulcorner \Box(\sigma_1 \to \sigma_2) \urcorner$ requires that in every possible world, if all the objects named in σ_1 exist and are thus and so (as required for the truth of σ_1) then all the objects named in σ_2 exist and are thus and so (as required for the truth of σ_2). In particular, since 'P_{10}' is (we suppose) an existence predicate, the sentence '$\Box(P_{10}m_1 \to P_{10}m_2)$' is true just in case in every possible world, if n_1 exists then n_2 exists.

This strong interpretation of '$\Box$' has very clear merits. (As in the case of the weak interpretation a certain amount of care is needed in constructing a truth theory for a language containing such an operator;

see e.g. Peacocke, 1978.) In fact, everything which can be expressed using '$\Box$' under the weak interpretation can also be expressed using '$\Box$' under this strong interpretation. For example, what under the weak interpretation is expressed by '$\Box P_1 m_1$' is expressed under the strong interpretation by '$\Box (P_{10} m_1 \rightarrow P_1 m_1)$' (cf. Hazen, 1976, p. 33). There are thus at least two views which a semantic theorist might take about the use of modal adverbs in English. On the one hand, he might hold that the modal adverbs are ambiguous, and in particular that 'necessarily' is ambiguous as between '$\Box$' under the weak interpretation (the preferred reading in claims about essential nature) and '$\Box$' under the strong interpretation (the preferred reading in modal claims about existence). On the other hand, he might hold that 'necessarily' is univocal, and that speakers do not quite say what they mean (s-mean) when they make essentialist claims. What a man who comes out with 'Whitlam is necessarily human' or 'Necessarily Whitlam is human' strictly and literally says is false (since 'necessarily' corresponds univocally to '$\Box$' under the strong interpretation). In order to say what he means (which is more arguably true) the man should come out with 'Necessarily, if Whitlam exists then he is human'.

It is not clear that we can choose between these views given only the facts which we have before us. But in any case there is a (final) feature of the use of modal adverbs to which neither view answers particularly well. Consider the two sentences

> Liza Minnelli was necessarily born of Judy Garland
> Judy Garland necessarily gave birth to Liza Minnelli.

Many speakers regard these sentences as requiring quite different things for their truth, even though 'was born of' is just the converse of 'gave birth to'. The first sentence is naturally heard as requiring for its truth that in every possible world in which Liza Minnelli exists Judy Garland also exists and Liza Minnelli was born of Judy Garland. The second sentence is naturally heard as requiring for its truth that in every possible world in which Judy Garland exists Liza Minnelli exists and Judy Garland gave birth to Liza Minnelli. The first view, upon which 'necessarily' in sentences such as these corresponds to '$\Box$' under the weak interpretation, clearly does not answer well to these facts about language use. The second view can be made to answer, but only by a relatively complicated story about speakers failing to say what they mean.

What this suggests, perhaps, is that modal adverbs are not simply sentence operators, and that in these last two sentences (and in 'Whitlam is necessarily human') the modal adverb operates only upon a predicate (in the first, 'was born of Judy Garland', and in the second, 'gave birth to Liza Minnelli'). David Wiggins (1976) has urged just this. On his view modal adverbs can modify whole sentences, in which case 'necessarily' corresponds to '$\Box$' under the strong interpretation. But they can also, without ambiguity, modify predicates, and a sentence made up of, say, a name and a necessitated predicate is true just in case in every possible world in which the named object exists it has the property associated with the predicate.

Clearly there are a number of things which a semantic theorist must do if he is to make progress on this issue. He must obtain (presumably from a linguist) data about the use of modal adverbs in natural languages. He must find a way to evaluate claims that the modal adverbs are ambiguous. And he must examine the semantic nature of the kind of expression (modifying sentences or predicates) of which, according to Wiggins, modal adverbs are examples. In particular, he must scrutinize the claim that there is no ambiguity in the use of such expressions to modify both sentences and predicates. Equally clearly, this is not the place to commence this massive task.

NOTES

In this chapter I am particularly indebted to Christopher Peacocke, Gareth Evans, and Stephen Williams. See Peacocke (1978), and for my earlier thoughts on this topic Davies (1978). Section VIII.3 relies very heavily upon an unpublished ancestor of Evans (forthcoming b), and upon numerous conversations with Gareth Evans and Christopher Peacocke (to whom the points in the last two paragraphs of the section are attributable). Section VIII.4 owes a great deal to conversations with Stephen Williams, to whom almost all the points in the last five paragraphs of that section are attributable.

The version of the Frege argument which is discussed in Section VIII.4 is not, perhaps, the most familiar version. See, for example, Davidson (1967, p. 3), Taylor (1976, pp. 266–74), and for Frege's version, 'On sense and reference' (1892, p. 64). On quantified modal logic in general, see Kripke (1963).

IX

ACTUALITY

1   ACTUALITY AND MODAL LOGIC

Consider the English sentence

> It is possible that everything which is actually red
> should have been shiny.

This sentence cannot, it seems, be represented in a quantified modal language such as L_{11}. Certainly

$$\Diamond(\forall x)(x \text{ is red} \rightarrow x \text{ is shiny})$$

will not do. For that sentence is true just in case there is a possible world in which everything which is red is also shiny, whereas the truth of the English sentence does not require that there be a possible world in which some things are both red and shiny. Equally certainly

$$(\forall x)(x \text{ is red} \rightarrow \Diamond(x \text{ is shiny}))$$

will not do. For that sentence is true just in case, for each thing which is (actually) red, there is a possible world in which that thing is shiny, whereas the truth of the English sentence requires that there be a possible world in which all the things which are actually red are shiny together. It is not merely lack of ingenuity which prevents us from finding a way to represent the English sentence. In order to avoid the inadequacy of the second candidate it is crucial that the universal quantifier occur within the scope of the modal operator '$\Diamond$'. But once the modal operator has wider scope than the quantifier a different inadequacy (that of the first candidate) is inevitable.

We need to extend our modal language by the addition of an operator '*A*' corresponding to the adverb 'actually'. The main semantic feature of such an operator is that for any sentence σ, $\ulcorner A\sigma \urcorner$ is true with respect to a given possible world just in case σ is true with respect to the actual world (that is, just in case σ is actually true). Using this operator we can represent the English sentence (with a proviso to be mentioned in a moment) as follows.

$$\Diamond (\forall x) (A (x \text{ is red}) \rightarrow x \text{ is shiny})$$

This sentence is true just in case there is some possible world w with respect to which the sentence which follows '$\Diamond$' is true. That latter sentence is true with respect to a world w just in case, for each object x (in w), if γ is a name of that object and $\ulcorner A(\gamma \text{ is red})\urcorner$ is true with respect to w then $\ulcorner \gamma \text{ is shiny}\urcorner$ is true with respect to w. The sentence $\ulcorner A(\gamma \text{ is red})\urcorner$ is true with respect to w just in case $\ulcorner \gamma \text{ is red}\urcorner$ is true with respect to the actual world, that is, just in case x is actually red, while $\ulcorner \gamma \text{ is shiny}\urcorner$ is true with respect to w just in case x is shiny in w. Thus, the modal sentence is true just in case there is a possible world w such that every object (in w) which is red in the actual world (is actually red) is shiny in w. The proviso is this. Because the domain of quantification varies from world to world, and in particular because in some possible worlds objects which exist in the actual world may fail to exist, the modal sentence containing '*A*' is not quite equivalent to the English sentence with which we began. For the sentence

$$(\forall x) (A (x \text{ is red}) \rightarrow x \text{ is shiny})$$

may be true with respect to a world in which some or all of the objects which exist (and are red) in the actual world fail to exist. But intuitively what is required for the truth of the English sentence is that there be a world in which all the objects which exist in the actual world and are red in the actual world exist and are shiny. Evidently some alteration is needed in our account of the conditions for the truth with respect to possible worlds of quantified sentences. But any alteration must leave it the case that what is required for the truth of

$$\Diamond (\forall x) (\sim (x \text{ is red}) \rightarrow x \text{ is shiny})$$

for example, is just that there be a possible world w such that everything in w which is not red in w is shiny in w. It is quite difficult to see exactly what alteration is called for, and the difficulty is not reduced by considering (as ultimately one must) modal languages with binary quantifiers instead of '$\forall$' and '$\exists$'.

221

The semantic importance of the 'actually' operator is, however, largely independent of these problems. Let us resort again to the pretence that the domain does not vary from world to world, and in particular that everything which exists in the actual world exists in every possible world. Then, even given this pretence, the English sentence with which we began cannot be represented in a quantified modal language such as L_{11}, for the inadequacies in the two candidates which we considered had nothing to do with the merely contingent existence of red objects. But that English sentence can be represented with the help of 'A' and, given the pretence, no proviso is required. (The example employed in these paragraphs, and much else in this section, is borrowed from Crossley and Humberstone, 1977; see also Hazen, 1976, pp. 35-41.)

Let us now consider some of the more formal properties of the 'actually' operator. Suppose that we wanted to give a truth theory for a simple modal language (without quantifiers) containing the operator 'A'. Then the theory would be cast in a *ML* the background logic of which contained axioms for 'A'. Indeed, the modal component of the background logic would be the system *S5A* which contains the axioms and rules of *S5* (cf. Section VIII.1) together with the following four axiom schemata for 'A':

(A1) $A(\alpha \rightarrow \beta) \rightarrow (A\alpha \rightarrow A\beta)$
(A2) $A\alpha \leftrightarrow \sim A\sim\alpha$
(A3) $\Box\alpha \rightarrow A\alpha$
(A4) $A\alpha \rightarrow \Box A\alpha$.

The schema (A4) may seem a little surprising, but it answers to the fact that since the truth of $\ulcorner A\sigma \urcorner$ with respect to any possible world depends only upon the truth of σ with respect to the actual world, if $\ulcorner A\sigma \urcorner$ is true with respect to any world then it is true with respect to every world. The other axiom schemata are clearly faithful to the intended meaning of 'A'.

As a consequence of (A2) and (A3) we have the theorem schema

$$\Box(\alpha \leftrightarrow \beta) \rightarrow (A\alpha \leftrightarrow A\beta)$$

and thence, via the *S4* axiom and *Nec* (or via (A1), (A4), and *Nec*), the schema

$$\Box(\alpha \leftrightarrow \beta) \rightarrow \Box(A\alpha \leftrightarrow A\beta).$$

This is enough to ensure that in a truth theory containing the axiom

$$\Box\, (\,\forall\sigma)\, [\mathit{Tr}(\ulcorner A\sigma\urcorner) \leftrightarrow A\, \mathit{Tr}(\sigma)]$$

(with the language parameter suppressed), strict truth condition specifying biconditionals for sentences containing '*A*' are forthcoming.

On the side of model theory, also, the introduction of '*A*' is relatively straightforward. As before, a model is a triple $<W,\, w^*,\, V>$ where W is a set, w^* is a particular designated member of W, and V assigns to each ordered pair of a member of W and an atomic sentence a truth value. The function V is extended to V^+, and the clause for '*A*' is, of course,

$$V^+(w,\, \ulcorner A\sigma\urcorner) = \text{T iff } V^+(w^*,\, \sigma) = \text{T}.$$

A little care is needed with the notion of validity, however. In the case of a modal language without '*A*' (such as L_{10}), if a sentence is true with respect to the designated world (w^*) in every model then the sentence is true with respect to every world in every model. (Recall that for the purposes of model theory the members of W, the 'worlds', can be assumed to be set theoretic objects.) For suppose that w_1 and w_2 are both members of W and that a sentence σ is true with respect to w_1 in the model $<W,\, w_1,\, V>$. Then σ is also true with respect to w_1 in the model $<W,\, w_2,\, V>$, since the truth of a sentence (not containing '*A*') with respect to a world, in a model, is independent of which world is designated. But for sentences containing '*A*' this is no longer the case. Suppose that $V(w_1,\, \sigma) = \text{T}$ and $V(w_2,\, \sigma) = \text{F}$. Then $\ulcorner A\sigma\urcorner$ is true with respect to w_1 in the model $<W,\, w_1,\, V>$, but not true with respect to w_1 in the model $<W,\, w_2,\, V>$. Thus, for such sentences we have to distinguish two notions of validity. A sentence is *generally valid* just in case it is true with respect to every world in every model. A sentence is *real world valid* just in case it is true with respect to the designated world in every model. The axioms of the system *S5A* are geared to the notion of general validity. (They are complete in the sense that they yield as theorems all sentences which are generally valid.) A system geared to the notion of real world validity would have as a theorem schema

$$A\alpha \leftrightarrow \alpha$$

since sentences of that form, while clearly not generally valid, are certainly real world valid (and provide the best example of the distinction). And it would impose some restriction upon the rule *Nec*, for it would not have as a theorem schema

$$\Box\,(A\alpha \leftrightarrow \alpha)$$

since sentences of that form are not, in general, even real world valid. This is not the place to argue the relative merits of these two notions of validity. It is enough that they be distinguished.

2   ACTUALITY, FIXED ACTUALITY, AND NECESSITY

We noted (in Section IX.1) that at first glance the axiom schema $(A4)$ may seem surprising. Let us reflect upon it further. The sentence s_2 means that the earth moves. It expresses a truth, but a truth which can be known only *a posteriori*. One cannot know *a priori* that the earth moves. Nor can one know *a priori* that actually the earth moves. So the sentence $\ulcorner As_2 \urcorner$ expresses a truth, but a truth which can be known only *a posteriori* (that is, an *a posteriori* truth). On the other hand, since $\ulcorner As_2 \urcorner$ is true so also, $(A4)$ assures us, is $\ulcorner \Box As_2 \urcorner$. The sentence $\ulcorner As_2 \urcorner$ is necessarily true. Kripke (1972, pp. 260-3) has urged that philosophers should not confuse the distinction between the necessary and the contingent with that between the *a priori* and the *a posteriori*. In $\ulcorner As_2 \urcorner$ we have a very clear example of a sentence which expresses a necessary but *a posteriori* truth. Rather similarly we have in $\ulcorner As_2 \leftrightarrow s_2 \urcorner$ a very clear example of a sentence which expresses a contingent but *a priori* truth. One can know *a priori* that the earth actually moves iff the earth moves. (Such knowledge is constitutive of mastery of the concept of actuality.) But the sentence $\ulcorner As_2 \leftrightarrow s_2 \urcorner$ is not necessarily true. For suppose that it were, that is, suppose that $\ulcorner \Box(As_2 \leftrightarrow s_2) \urcorner$ were true. Then $\ulcorner \Box As_2 \rightarrow \Box s_2 \urcorner$ would be true also, and so (by $(A4)$) would $\ulcorner As_2 \rightarrow \Box s_2 \urcorner$. But $\ulcorner As_2 \urcorner$ is true while $\ulcorner \Box s_2 \urcorner$ is false.

There is more that can, and should, be said about these examples. Certainly $\ulcorner As_2 \urcorner$ is necessarily true in the sense of 'necessarily' which is expressed by '$\Box$'. But, it is natural to say, in some sense of 'necessarily' (yet to be made precise) the sentence $\ulcorner As_2 \urcorner$ is not necessarily true. That sentence is true because s_2 is true with respect to the actual world; it would have been false if another possible world (in which the earth does not move) had been actual. The problem with the modal languages which we have considered so far is that they make no provision for the idea that another possible world might have been actual. In the model theory for $S5A$, for example, this is reflected in the fact that in each model a single world is designated and for no sentence do we, in evaluating its truth or falsity in one model, consider variant models in which other worlds are designated. What is needed to overcome the problem is not a replacement for '□', for it was precisely for its inter-action with '□' that '*A*' was introduced. What is needed, rather, is a further operator (along with '□' and '*A*') which takes a sentence to make a sentence which is true with respect to a possible world w just in case the contained sentence is true with respect to w whichever world plays the role of the actual world. Let us say that, in that case, the contained sentence is *fixedly* true with respect to w. Suppose now that '$\mathscr{F}$' is such an operator and consider the combination of oper-ators '$\mathscr{F}A$'. Then, for any sentence σ, $\ulcorner \mathscr{F}A\sigma \urcorner$ is true with respect to w_2 just in case for every world w, $\ulcorner A\sigma \urcorner$ is true with respect to w_2 but with w playing the role of the actual world. This, in turn, is so just in case for every world w, σ is true with respect to w (with w also playing the role of the actual world). Thus, for example, $\ulcorner \mathscr{F}As_2 \urcorner$ is true (with respect to w_2 and with w_1 playing the role of the actual world) just in case for every world w, s_2 is true with respect to w (with w also playing the role of the actual world) that is, just in case in every possible world the earth moves. The sentence $\ulcorner \mathscr{F}As_2 \urcorner$ is equivalent to $\ulcorner \square s_2 \urcorner$. But consider, as a second example, the sentence $\ulcorner (\mathscr{F}A)(As_2) \urcorner$. This is true (with respect to w_2 and with w_1 playing the role of the actual world) just in case for every world w, $\ulcorner As_2 \urcorner$ is true with respect to w (with w also playing the role of the actual world), that is, just in case in every possible world the earth moves. The sentence $\ulcorner (\mathscr{F}A)(As_2) \urcorner$ is not equivalent to $\ulcorner \square As_2 \urcorner$. The former is false while the latter is true. The sentence $\ulcorner As_2 \urcorner$ is necessarily true (in the sense of 'necessarily' which is expressed by '□') but it is not fixedly actually true. There is, then, a sense of 'necessarily' in which $\ulcorner As_2 \urcorner$ is not necessarily true, namely the sense expressed by 'fixedly actually'.

The sentence $\ulcorner As_2 \leftrightarrow s_2 \urcorner$ expresses a contingent *a priori* truth. Certainly that sentence is not necessarily true in the sense of 'necess-arily' which is expressed by '□'. But, it is natural to say, in some sense of 'necessarily' the sentence $\ulcorner As_2 \leftrightarrow s_2 \urcorner$ is necessarily true. It is, indeed, fixedly actually true. For the sentence $\ulcorner (\mathscr{F}A)(As_2 \leftrightarrow s_2) \urcorner$ is true (with respect to w_2 and with w_1 playing the role of the actual world) just in case for every world w, $\ulcorner As_2 \leftrightarrow s_2 \urcorner$ is true with respect to w (with w also playing the role of the actual world) that is, just in case in every possible world the earth moves iff the earth moves.

One (informal but suggestive) way of stating the main semantic feature of '$\mathscr{F}A$' is this. For any sentence σ, $\ulcorner \mathscr{F}A\sigma \urcorner$ is true just in case every possible world has the property which the truth of σ requires of a world considered as actual. What the truth of $\ulcorner As_2 \urcorner$ requires of a world considered as actual is just what the truth of s_2 requires of a world (considered as actual), namely that in that possible world the earth move. So $\ulcorner(\mathscr{F}A)As_2\urcorner$ is not true. What the truth of $\ulcorner As_2 \leftrightarrow s_2\urcorner$ requires of a world considered as actual is, clearly enough, nothing at all. So $\ulcorner(\mathscr{F}A)(As_2 \leftrightarrow s_2)\urcorner$ is true.

With this much by way of informal motivation for considering languages containing the 'fixedly' operator '$\mathscr{F}$' alongside '$\Box$' and 'A', we must now set out some of the more formal properties of '$\mathscr{F}$'. As in the case of 'A' there are three areas which need attention. First, we give a system of axioms and rules for '$\mathscr{F}$'. Second, we give a truth theory for a language containing '$\mathscr{F}$', cast in a *ML* whose background logic contains the axioms and rules for '$\mathscr{F}$'. Third, we outline the model theory for '$\mathscr{F}$' and relate the axioms and rules to a model theoretic notion of validity. (Some readers may prefer to omit the formal development and proceed directly to Section IX.3.)

First, the system $S5A\mathscr{F}$ contains the axioms and rules of the system $S5A$ (cf. Section IX.1) together with the following six axiom schemata and one rule for '$\mathscr{F}$'.

($\mathscr{F}$1) $\mathscr{F}(\alpha \rightarrow \beta) \rightarrow (\mathscr{F}\alpha \rightarrow \mathscr{F}\beta)$
($\mathscr{F}$2) $\mathscr{F}\alpha \rightarrow \alpha$
($\mathscr{F}$3) $\mathscr{F}\alpha \rightarrow \mathscr{F}\mathscr{F}\alpha$
($\mathscr{F}$4) $\alpha \rightarrow \mathscr{F}\sim\mathscr{F}\sim\alpha$
($\mathscr{F}$5) $\alpha \rightarrow \mathscr{F}\alpha$ (provided 'A' does not occur in α)
($\mathscr{F}$6) $\mathscr{F}A\alpha \leftrightarrow \Box\alpha$ (provided 'A' does not occur in α)
Fix $\dfrac{\vdash \alpha}{\vdash \mathscr{F}\alpha}$

(In the rule of proof *Fix*, '$\vdash$' is read as 'there is a proof from the logic alone of . . .'.) The first four schemata and the rule *Fix* are formally analogous to the schema

$$\Box(\alpha \rightarrow \beta) \rightarrow (\Box\alpha \rightarrow \Box\beta)$$

the T axiom, the $S4$ axiom, the *Brouwerian* axiom, and the rule of necessitation (*Nec*), respectively, in the system $S5$. The fifth schema distinguishes '$\mathscr{F}$' very sharply from '$\Box$'. In the sense in which '$\Box$' is related to variations in the possible world with respect to which a sentence is evaluated (the actual world being held constant), so '$\mathscr{F}$' is related to variations in the possible world playing the role of the actual world (the world with respect to which a sentence is evaluated being held constant). Unless a sentence contains 'A', this latter variation is quite without consequence. The sixth schema answers to the fact that '$\mathcal{F}$' and '$\Box$' are related to variations over exactly the same range of possible worlds.

Second, as consequences of the axioms and rules of $S5A\mathcal{F}$ we have the theorem schemata

$$\mathcal{F}\Box\,(\alpha \leftrightarrow \beta) \rightarrow \mathcal{F}\Box\,(\Box\alpha \leftrightarrow \Box\beta)$$
$$\mathcal{F}\Box\,(\alpha \leftrightarrow \beta) \rightarrow \mathcal{F}\Box\,(A\alpha \leftrightarrow A\beta)$$
$$\mathcal{F}\Box\,(\alpha \leftrightarrow \beta) \rightarrow \mathcal{F}\Box\,(\mathcal{F}\alpha \leftrightarrow \mathcal{F}\beta).$$

These play a crucial role in the derivation of biconditionals in a truth theory for the language L_{12} which extends L_{10} by the addition of 'A' and '$\mathcal{F}$'. As axioms of such a truth theory we have

$$\mathcal{F}\Box\,[\,Tr(L_{12}, s_1) \leftrightarrow \text{snow is white}]$$

for s_1, and similar axioms for s_2 and s_3. We have

$$\mathcal{F}\Box\,(\,\forall\sigma)\,(\forall\tau)\,[\,Tr(L_{12}, \ulcorner\sigma\;\&\;\tau\urcorner) \leftrightarrow$$
$$(Tr(L_{12}, \sigma)\;\&\;Tr(L_{12}, \tau))]$$

for '&', and similar axioms for '∨' and '∼'. And we have

$$\mathcal{F}\Box\,(\,\forall\sigma)\,[\,Tr(L_{12}, \ulcorner\Box\sigma\urcorner) \leftrightarrow \Box Tr(L_{12}, \sigma)]$$

for '$\Box$', and similar axioms for 'A' and '$\mathcal{F}$'. From these axioms we can prove truth condition specifying biconditionals which themselves have the modal prefix '$\mathcal{F}\Box$'. Since the system $S5A\mathcal{F}$ has as theorem schemata

$$\mathcal{F}\Box\alpha \leftrightarrow \Box\mathcal{F}\alpha$$
$$\mathcal{F}\Box\alpha \rightarrow \mathcal{F}A\alpha$$
$$\mathcal{F}\Box\alpha \rightarrow \Box\alpha$$
$$\mathcal{F}\Box\alpha \rightarrow A\alpha$$
$$\mathcal{F}\Box\alpha \rightarrow \alpha$$

we can also prove, from the axioms of the truth theory, truth condition specifying biconditionals with the modal prefix '$\Box\mathcal{F}$' or '$\mathcal{F}A$' or '$\Box$', or with the prefix 'A', or with no prefix at all (bare material biconditionals).

There is something important to be gained by asking how the biconditionals which are theorems of this truth theory are related to the conditions for the TRUTH of utterances of sentences of L_{12}. Consider first the biconditionals beginning with '$\mathcal{F}\Box$'. These specify conditions for the truth of a sentence with respect to a possible world with, perhaps, another possible world playing the role of the actual world. The concept of truth involved is, in that sense, doubly world relative. The truth of the sentence $\ulcorner As_1 \urcorner$ with respect to a possible world depends upon the colour of snow in, perhaps, another possible world which is playing the role of the actual world. But the TRUTH of an utterance in a possible world of the sentence $\ulcorner As_1 \urcorner$ depends upon the colour of snow in that very possible world. If snow is not white in w_1, the possible world playing the role of the actual world, and snow is white in w_2, then although the sentence s_1 is true with respect to w_2 the sentence $\ulcorner As_1 \urcorner$ is not true with respect to w_2. But an utterance in w_2 of $\ulcorner As_1 \urcorner$, like an utterance of s_1, would be TRUE. The concept of TRUTH is only singly world relative, for from the point of view of a speaker making an utterance in a certain possible world w the actual world is just that world w. The concept of actuality is grounded in the schema

$$A\alpha \leftrightarrow \alpha$$

(where, crucially, '$\leftrightarrow$' is the material biconditional). (Cf. Lewis, 1973, pp. 85–6. Some writers speak of the *indexicality* of 'actually'. That terminology is helpful provided that indexicality is not then equated with context dependence; cf. Section VIII.3.)

The biconditionals which are most closely related to the conditions for the TRUTH of utterances are the biconditionals beginning with '$\mathscr{F}A$'. These specify conditions for the truth of a sentence with respect to a possible world considered as actual. If the doubly world relative concept of truth (of sentences) is truth relative to ordered pairs of worlds $\langle w_1, w_2 \rangle$ then the TRUTH of utterances is most closely related to truth relative to ordered pairs of worlds $\langle w, w \rangle$ (a singly world relative concept). The doubly relativized concept is, one might say, 'purely internal to the semantic theory' (Evans, 1979, p. 181). Yet even if we focus upon the TRUTH of utterances we cannot do without the doubly relativized concept. For in order to work out the conditions for the TRUTH of an utterance, in a possible world w, of a sentence '$\Box(\ldots A \ldots)$' in which 'A' occurs within the scope of '$\Box$', for example, we must consider the truth of the contained sentence '$\ldots A \ldots$' with respect to other possible worlds while w continues to play the role of the actual world.

Third, in the model theory for '$\mathscr{F}$' we make use of the notion of a variant model: $\langle W_2, w_2{}^*, V_2 \rangle$ is a variant of $\langle W_1, w_1{}^*, V_1 \rangle$ just in case $W_2 = W_1$ and $V_2 = V_1$. Then, for any model $\langle W_1, w_1{}^*, V_1 \rangle$,

$$V_1^+ (w, \ulcorner \mathscr{F}\sigma \urcorner) = \text{T iff for every variant model}$$
$$<W_2, w_2*, V_2>, V_2^+ (w, \sigma) = \text{T}.$$

Consequently

$$V_1^+ (w, \ulcorner \mathscr{F}A\sigma \urcorner) = \text{T iff for every variant model}$$
$$<W_2, w_2*, V_2>, V_2^+ (w_2*, \sigma) = \text{T}$$

and

$$V_1^+ (w, \ulcorner \mathscr{F}\Box\sigma \urcorner) = \text{T iff for every variant model}$$
$$<W_2, w_2*, V_2> \text{ and every } w' \text{ in } W_2 \text{ (that is, in } W_1)$$
$$V_2^+ (w', \sigma) = \text{T}.$$

Once again we must distinguish the two notions of validity. The axioms of the system $S5A\mathscr{F}$ are geared to the notion of general validity. A system geared to the notion of real world validity would have as a theorem schema

$$\mathscr{F}A\alpha \rightarrow \alpha$$

whereas the system $S5A\mathscr{F}$ has only the schema

$$A(\mathscr{F}A\alpha \rightarrow \alpha)$$

and its equivalent

$$\mathscr{F}A\alpha \rightarrow A\alpha.$$

The general validity of this last schema is arguably enough to justify the claim that '$\mathscr{F}A$' expresses a sense of 'necessarily'.

There is a slightly different way of setting out this model theory, which deserves a brief mention. A model is taken to be an ordered pair $<W, V>$ where W is a set and V assigns to each triple consisting of two members of W and an atomic sentence a truth value. The function V is extended to V^+ by obvious clauses for '&', 'v', and '~', and by

$$V^+ (w_1, w_2, \ulcorner \Box\sigma \urcorner) = \text{T iff for every } w_2' \text{ in } W,$$
$$V^+ (w_1, w_2', \sigma) = \text{T}$$
$$V^+ (w_1, w_2, \ulcorner A\sigma \urcorner) = \text{T iff } V^+ (w_1, w_1, \sigma) = \text{T}$$
$$V^+ (w_1, w_2, \ulcorner \mathscr{F}\sigma \urcorner) = \text{T iff for every } w_1' \text{ in } W,$$
$$V^+ (w_1', w_2, \sigma) = \text{T}.$$

A sentence σ is generally valid just in case for every model $<W, V>$ and every w_1 and w_2 in W, $V^+ (w_1, w_2, \sigma) = \text{T}$, while σ is real world valid just in case for every model $<W, V>$ and every w in W, $V^+ (w, w, \sigma) = \text{T}$.

This way of presenting the model theory makes it very clear why the study of systems like *S5A$\mathscr{F}$* is called *'two dimensional modal logic'*.

3 ACTUALITY AND THE CONTINGENT *A PRIORI*

After drawing the distinction between necessity and *a priority*, Kripke (1972, p. 274) gave the following example of a contingent but *a priori* truth:

> We could [stipulate] that one meter is to be the length of [stick] *S* at a fixed time t_0. Is it then a necessary truth that stick *S* is one meter long at time t_0? Someone who thinks that everything one knows *a priori* is necessary might think: 'This is the definition of a meter. By definition stick *S* is one meter long at t_0. That's a necessary truth.' But there seems to me to be no reason so to conclude, even for a man who uses the stated definition of 'one meter'. For he's using this definition not to give the meaning of what he called the 'meter', but to fix the reference. . . . There is a certain length which he wants to mark out. He marks it out by an accidental property, namely that there is a stick of that length. . . .
>
> [H]e can still say, 'if heat had been applied to this stick *S* at t_0, then at t_0 stick *S* would not have been one meter long.'

Given the stipulation by which the expression 'one meter' is introduced, one can know *a priori* that stick *S* is one metre long at t_0. Yet the sentence

$$\Box(\text{Stick } S \text{ is one metre long at } t_0)$$

is false; the sentence which follows '$\Box$' expresses a merely contingent truth. The description which is used to fix the reference of the expression 'one metre' does not give that expression's meaning since the sentence

$$\Box(\text{Stick } S \text{ is, at } t_0, \text{ the length of stick } S \text{ at } t_0)$$

is true.

The idea that one can use a definite description to fix the reference of an expression and so give rise to contingent *a priori* truths has not been universally welcomed. Kripke (1972, p. 263) himself recognized that the idea of an *a priori* but contingent truth is, at least initially, puzzling:

I guess it's thought that . . . if something is known *a priori* it must be necessary, because it was known without looking at the world. If it depended on some contingent feature of the actual world, how could you know it without looking?

Dummett (1973, p. 121) expressed outright rejection of the idea:

> Kripke expresses some uneasiness about the claim that there are statements which are known *a priori* but are not necessarily true. He thinks that the generally accepted principle that everything *a priori* is necessary is incorrect as it stands . . . but he thinks also that there may be a case for reformulating the principle so as to make it correct. . . . His reason for suspecting that such reformulation may be desirable is that it is counter-intuitive to suppose that someone who has fixed a system of measurement . . . has thereby acquired some information about the world. . . . Counter-intuitive it undoubtedly is, but it appears to follow from Kripke's arguments: something must, therefore, be amiss with those arguments.

And others have attempted to show that, in examples such as that provided by Kripke, the truth in question is either not *a priori* or else not contingent.

We have seen (in Section IX.2) how, in at least some cases, any initial puzzlement over the contingent *a priori* can be dispelled once we distinguish between two notions of necessity (and so, between two notions of contingency). One can know *a priori* that snow is actually white iff snow is white (where 'iff' expresses material equivalence). What is initially puzzling is (in Kripke's terminology) how the truth of the sentence $\ulcorner As_1 \leftrightarrow s_1 \urcorner$ could depend on some contingent feature of the actual world. The initial puzzlement is dispelled once we distinguish the notion of contingency related to '$\Box$' from that related to '$\mathscr{F}A$'. If w_1 is the actual world then the truth of $\ulcorner As_1 \leftrightarrow s_1 \urcorner$ with respect to w_2 requires that snow is white in w_2 just in case snow is white in w_1. That sentence is true with respect to w_1, but false with respect to some other worlds. The truth of that sentence depends on a feature which the actual world w_1 has, but which other worlds lack, namely the feature of agreement with w_1 as to whether snow is white. The sentence $\ulcorner \Box (As_1 \leftrightarrow s_1) \urcorner$ is false; $\ulcorner As_1 \leftrightarrow s_1 \urcorner$ is contingent in the first sense. But the truth of $\ulcorner As_1 \leftrightarrow s_1 \urcorner$ with respect to a world w considered as actual requires nothing at all of w. So there is no world which lacks the feature on which the truth (in this sense) of $\ulcorner As_1 \leftrightarrow s_1 \urcorner$ depends. The sentence $\ulcorner \mathscr{F}A\,(As_1 \leftrightarrow s_1) \urcorner$ is true; $\ulcorner As_1 \leftrightarrow s_1 \urcorner$ is not contingent in the second sense.

The reason why one can know 'without looking' that snow is actually white iff snow is white is that one can know without looking in what the actuality of the actual world consists (cf. Section VIII.2). The combination, in this example, of *a priority* and contingency (in the first sense) is not persistently puzzling. Perhaps the combination of *a priority* and contingency in the second sense would be persistently puzzling. For it is the second notion of contingency which is tied to the concept of truth relative to ordered pairs of worlds $<w, w>$, that is, the truth most closely related to the TRUTH of utterances, the truth at which sincere assertion aims, the truth (one might say) which really matters. But we do not have in the present (nor, it seems, in any other) example the combination of *a priority* and contingency in that second sense (see Evans, 1979, p. 161).

Let us now attempt to extend this strategy for dispelling the initial puzzlement which surrounds very simple examples of the contingent *a priori*, so as to dispel such initial puzzlement as may surround examples of the kind which Kripke gave. Here is an example of that kind. Suppose that a group of philosophers come to be impressed by the illumination provided by two dimensional modal logic, but lack any knowledge at all as to the origins of that discipline. Suppose that they nevertheless believe that there is some member of the past or present philosophical community who can reasonably be regarded as the inventor of two dimensional modal logic. And suppose that they introduce the expression (with the syntactic form of a name) 'Bruce Fix' with its reference fixed by the description 'the inventor of two dimensional modal logic'. According to Kripke those philosophers are in a position to know *a priori* that if anyone uniquely invented two dimensional modal logic then Bruce Fix invented two dimensional modal logic. Yet the sentence

(*BF*) If anyone uniquely invented two dimensional modal logic
      then Bruce Fix invented two dimensional modal logic

is only contingently true since the sentence which results from prefixing (*BF*) with '□' is false; if Gough Whitlam had been a philosopher he might have invented two dimensional modal logic. (This example is simply a variant of that discussed in Evans, 1979, see p. 163 and pp. 170-1. Cf. also Kripke, 1972, pp. 347-8, note 33.)

To see how such initial puzzlement as surrounds this example may be dispelled, imagine for a moment that the philosophers had instead introduced the expression 'Bruce Fix' as an abbreviation for the definite description 'the actual inventor of two dimensional modal logic'. One can certainly know *a priori* that if anyone uniquely invented two dimensional modal logic then the actual inventor of two dimensional modal logic invented it. There is nothing more puzzling about that piece of *a priori* knowledge than there is about *a priori* knowledge that snow is actually white iff snow is white. And the sentence

(*BF'*) If anyone uniquely invented two dimensional modal logic then the actual inventor of two dimensional modal logic invented two dimensional modal logic

is contingent in the sense related to '□'. If w_1 is the actual world then (*BF'*) is true with respect to w_2 just in case if anyone uniquely invented two dimensional modal logic in w_2 then whoever invented it in w_1 invented it in w_2. Since in some possible worlds Whitlam or Tiny Tim invented two dimensional modal logic, the sentence which results from prefixing (*BF'*) with '□' is false. There is nothing more puzzling about that contingency than there is about the contingency (in the sense related to '□') of $\ulcorner As_1 \leftrightarrow s_1 \urcorner$. And the persistent intuition that all *a priori* truths are, in some sense, necessary is answered to by the fact that (*BF'*) is indeed true with respect to every possible world considered as actual, so that the sentence which results from prefixing (*BF'*) with '$\mathscr{F}A$' is true.

Had the philosophers introduced the expression 'Bruce Fix' as an abbreviation of the description 'the actual inventor of two dimensional modal logic' then they would have provided themselves with a clear, and not persistently puzzling, example of the contingent *a priori*. The philosophers in the example introduced the expression 'Bruce Fix' with its reference fixed by the description 'the inventor of two dimensional modal logic'. All that is required in order that this and other Kripkean examples should not be persistently puzzling is that Kripke's notion of reference fixing should be interpretable in such a way that fixing the reference of an expression by a description has the same net effect (in point of *a priority* and contingency) as introducing the expression as an abbreviation for the corresponding description beginning with 'the actual . . .' instead of 'the . . .'.

There are two features of the description 'the actual inventor of two dimensional modal logic' which are crucial in point of *a priority* and contingency. The first is that the man, Frank Vlach, to whom the description applies is tc-salient. The second is that that man is not e-salient. First, the concept of tc-salience was introduced in respect of the objects referred to by genuine singular referring expressions (cf. Section V.2). If a name refers to a certain object then the truth (with respect to actual and counterfactual situations) of sentences containing the name depends upon how things are (in those situations) with that object. And tc-salience was explicitly related to the substitutability of co-referring names *salva veritate* within the scope of the modal operators '□' and '◇'. We did not, at that stage, consider such operators as '*A*' and '*ℱ*'. But we can now say, with a little more precision, that an object is tc-salient for sentences containing a certain expression just in case the truth of those sentences with respect to possible worlds (the actual world being held constant) depends upon how things are with that object in those possible worlds. It is a consequence of this definition that the man Frank Vlach is tc-salient for sentences containing the expression 'the actual inventor of two dimensional modal logic' and for sentences containing the genuine singular referring expression 'Frank Vlach'. Thus any sentence

□ (the actual inventor of two dimensional modal logic
is thus and so)

has the same truth value as

□ (Frank Vlach is thus and so)

and any sentence

◇ (the actual inventor of two dimensional modal logic
is thus and so)

has the same truth value as

◇ (Frank Vlach is thus and so).

(Thus the special kind of definite description beginning with 'the*', mentioned in Section V.3, is equivalent to a definite description beginning with 'the actual'.) It is the tc-salience of the object to which an 'actualized' description applies that is crucial in point of contingency (in the sense related to '□'). The sentence (BF') is contingent (in that sense) for the same reason that the sentence

If anyone uniquely invented two dimensional modal logic
then Frank Vlach invented two dimensional modal logic

is contingent (in that sense). (See Evans, 1979, pp. 184-5.)

Second, the concept of e-salience was also introduced in respect of the objects referred to by genuine singular referring expressions. If a name refers to a certain object then the beliefs expressed by sentences containing the name are not indifferent to the existence or non-existence of that object. (They are existence dependent.) And e-salience was explicitly related to the obtaining of appropriate (information yielding) causal relations between the (medium-sized material) object referred to and the person who has the beliefs. If the man Frank Vlach were e-salient for sentences containing the expression 'the actual inventor of two dimensional modal logic' then it would not be possible for the philosophers in the example (who do not stand in an appropriate causal relation to that man) to know *a priori*, or even to believe, that if anyone uniquely invented two dimensional modal logic then the actual inventor of two dimensional modal logic invented two dimensional modal logic. If the man Frank Vlach were e-salient then the philosophers in the example could know (perhaps *a priori*) that the sentence (BF') expresses a truth, but they could not know (*a priori* or any other way) the truth which it expresses (cf. Donnellan, 1977, p. 18 and Evans, 1979, p. 172). But that man is not e-salient. Nothing more in the way of causal interaction is required for knowledge (or belief) that the actual inventor of two dimensional modal logic is thus and so than is required for knowledge (or belief) that the inventor of two dimensional modal logic is thus and so. All that is required in addition is knowledge (available *a priori*) of what the actuality of the actual world consists in. (See Evans, 1979, p. 178.)

The Kripkean examples of the contingent *a priori* will not be persistently puzzling provided that the notion of reference fixing used in those examples is interpretable in such a way that if the reference of an expression is fixed by description then the object to which the description applies is tc-salient but not e-salient for sentences containing that expression. That the object is tc-salient is quite explicit in Kripke's account. Where we have said that an object is tc-salient for sentences containing an expression, Kripke would say that the expression *rigidly designates* the object. After giving his example of the contingent *a priori* he said the following (Kripke, 1972, pp. 274-5):

> [T]here is an intuitive difference between the phrase 'one meter' and the phrase 'the length of S at t_0'. The first phrase is meant to designate rigidly a certain length in all possible worlds, which in

the actual world happens to be the length of the stick S at t_0. On the other hand 'the length of S at t_0' does not designate anything rigidly.

That the object is not e-salient seems, at least, to be implicit in Kripke's account. He offered as an example the expression 'Jack the Ripper' (ibid. p. 291):

> Another case . . . might be when the police in London use the name 'Jack' or 'Jack the Ripper' to refer to the man, whoever he is, who committed all these murders, or most of them. Then they are giving the reference of the name by a description.

And he drew a contrast between the case of an ordinary proper name and the case of a name with its reference fixed by description. In the former case 'it's in virtue of our connection with other speakers in the community, going back to the referent himself, that we refer to a certain man' (ibid. p. 301). In the latter case (ibid.):

> some man really gives a name by going into the privacy of his room and saying that the referent is to be the unique thing with certain identifying properties. 'Jack the Ripper' was a possible example which I gave.

The expression 'reference fixing' is, perhaps, potentially misleading since an expression which is introduced with its reference fixed by description is not a genuine singular referring expression. But what is more important is that we have an interpretation of the notion of reference fixing such that introduction of an expression with its reference fixed by description gives rise to clear, but not persistently puzzling, cases of the contingent *a priori*. (And this interpretation seems to be consistent with Kripke's own use of the notion.)

There are two other possible interpretations of the notion of reference fixing which deserve mention. On each of these interpretations, the allegedly contingent *a priori* truths provided in Kripkean examples are either not contingent or else not *a priori*. On the first alternative interpretation a name with its reference fixed by description is a genuine singular referring expression. In that case, the sentences in Kripkean examples are contingently true (in the sense related to '$\Box$') but the truths which are expressed by those sentences are not *a priori*. All that can be known *a priori* is that those sentences express truths. (This is the interpretation offered in Donnellan, 1977.) Given this

236

interpretation, it is tempting to draw an analogy between the sentences in Kripkean examples and the context dependent sentence 'I am here', and to point to the contrast between knowing *a priori* that relative to any context of utterance, that sentence expresses a truth, and (what is impossible) knowing *a priori* where one is (see e.g. Blackburn, 1981, Section 3.3.3, and Dummett, 1973, p. 122). But this first alternative interpretation of the notion of reference fixing, even if it were the only interpretation possible, would leave many examples of contingent *a priori* truths (those in which there is explicit use of 'actually') quite untouched. And, as we have seen, it is not the only interpretation possible. There is, indeed, a contrast between knowing *a priori* that the sentence (*BF*), for example, expresses a truth and knowing *a priori* the truth which it expresses. But the second kind of *a priori* knowledge is far from impossible.

On the second alternative interpretation, a name with its reference fixed by description is not a genuine singular referring expression but simply an abbreviation of the reference fixing description, governed by a convention that sentences containing the name are always heard as though the description has wider scope than the modal operators '□' and '◇'. In that case the sentences in the Kripkean examples express *a priori* truths but are not contingently true (in the sense related to '□'). For suppose that the expression 'Fred' is an abbreviation of 'the *F*', governed by that convention. Then the sentence

> If anything is uniquely *F* then Fred is *F*

is, since it does not contain '□' or '◇', an abbreviation of

> If anything is uniquely *F* then the *F* is *F*

and so expresses an *a priori* truth. But that sentence is not merely contingently true; it is necessarily true. The appearance of contingency results from the fact that the sentence

> □ (If anything is uniquely *F* then Fred is *F*)

is indeed false. But this sentence is a (rather misleading) abbreviation of

> The *F* is an object *x* such that □ (if anything is
> uniquely *F* then *x* is *F*)

and so it is not, properly speaking, the sentence on whose truth or falsity the contingency of the original sentence turns (cf. Dummett, 1973, pp. 112–28).

In order to deal with all the examples of the contingent *a priori* which we have discussed, this alternative interpretation would need to be coupled with the claim that 'actually' is itself simply a conventional indicator of scope (rather like 'any' or 'a certain' (cf. Section VI.2) so that, for example,

□ (Snow is actually white iff snow is white)

is false only because it is a (rather misleading) version of

Snow is white iff □(snow is white).

Similarly, according to that claim, the sentence which results from prefixing (BF') with '□' is false only because it is a version of

The inventor of two dimensional modal logic is an
object x such that □(if anyone uniquely invented two
dimensional modal logic then x invented two
dimensional modal logic).

But the claim that 'actually' is simply a scope indicating device (so that everything which can be said using 'actually' can be said without it provided that one is careful about scope distinctions) is incorrect. That was the point of the original example

It is possible that everything which is actually red
should have been shiny.

And, even if the claim were correct, it would still be theoretically possible to introduce an operator with the semantic properties of our 'A' and so to provide a host of examples of the contingent *a priori*. So this second alternative interpretation of the notion of reference fixing, even if it were the only interpretation possible, would leave many examples of contingent *a priori* truths quite untouched. And, as we have seen, it is not the only interpretation possible.

4   ACTUALITY AND THE NECESSARY *A POSTERIORI*

Let us say that an expression which has the syntactic form of a name and is introduced either with its reference fixed by description or else as an abbreviation of an 'actualized' description is a *descriptive name*. (This is the terminology of Evans, 1979.) The two ways of introducing a descriptive name have the same net effect in point of contingency and *a priority*. We can leave it open whether such descriptive names as may occur in natural languages are best regarded as explicitly abbreviatory devices.

The expression 'Bruce Fix' is a descriptive name of a man and 'Frank Vlach' is an ordinary proper name of that same man. One can know only *a posteriori* that Bruce Fix is Frank Vlach. (And one can know only *a posteriori* that if anyone uniquely invented two dimensional modal logic then Bruce Fix is Frank Vlach.) Yet the sentence

> Bruce Fix is Frank Vlach

is (with a certain proviso) necessarily true in the sense of 'necessarily' expressed by '$\Box$'. (The proviso is that we ignore two problems which arise because men exist only contingently. One problem (related to the occurrence of the ordinary proper name) is whether '$\Box$' is to be given a weak or a strong interpretation (cf. Section VIII.4). The other problem (related to the occurrence, in effect, of a description containing 'actually') is how, exactly, quantifiers are to be interpreted when they occur within the scope of '$\Box$' or '$\Diamond$' and have 'A' occurring within their scope (cf. Section IX.1).) Thus descriptive names provide clear examples of identity statements which express necessary *a posteriori* truths.

The identity statement is not, however, necessarily true in the sense of 'necessarily' expressed by '$\mathscr{F}A$'. For the truth of that sentence with respect to a world w considered as actual requires that Frank Vlach invented two dimensional modal logic in w. If, in w, Tiny Tim invented two dimensional modal logic then the sentence

> Bruce Fix is Tiny Tim

is true with respect to w considered as actual, and an utterance in w of that sentence would be a TRUE utterance (while an utterance in w of 'Bruce Fix is Frank Vlach' would be a FALSE utterance). This provides a sharp contrast with identity statements in which two genuine singular referring expressions are used. Consider, for example, the two names 'm_1' and 'm_2' (in the language L_6) and suppose that 'R_1' is an identity predicate. Let us write '$m_1 = m_2$' instead of '$R_1(m_1, m_2)$'. Then if '$m_1 = m_2$' is true it is necessarily true in the sense of 'necessarily' expressed by '$\Box$' and in the sense expressed by '$\mathscr{F}A$'. That it is necessarily true in the first sense is, of course, guaranteed by the tc-salience of the objects n_1 and n_2. That it is necessarily true in the second sense is a consequence of the fact that there is nothing in the semantic properties of 'm_1', for example, to allow that the reference of 'm_1' could vary with a variation in which possible world is considered as actual. If in world w the object n_1 is not Q_1 but the object n_3 is Q_1, then the sentence '$P_1 m_1$' is false with respect to w considered as actual and an utterance in w of that sentence is a FALSE utterance. What is more, the belief expressed in an utterance, in that world, of that sentence is a belief which it would be impossible to have if n_1 were not to exist. If an utterance in w of the sentence '$P_1 m_1$' is TRUE in some language, and expresses a belief which it would be possible to have if n_1 were not to exist but would be impossible to have were n_3 not to exist, then that language is a different language and in it the expression 'm_1' has quite different semantic properties from those which it has in L_6. The relation of genuine singular reference is not at all world relative. The relation between a descriptive name and its bearer is singly world relative: it varies only with which possible world plays the role of the actual world. In general, the relation between a definite description and the object to which it applies is doubly world relative. As such an example as

> the best friend of everyone who actually came to
> the party

shows, the relation varies both with which possible world plays the role of the actual world and with which possible world it is with respect to which sentences are evaluated.

True identity statements which contain a descriptive name and a genuine singular referring expression are necessarily true in the sense of 'necessarily' expressed by '$\Box$' but not in the sense expressed by '$\mathscr{F}A$', and they express *a posteriori* truths. True identity statements which contain two genuine singular referring expressions are necessarily true in both senses (and, indeed, in a third sense of 'necessarily' expressed by '$\mathscr{F}\Box$'). But they may still express *a posteriori* truths if the two names, for example, are not synonymous. Thus we cannot hope to establish that all and only sentences which are necessarily true in the sense of 'necessarily' expressed by '$\mathscr{F}A$' express *a priori* truths. The sentences which constitute exceptions to this neat equivalence have to be accounted for, and in the case of identity statements they can be accounted for in terms of the evident possibility that two genuine singular referring expressions might be conventionally associated with quite different ways of thinking about the same object (cf. Section V.3 and Appendix 4).

Many putative examples of the necessary *a posteriori* can, however, be illuminated by the distinction between two notions of necessity. One example to which the distinction might be applied is that of 'Hesperus' and 'Phosphorus'. These names provide the most favoured case for a description theorist of names just because it is not wildly implausible that they are descriptive names with their references fixed by descriptions which contain (conceptually modest) predicates furnished by our two ways of thinking about the planet Venus (cf. Section V.3). Other examples concern expressions which seem to be names of natural kinds. Kripke (1972, p. 323) discusses the case of 'water' and 'H_2O' among others. Suppose that 'water' is a descriptive name of a natural kind (in this case a chemical kind) with its reference fixed by some such description as 'the kind of stuff which falls from the clouds as rain, flows in rivers, is colourless, odourless and tasteless (when pure), is drinkable. . .'. And suppose that 'H_2O' is an ordinary proper name of that same chemical kind. Then the sentence 'Water is H_2O' is necessarily true in the sense of 'necessarily' expressed by '$\square$' and expresses an *a posteriori* truth. But it is not necessarily true in the sense expressed by '$\mathscr{F}A$'. An utterance, in a possible world in which chemically quite different stuff fell from the clouds as rain and so on, of the sentence 'Water is H_2O' would be a FALSE utterance. This brief account certainly seems to accord well with intuition; it has the consequence, for example, that mastery of the word 'water' does not require any knowledge of chemistry. The main alternative account is one on which both 'water' and 'H_2O' are genuine singular referring expressions; on which, for example, an utterance of 'Water is H_2O' is TRUE whatever falls from the clouds, unless 'water' has a meaning different from that which it has in our language (cf. Putnam, 1973, pp. 700-4 and 1975, pp. 139-52). Which of the two accounts is ultimately preferable depends in part upon what is required for mastery of a name of something (a chemical kind) which is not a medium-sized material object, and so upon what is required if a person is to have singular beliefs concerning such a thing. But this is not the point at which to answer that (difficult) question nor, more generally, to embark upon an investigation of the semantic properties of natural kind words. It is enough that we have seen how the ideas of descriptive names and of a distinction between two notions of necessity (and of contingency) might have application in that area.

NOTES

Lloyd Humberstone introduced me to the logic of 'actually' in 1974. Gareth Evans's elegant and convincing solution of the puzzle of the contingent *a priori* in 'Reference and contingency' (1979) persuaded me to return to the topic. For towards the end of his paper (p. 183) he points out (what is decisive against some purported solutions of the puzzle) that the 'actually' operator generates examples of contingent *a priori* truths. While I was visiting Monash University in 1979, Lloyd Humberstone and I wrote 'Two notions of necessity' (1980), in which Evans's solution is located against a background of modal logic with 'actually' and 'fixedly'. The main points of this chapter are drawn immediately from that joint paper. We also announced as forthcoming a more formal paper, 'The logic of "fixedly"'. This appears as Appendix 10. I am grateful to Lloyd Humberstone for suggesting that I incorporate that material into the present book.

The tense logical analogue of 'actually' is, of course, 'now'; see Kamp (1971). My claim that Frank Vlach can be regarded as the inventor of two dimensional modal logic is based upon testimony of David Lewis. Vlach was, in fact, working on tense logic. In his doctoral thesis (1973) he introduced an operator whose analogue in modal logic '†' has the property that $\ulcorner †\sigma \urcorner$ is true with respect to world w_2 with w_1 playing the role of the actual world just in case σ is true with respect to w_2 with w_2 also playing the role of the actual world. The modal prefix '□†' is equivalent to our '$\mathscr{F}A$'; for the suggestion that '□†' is the *a priori* truth operator see Stalnaker (1978, p. 320).

For a fully general account of two dimensional modal logic see Segerberg (1973). See also Åqvist (1973), van Fraassen (1977) and Kaplan (1978). Interesting questions arise when two dimensional modal or tense logic is generalized to more than two dimensions (and ultimately to infinitely many dimensions). Such a generalization was outlined in Vlach's thesis. For a discussion see, for example, van Benthem (1977).

On the contingent *a priori* see e.g. Donnellan (1977) and Schiffer (1977). For some more applications of 'actually' and 'fixedly', see Davies and Humberstone (1980).

APPENDICES

APPENDIX 1

In the Preface to *Truth and Other Enigmas* (1978, p. xxiii), Dummett says:

> I am inclined at present to believe that it is not merely that a non-classical theory of meaning will always *admit* a suitable notion of truth, that is, allow a notion of truth to be defined such that the condition for an assertion to be correct will be that for the sentence asserted to be true, but that, while the notion of truth will not be *fundamental* . . . it will be *crucial*; that is, that it will play an essential role in the account of the connection between the way in which the meaning of a sentence is given and the use that is made of it.

To allow, as Dummett does, that the concept of truth can be introduced via the concept of meaning is not necessarily to allow that the concept of truth is such that truth may transcend all possibilities of verification (cf. Dummett, 1976, and Wright, 1976). So, in particular, to introduce the concept of truth via rule (T) is not necessarily to allow that the concept of truth has that feature. We might agree with Wiggins (1980a, p. 208) that truth is a property such that 'every statement which lacks it lacks it independently of a speaker's means of recognizing it; and every statement which possesses it possesses it independently of a speaker's means of recognizing it'. (This is his third mark of truth.) For, in general, a speaker's believing that p is both ways independent of its being the case that p. But (as Wiggins points out) this mark of truth does not require that truth may transcend all possibilities of verification. Nor, of course, does it rule it out.

APPENDIX 2

In 'Logical form, meaning, translation' (1978), Wallace begins by pointing out that 'A translation manual cannot be a theory of meaning; neither can a theory of truth', (p. 45) and goes on to construct a theory$_1$ of meaning of a kind slightly different from $M\theta$. His main idea is to introduce an operator 'It is a matter of meaning alone that'. As an axiom for s_1, for example, he would have

It is a matter of meaning alone that $[s_1$ is true (in L_1) $\leftrightarrow$ snow is white]

and as an axiom for '&'

It is a matter of meaning alone that $[(\forall \sigma)(\forall \tau)$ ($\ulcorner \sigma \& \tau \urcorner$ is true in $(L_1) \leftrightarrow (\sigma$ is true (in L_1) & τ is true (in L_1)))].

From axioms such as these one would proceed, by rules which are not specified by Wallace, to

(i) It is a matter of meaning alone that $[\ulcorner s_1 \& s_2 \urcorner$ is true (in L_1) $\leftrightarrow (s_1$ is true (in L_1) & s_2 is true (in L_1))]

and thence to

(ii) It is a matter of meaning alone that $[\ulcorner s_1 \& s_2 \urcorner$ is true (in L_1) $\leftrightarrow$ snow is white & the earth moves].

The fact that both (i) and (ii) are theorems shows that, in general,

It is a matter of meaning alone that $[s$ is true (in L) $\leftrightarrow p]$

is not equivalent to

> s means (in L) that p.

What Wallace (1978, p. 50) offers as a definition of 's means that p' is the following:

> It is a matter of meaning alone that s is true if and only if p and for all q, if it is a matter of meaning alone that s is true if and only if q, then it is a matter of the laws of meaning applied in the left-right direction only that if q, then p.

This definition allows one to proceed from (ii) to

> $\ulcorner s_1 \ \& \ s_2 \urcorner$ means (in L_1) that (snow is white & the earth moves)

but does not allow one to proceed from (i) to

> $\ulcorner s_1 \ \& \ s_2 \urcorner$ means (in L_1) that (s_1 is true (in L_1) & s_2 is true (in L_1)).

There is little to choose between Wallace's proposal and the proposal which leads to $M\theta$. It might be thought to be an advantage for Wallace's proposal that his axioms do not contain the (slightly) controversial '($\forall p$)' and '($\forall q$)' quantifiers. But this apparent advantage is neutralized by the fact that those axioms do not by themselves yield meaning specifications. For that one needs the definition of 's means that p'. And in that definition just such a quantifier ('for all q') does appear. So it seems that it cannot be a mistake not to prefer Wallace's theory over $M\theta$.

APPENDIX 3

The very simple examples discussed in the text may suggest (what is false) that the application of *SC* to semantic theories for natural languages is quite straightforward. Here are three complicating factors (among many):

(1) The question as to what is the business of semantics and what is the business, rather, of etymology is not always easily answered. It is relatively easy to decide that 'hydro-', for example, does not make a uniform contribution to the meanings of words, such as 'hydrophobia' and 'hydro-electricity', in which it occurs. The occurrence of 'hydro-' in those words is the business of the etymologist rather than the semantic theorist. But the prefix 're-', for example, provides a more difficult case. It does seem to make a uniform contribution to the meanings of 're-evaluate', 're-examine', 'rekindle', 'rewire', and so its occurrence in those words seems to be the business of the semantic theorist. It is not clear, however, that 're-' makes the same contribution to 're-enter' (since a spacecraft which re-enters the earth's atmosphere may well not have entered the earth's atmosphere before). So it is not clear that the occurrence of 're-' in that word is the business of the semantic theorist, rather than of the etymologist. And while 're-' as it occurs in 'revise' is etymologically the same as 're-' as it occurs in 'rekindle', its occurrence in 'revise' is not the business of the semantic theorist since 'vise' is not a verb which can be used on its

248

own, and whose meaning (together with the meaning of 're-') determines the meaning of 'revise'.

(2) An answer to the question whether, in a given case, the level of input to a semantic theory is to come apart from the level of surface syntax may depend upon answers to large questions about syntactic theory. Consider, for example, the sentence

> Mary wants John to dance the polka.

The content of Mary's want (desire) is specifiable by the sentence

> John dances the polka

and it is very natural to regard 'Mary wants (that)' as a sentence operator which is semantically similar to 'Mary believes that'. But then the sentence

> Mary wants to dance the polka

presents a *prima facie* difficulty. For what follows 'Mary wants' is more like a verb phrase than like a sentence. One response to this difficulty is as follows. If the sentence is true then what Mary wants is that she (herself) should dance the polka. The content of her want (desire) is specifiable by a sentence. A sentence which Mary could use to specify that content is

> I dance the polka.

A sentence which others could use to go some way towards specifying that content is

> Mary dances the polka.

(This does not give a fully accurate specification since

> Mary wants to dance the polka

is not equivalent to

> Mary wants Mary to dance the polka.)

So according to this response the appearance of a verb phrase rather than a full sentence after 'Mary wants' is 'so much misleading surface structure'.

Such a response might well be accompanied by the suggestion that the surface sentence

Mary wants to dance the polka

corresponds to a sentence, at the level of input to a semantic theory, something like

Mary wants Mary to dance the polka

(although not exactly like it), and that the syntactic rule relating the two is the deletion rule *Equi-NP Deletion*. Indeed, this suggestion would seem to offer some prospect of an account of the grammatical correctness of 'herself' rather than 'her' in

Mary wants to improve herself

and of 'her' rather than 'herself' in

Mary wants John to dance with her.

But *Equi-NP Deletion* may itself come under attack for reasons having to do with syntactic theory. And, if the constraints upon syntactic theory will not allow the rules which would bridge the gap between surface sentences and sentences at the level of input to a semantic theory, then the semantic theorist must think again about allowing such a gap to open. In the case which we are considering he must reconsider the response to the original *prima facie* difficulty.

(3) The answer to a question as to whether a certain language is impoverished may be sensitive to quite small variations in the meaning specifications. It is possible to imagine cases in which (i) a language L' contains all the sentences of L and some sentences which are not in L, (ii) the sentences in common to the two languages would be used in just the same kinds of circumstances by speakers of L and by speakers of L', (iii) given what the shared sentences mean in L' it is possible to project from their meanings to the meanings of sentences of L' which are not in L, but (iv) given what the shared sentences mean in L it is not possible to project from their meanings to the meanings of any sentences other than those in L. In such an imaginable case the facts about a population's linguistic behaviour which might suggest that they speak an impoverished fragment of L' would also suggest (and *ceteris paribus* suggest more strongly) that they speak not L' but L. The structure of the linguistic competence of speakers is one

crucial source of evidence as to what conceptual resources they employ, and so, as to what their sentences mean. (See also Davies, 1981, Section 8.)

(In this appendix I am indebted to Simon Blackburn, Geoffrey Pullum, and Deirdre Wilson.)

APPENDIX 4

The notion of a way of thinking about an object has its home in theories about the content of beliefs which are expressed using demonstratives (see e.g. Evans, forthcoming b). The idea would be that if two beliefs, concerning the same object, to the effect that it is thus and so, involve precisely the same way of thinking about the object then the two beliefs have the same content. A name is not associated with such a precise way of thinking about the object named, but with a relatively unspecific way, or a range of precise ways, of thinking about it. This may suggest that a resolution of the puzzle about belief, in the case of beliefs expressed using names, will involve distinguishing the contents of beliefs each of which is a belief that, say, Harry is modest. (The suggestion would be all the more attractive if it were independently plausible that any belief which can be expressed using a proper name can also be expressed using a demonstrative.) Suppose that the puzzle were resolved in this way. Then, someone might say, we should no longer need to claim that 'Hesperus' and 'Phosphorus', for example, are non-synonymous names. For we should have another explanation of the apparent failure of substitutivity *salva veritate* within the scope of hyperintensional operators such as 'John believes that'. But, while it is correct that, in a certain sense, we should not 'need' to claim that 'Hesperus' and 'Phosphorus' are non-synonymous, we should nevertheless, still claim that. For it is not just an accident that a speaker who expresses one belief using 'Hesperus' and another using 'Phosphorus' thinks about the planet Venus in two different ways. The different (ranges of) ways of thinking are, in the case imagined, conventionally associated with the different names (McDowell, 1977, p. 176):

252

Such connections, between the use of a name and the sort of situation which prompts the beliefs it helps to express, can be, not merely idiosyncratic facts about individuals, but partly constitutive of a shared language.

To retreat to the idea that all co-referring names have the same meaning would be to ignore the difference between idiosyncratic variations in ways of thinking and conventional variations. (In this appendix I am indebted to Christopher Peacocke.)

APPENDIX 5

The axiom for '$\forall$' in a theory of meaning for L_6

$$(\forall\Phi)(\forall Y)\,[MCorr\,(\Phi,\,Y)\to$$
$$\ulcorner(\forall v_i)\Phi v_i\urcorner \text{ means that } (\forall x)Yx]$$

is true even though the '$(\forall\gamma)$' quantifier in the expression which '$MCorr\,(\Phi,\,Y)$' abbreviates ranges only over names in L_6. This is in sharp contrast to the following putative axiom for a truth theory for L_6, which is in general not true:

$$(\forall\Phi)(\forall Y)\,[(\forall\gamma\in L_6)(\forall x)\,(Ref(L_6,\gamma)=x\to$$
$$(Tr\,(L_6,\ulcorner\Phi\gamma\urcorner)\leftrightarrow Yx))\to(Tr(L_6,\ulcorner(\forall v_i)\Phi v_i\urcorner)\leftrightarrow(\forall x)\,Yx)]\,.$$

But there is one sort of case in which an axiom for a theory of meaning of the sort just offered is incorrect. Suppose that a language contains just one name 'Whitlam' and that 'Whitlam likes Whitlam' is a sentence. Consider the result of removing the first occurrence of 'Whitlam' from this sentence. Then the following are both true:

$$(\forall\gamma)(\forall v)\,[MRef(\gamma,\,v)\to$$
$$\ulcorner\gamma \text{ likes Whitlam}\urcorner \text{ means that } v \text{ likes Whitlam}]$$
$$(\forall\gamma)(\forall v)\,[MRef(\gamma,\,v)\to$$
$$\ulcorner\gamma \text{ likes Whitlam}\urcorner \text{ means that } v \text{ likes } v]\,.$$

Yet it cannot be that '$(\forall v_1)\,v_1$ likes Whitlam' means both that everything likes Whitlam and that everything likes itself. In such a case we need to invoke an extended language when expanding abbreviations of the form '$MCorr\,(\Phi,\,G)$' (see p. 123).

APPENDIX 6

Let us consider a language containing, instead of the quasi-predicates 'X_1', ..., 'X_{10}' ten *pseudo-predicates* 'Y_1', ..., 'Y_{10}' which introduce opacity of the second kind. One might be tempted to provide a theory in the Kripkean style for such a language. The notion of *MRef* cannot be put to use this time because if 'm_1' and 'm_2' are synonymous then *MRef* ('m_1', m_2) while it is in general false that

$$Tr \, (`Y_1 m_1') \leftrightarrow Y_1 m_2$$

since 'm_1' and 'm_2' are syntactically different. So in the axioms for names a new primitive theoretical notion *PRef* is needed (cf. Kripke, 1976, p. 360). It might then seem that a theory meeting *SC* could be provided simply by replacing *MRef* by *PRef* in the theory for L_9 (and, of course, replacing 'X_1' by 'Y_1', ..., 'X_{10}' by 'Y_{10}'). But this thought would be mistaken. In such a theory 'm_1' is governed by a single axiom which is employed in the canonical derivations of biconditionals for both '$P_1 m_1$' and '$Y_1 m_1$'. But, *ex hypothesi*, 'm_1' does not contribute to the meaning of '$Y_1 m_1$' by its semantic properties but merely by its syntactic form. Since it is not possible to come to know what '$P_1 m_1$' means on the basis of knowing what '$Y_1 m_1$' means and what some sentences containing 'P_1' such as '$P_1 m_2$' mean, the suggested theory would infringe *SC*.

A second thought might be to provide two axioms for each name, one axiom to be used in the canonical derivations of biconditionals for sentences containing predicates and the other in canonical derivations of biconditionals for sentences containing pseudo-predicates. But this thought would be mistaken for two reasons. First, the suggestion involves the utterly implausible claim that names in such a language are ambiguous. It is a very special kind of perversity that would encourage one to maintain that the expression 'Hesperus' as it occurs in

'Hesperus' contains eight letters

or

'Hesperus' is an eight-lettered name of a planet

has the same syntactic form but quite different semantic properties from that expression whose semantic properties involve naming the planet Venus. Second, if 'Y_1' has the meaning of

' . . . ' is a short expression

for example, then it is surely possible to know the meaning of 'Y_1P_1' on the basis of knowing the meaning of 'Y_1m_1', whereas 'Y_1P_1' is not even admitted as well formed on the present suggestion.

The most natural way of avoiding these difficulties is to recognize the occurrence within such expressions as

' . . . ' contains eight letters

of the quotation functor. Pseudo-predicates (such as 'Y_1') are composed of genuine predicates ('Y_1^*'), true of expressions and perhaps other objects as well, and that functor. The quotation functor is governed by a very simple axiom involving objectual quantification over expressions.

$$(\forall \alpha) \, (Ref(\ulcorner `\alpha' \urcorner) = \alpha)$$

The net effect of this axiom and an axiom for 'Y_1^*' is the following theorem which makes it clear that the semantic properties of names are irrelevant to the meanings of atomic sentences containing pseudo-predicates.

$$(\forall \alpha) \, [Tr(\ulcorner Y_1 \alpha \urcorner) \leftrightarrow Y_1^* \alpha]$$

The canonical derivation of a biconditional for the sentence '$(Ev_1)(Y_1v_1 \, \& P_1v_1)$', for example, proceeds as follows (we consider just the left-to-right direction; the converse is similar):

$$Tr(`(Ev_1)(Y_1v_1 \, \& P_1v_1)')$$
$$(\exists \gamma) \, Tr(\ulcorner Y_1 \gamma \, \& P_1 \gamma \urcorner)$$

(by the axiom for 'E'). Suppose the name is γ_0. Then

Appendix 6

$$Tr\,(\ulcorner Y_1\gamma_0 \ \& \ P_1\gamma_0\urcorner)$$
$$Tr\,(\ulcorner Y_1\gamma_0\urcorner) \ \& \ Tr\,(\ulcorner P_1\gamma_0\urcorner)$$

(by the axiom for '&'). From the first conjunct we have $Y_1^*\gamma_0$ by the theorem just mentioned. From the second conjunct we have $P_1\,(Ref\,(\gamma_0))$ by the axiom for the predicate 'P_1'. (Since 'P_1', ..., 'P_{10}' are predicates the theory need include just reference axioms for names.) The next step requires one of a pair of axioms relating objectual quantification over names and substitutional quantification in the ML, namely

$$(\forall\gamma)\,(Ex)\,(\gamma = \text{'x'} \ \& \ Ref(\gamma) = x).$$

(For the right-to-left direction the other member of the pair, namely

$$(Ax)\,(\exists\gamma)\,(\gamma = \text{'x'} \ \& \ Ref(\gamma) = x)$$

is needed.) Using that axiom we have from

$$Y_1^*\gamma_0 \ \& \ P_1\,(Ref(\gamma_0))$$

the substitutionally quantified

$$(Ex)\,(Y_1^*\text{'x'} \ \& \ P_1 x)$$

that is

$$(Ex)\,(Y_1 x \ \& \ P_1 x).$$

The difference which in general is crucial for the truth of quantified sentences of this language is that between one ordered pair of an object and a name of that object and two such ordered pairs. The quantification is quantification over such pairs. If 'Y_1' has the meaning of

'...' is a short expression

and 'P_1' has the meaning of 'is modest' then we might specify the meaning of '$(Ev_1)\,(Y_1 v_1 \ \& \ P_1 v_1)$' as that there is an object and a name (in the language) of that object such that the name is a short expression and the object is modest. Similarly, if the base language were to contain predicates, quasi-predicates, and pseudo-predicates then substitutional quantification would be quantification over ordered pairs of names and their meanings.

We are now in a position to tie up some ends which were left loose in the discussion of the '$(\forall p)$' and '$(\forall q)$' quantifiers (in Section II.3), the '$(\forall v)$' quantifier (in Section V.1), and the '$(\forall Y)$' quantifier

257

Appendices

(in Section VI.1). It is implicit in Section VI.4 that the '($\forall v$)' quantifier which was used in the *ML* can be interpreted as a substitutional quantifier. Since the opaque contexts into which quantification using '($\forall v$)' takes place involve opacity of only the first kind the quantification is over the meanings of names (in the *ML*). Similarly, the quantification using '($\forall Y$)', and using '($\forall p$)' and '($\forall q$)', can be interpreted as substitutional quantification into predicate position and into sentence position, respectively. In the latter case, for example, it would suffice to take as the substitution class the class of *ML* sentences which themselves contain neither semantic vocabulary (such as 'means that' or 'is true') nor substitutional quantification. The quantification would be quantification over the meanings of sentences in the substitution class. (For the conditions which must be imposed upon the substitution class in these cases see Kripke, 1976, pp. 331 and 368.)

At the end of Section II.3 (at (2)) quantification 'in and out of quotes' was mentioned. We have just discussed such quantification into name position. Similar remarks apply to such quantification into sentence position, as in what we should now write as

(Ap) ('p' means that p).

We suppose that the *OL* is included in the *ML* and that the substitution class for the substitutional quantification in the *ML* is the class of *OL* sentences. Since one sentence position is within quotation and the other within the scope of the hyperintensional operator 'means that' this quantification is over ordered pairs of *OL* sentences and their meanings. We might specify the meaning of the universally quantified *ML* sentence as that for every *OL* sentence *s* which means that *p*, *s* means that *p*. This shows why the acceptability of the '($\forall p$)' and '($\forall q$)' quantifiers (in the theory $M\theta$, for example) does not turn upon the acceptability in a theory of meaning of that universally quantified sentence.

APPENDIX 7

The reason for the parenthetical 'almost' in the claim about the privileges of occurrence of definite descriptions and proper names is this. It is a familiar point that a definite description (such as 'the elephant') can be followed by a restrictive relative clause as in

> The elephant that fell down did little damage

while

> Jumbo that fell down did little damage

is not a grammatical sentence. In fact, however, this is not a serious exception to the claim that definite descriptions and proper names have the same privileges of occurrence. For, in this example, the expression 'the elephant' is not functioning as a definite description. Rather, the restrictive relative clause attaches to the common noun 'elephant' to form a common noun phrase, and the only definite description is 'the elephant that fell down'. And a proper name can occupy the position occupied by that definite description. Similarly, it would be misleading to say that in

> Every elephant that fell down did little damage

a quantifier phrase 'every elephant' occurs as antecedent to a restrictive relative clause.

APPENDIX 8

The sentence

(MOST x) [(Woman whom John admires) x;
John loves x]

surfaces as

John loves most women whom he (John) admires.

In this sentence the first name position occupied by 'John' governs the second. So we expect that surface sentences in which a quantifier phrase occupies the first name position and a pronoun occupies the second will be naturally interpreted as corresponding to sentences of the form

(Qy) [Fy; (MOST x) ((Woman whom y admires) x;
y loves x)] .

And it is easy to check that this expectation is correct. The sentence

(EVERY x) [(Man who loves Mary) x; x loses Mary]

surfaces as

Every man who loves Mary loses her (Mary).

In this sentence the first name position occupied by 'Mary' does not govern the second. So we expect that surface sentences in which a quantifier phrase occupies that first name position and a pronoun occupies the second will not be naturally interpreted as corresponding to sentences of the form

260

(Qy) $[Fy$; $(\text{EVERY } x)$ $((\text{Man who loves } y)$ x; x loses $y)]$.

Rather, we expect that the sentence

> Every man who loves a woman loses her

will be naturally interpreted as equivalent to

> Every man who loves a woman loses the woman whom
> he loves.

It is easy to check that these expectations, too, are correct. Someone might suggest that, simply on the basis of word order, we could expect that

> Every man who loves a woman loses her

would not be interpreted as though it corresponds to a sentence at the level of input in which the 'a' quantifier has wider scope than the 'every' quantifier. But this suggestion, unless it is accompanied by a general account of the anaphoric use of pronouns, simply leaves the occurrence of the pronoun 'her' in the surface sentence a semantic mystery. (For some more examples, see Evans, 1977, p. 496.)

APPENDIX 9

Suppose that the cardinality of the set of fully determinate counter-factual states of affairs (possible worlds) is κ. Each subset of this set determines (or, on some accounts, is) a proposition, namely the proposition which would be expressed by a sentence which was true with respect to precisely the possible worlds in that subset. There are thus 2^{κ} such propositions, and 2^{κ} is strictly greater than κ (by Cantor's theorem). Consider some man X and time t. For each proposition it is possible that X should have been thinking a thought at t whose content would be specifiable by a sentence expressing that proposition. So there is a distinct possible situation corresponding to each such proposition, and so there are at least 2^{κ} possible worlds. But we began by assuming that there are precisely κ possible worlds. (I am indebted here to David Kaplan and Christopher Peacocke.) There are, of course, things which can be said in response to this apparent paradox. But it does raise a doubt about the coherence of the notion of a fully deter-minate counterfactual state of affairs.

APPENDIX 10

THE LOGIC OF 'FIXEDLY'

(1) The axiomatization of $S5A\mathscr{F}$ was chosen as the most convenient for a completeness proof, but it has a feature which may suggest that it is not ideal. For consider the schema

$$(C)\quad \mathscr{F}\Box\alpha \leftrightarrow \Box\mathscr{F}\alpha.$$

It is easy to see that (C) is valid (that is, generally valid). What is more, the reasoning which shows that (C) is valid does not depend in any way on the particular structure of α. But (C) is a theorem-schema without a corresponding proof-schema. There is no uniform way of deriving the instances of (C); the proof in any case depends crucially upon the structure of the α in question. For example, a proof of

$$\mathscr{F}\Box s_1 \leftrightarrow \Box\mathscr{F}s_1$$

makes essential use of ($\mathscr{F}5$) and no use of ($\mathscr{F}6$), while a proof of

$$\mathscr{F}\Box As_1 \leftrightarrow \Box\mathscr{F}As_1$$

requires ($\mathscr{F}6$) and ($A4$) but not ($\mathscr{F}5$). It is possible to prove that all instances of (C) are theorems, without appealing to the completeness theorem. The proof, which makes use of the Elimination Theorem for '$\mathscr{F}$' (see (3) below), is rather tedious and we omit it. We leave as an open question how the axiomatization of $S5A\mathscr{F}$ might be improved.

263

(2) The T axiom for '$\mathscr{F}A$'

$$\mathscr{F}A\alpha \to \alpha$$

is not a generally valid schema. But the $S4$ axiom for '$\mathscr{F}A$'

$$\mathscr{F}A\alpha \to \mathscr{F}A\,\mathscr{F}A\alpha$$

and the $S5$ axiom for '$\mathscr{F}A$'

$$\sim\mathscr{F}A\sim\alpha \to \mathscr{F}A\sim\mathscr{F}A\sim\alpha$$

are both generally valid schemata. Without appealing to the completeness theorem we can show that all instances of the $S4$ axiom for '$\mathscr{F}A$' (strengthened to a biconditional) are provable in $S5A\mathscr{F}$. We make use of the Elimination Theorem (see (3) below) to guarantee, for each sentence σ, the existence of an equivalent σ_1 in which '$\mathscr{F}$' does not occur. And we make use of the following fact (which is an immediate consequence of a result proved in Crossley and Humberstone, 1977, p. 16):

> (D) For any sentence σ not containing '$\mathscr{F}$' there is an 'A'-free sentence σ' such that $S5A\mathscr{F} \vdash A\sigma \leftrightarrow A\sigma'$

Then the following are equivalent:

$\mathscr{F}A\sigma$	
$\mathscr{F}A\sigma_1$	
$\mathscr{F}A\sigma_1'$	where σ_1' is 'A'-free, by (D)
$\Box\sigma_1'$	by ($\mathscr{F}6$)
$\Box\Box\sigma_1'$	by $S4$ and T axioms for '$\Box$'
$\mathscr{F}A\Box\sigma_1'$	by ($\mathscr{F}6$)
$\mathscr{F}A\,\mathscr{F}A\sigma_1'$	by ($\mathscr{F}6$)
$\mathscr{F}A\,\mathscr{F}A\sigma_1$	by (D)
$\mathscr{F}A\,\mathscr{F}A\sigma.$	

(3) *Elimination Theorem*: For any sentence σ there exists an '$\mathscr{F}$'-free sentence σ' such that $S5A\mathscr{F} \vdash \sigma \leftrightarrow \sigma'$.
Proof: We consider innermost occurrences of '$\mathscr{F}$'. Let $\ulcorner\mathscr{F}\tau\urcorner$ be any subsentence of σ such that '$\mathscr{F}$' does not occur in τ. Then (by Crossley and Humberstone, 1977, p. 15) τ is provably equivalent to a conjunction of disjunctions of the form

$$\Box\gamma_1 \lor \ldots \lor \Box\gamma_n \lor \Diamond\delta \lor A\epsilon \lor \theta$$

where $\gamma_1, \ldots, \gamma_n, \delta, \epsilon$, and θ are purely truth functional sentences. We then use the following two schemata which follow from $(\mathscr{F}1)$–$(\mathscr{F}4)$:

(I) $\mathscr{F}(\alpha \ \& \ \beta) \leftrightarrow (\mathscr{F}\alpha \ \& \ \mathscr{F}\beta)$
(II) $\mathscr{F}(\alpha \ \vee \ \mathscr{F}\beta) \leftrightarrow (\mathscr{F}\alpha \ \vee \ \mathscr{F}\beta)$

By (I), $\ulcorner \mathscr{F}\tau \urcorner$ is equivalent to a conjunction of sentences of the form

$$\mathscr{F}(\Box\gamma_1 \ \vee \ldots \vee \ \Box\gamma_n \ \vee \ \Diamond\delta \ \vee \ A\epsilon \ \vee \ \theta).$$

By $(\mathscr{F}2)$ and $(\mathscr{F}5)$ each such sentence is equivalent to

$$\mathscr{F}(\mathscr{F}\Box\gamma_1 \ \vee \ldots \vee \ \mathscr{F}\Box\gamma_n \ \vee \ \mathscr{F}\Diamond\delta \ \vee \ A\epsilon \ \vee \ \mathscr{F}\theta).$$

By $(\mathscr{F}3)$, (II), and $(\mathscr{F}6)$ each such sentence is equivalent to

$$(\mathscr{F}\Box\gamma_1 \ \vee \ldots \vee \ \mathscr{F}\Box\gamma_n \ \vee \ \mathscr{F}\Diamond\delta \ \vee \ \Box\epsilon \ \vee \ \mathscr{F}\theta).$$

By $(\mathscr{F}2)$ and $(\mathscr{F}5)$ all the remaining occurrences of '$\mathscr{F}$' can be deleted, to yield a provably equivalent sentence containing no occurrences of '$\mathscr{F}$'. By repeating this procedure all occurrences of '$\mathscr{F}$' in σ can be eliminated.

Corollary: For any sentence of the form $\ulcorner \mathscr{F}\tau \urcorner$, there exists a sentence τ' containing neither '$\mathscr{F}$' nor 'A' such that $S5A\mathscr{F} \vdash \mathscr{F}\tau \leftrightarrow \tau'$ (by inspection of the above proof).

(4) In order to prove the completeness of $S5A\mathscr{F}$ we shall use the notion of a canonical model. In a canonical model, the set of 'worlds' is the set of all maximal consistent sets of sentences of the language in question. Instead of there being a single designated world, the set of worlds is partitioned by an equivalence relation R and there is a designated world within each equivalence class. Thus, for the purposes of this proof, a model will be a quadruple $<W, R, f, V>$ where R is an equivalence relation on W, for each w in W, $[w]$ is the R-equivalence class containing w, and $f([w]) \in [w]$. If X and Y are equivalence classes then we say that $X \approx Y$ just in case there is a one-to-one function g from X onto Y such that, for every w in X, w and $g(w)$ agree on the truth values of all atomic sentences. To indicate that g is the function in question, we write '$X \overset{g}{\approx} Y$'. Instead of considering variant models, we consider $\approx$-related equivalence classes within a single model.

The function V is extended to V^+ by obvious clauses for the truth functional connectives and by

$V^+(w, \ulcorner \Box \sigma \urcorner) = $ T iff for every w' such that
$R(w, w')$, $V^+(w', \sigma) = $ T
$V^+(w, \ulcorner A\sigma \urcorner) = $ T iff $V^+(f([w]), \sigma) = $ T
$V^+(w, \ulcorner \mathcal{F}\sigma \urcorner) = $ T iff for every Y and every g
such that $Y \overset{g}{\lessapprox} [w]$, $V^+(g(w), \sigma) = $ T.

Finally, we impose the following condition on models.

(U) For every equivalence class X and every w in X,
there is an equivalence class Y and a function g
such that $Y \overset{g}{\lessapprox} X$ and $f(Y) = g(w)$.

It is not difficult to confirm that the axioms of $S5A\mathcal{F}$ are
valid with respect to this modified model theory, and that the rules
preserve validity. (In the cases of ($\mathcal{F}5$) and ($\mathcal{F}6$) we appeal
to condition (U).)

We now define the canonical model. The set W is the set
of all maximal consistent sets of sentences of the language
in question. (Consistency is, of course, consistency with
respect to $S5A\mathcal{F}$.) If x and y are in W then $R(x, y)$ iff for
every sentence σ, if $\ulcorner \Box \sigma \urcorner$ is in x then σ is in y. If w is in W
then $f([w])$ is the set of sentences σ such that $\ulcorner A\sigma \urcorner$ is in w.
If w is in W and σ is an atomic sentence then $V(w, \sigma) = $ T iff
σ is in w. That R is an equivalence relation can be established
by a familiar argument (cf. Lemmon and Scott, 1977). That
f has the required properties is a consequence of the fact that
$S5A\mathcal{F}$ includes the axioms ($A1$)–($A4$) for 'A'. And it can be
checked that the canonical model meets condition (U).

It remains to show that, for every sentence σ and every w
in W, $V^+(w, \sigma) = $ T iff σ is in w. Suppose that we can establish
that. Then, if σ is a sentence which is not a theorem of $S5A\mathcal{F}$
then $\ulcorner \sim \sigma \urcorner$ is a member of a maximal consistent set w. Consequently, $V^+(w, \sigma) = $ F and σ is not valid with respect to the
modified model theory. Furthermore, σ is not valid with
respect to the original model theory, for the triple
$< [w], f([w]), V'>$ (where V' is the restriction of V to $[w]$)
is a falsifying model in the original sense.

In order to prove that for every σ and w, $V^+(w, \sigma) = $ T
iff σ is in w, we first restrict attention to sentences which do
not contain '$\mathcal{F}$'. We proceed by induction on the complexity

of sentences. The basis case and the induction cases for the truth functional connectives and for '□' are as in a completeness proof for *S5* (cf. Lemmon and Scott, 1977). So we omit them.

Suppose that σ is $\ulcorner A\tau \urcorner$ and that $V^+(w, \sigma) = \text{T}$. Then $V^+(f([w]), \tau) = \text{T}$. By the induction hypothesis τ is in $f([w])$. Thus $\ulcorner A\tau \urcorner$ is in w. The converse is similar. Thus we have a completeness theorem for *S5A*.

Now suppose that σ does contain '$\mathscr{F}$'. By the Elimination Theorem there is a provably equivalent sentence σ', not containing '$\mathscr{F}$'. Suppose that $V^+(w, \sigma) = \text{T}$. Then $V^+(w, \sigma') = \text{T}$ and since σ' is '$\mathscr{F}$'-free, σ' is in w. But $S5A\mathscr{F} \vdash \sigma' \rightarrow \sigma$. So σ is in w. The converse is similar. Thus we have a completeness theorem for *S5A$\mathscr{F}$*.

(This appendix is almost entirely attributable to Lloyd Humberstone.)

BIBLIOGRAPHY

Altham, J. and Tennant, N. (1975), 'Sortal quantification', in Keenan, E. L. (ed.), *Formal Semantics of Natural Language* (Cambridge University Press, 1975), pp. 46–60.
Åqvist, L. (1973), 'Modal logic with subjunctive conditionals and dispositional predicates', *Journal of Philosophical Logic*, 2 (1973), pp. 1–76.
Baldwin, T. (1975), 'Quantification, modality and indirect speech', in Blackburn, S. (ed.), *Meaning, Reference and Necessity* (Cambridge University Press, 1975), pp. 56–108.
Bennett, J. F. (1973), 'The meaning-nominalist strategy', *Foundations of Language*, 10 (1973), pp. 141–68.
— (1976), *Linguistic Behaviour* (Cambridge University Press, 1976).
Bigelow, J. (1978), 'Semantics of thinking, speaking and translation', in Guenthner, F. and Guenthner-Reutter, M. (eds), *Meaning and Translation* (Duckworth, 1978), pp. 109–35.
Blackburn, S. (1979), 'Thoughts and things', *Proceedings of the Aristotelian Society*, supp. vol. 80 (1979), pp. 23–41.
— (1981), *Philosophical Logic* (Open University Course A 313, Units 10–11, 1981).
Boolos, G. (1975), 'On second-order logic', *Journal of Philosophy*, 72 (1975), pp. 509–27.
Burge, T. (1975), 'On knowledge and convention', *Philosophical Review*, 84 (1975), pp. 249–55.
— (1978), 'Belief and synonymy', *Journal of Philosophy*, 75 (1978), pp. 119–38.
Camp, J. L. (1975), 'Truth and substitution quantifiers', *Noûs*, 9 (1975), pp. 165–85.
Chomsky, N. (1965), *Aspects of the Theory of Syntax* (MIT Press, 1965).
— (1969), 'Comments on Harman's reply', in Hook, S. (ed.), *Language and Philosophy* (New York University Press, 1969), pp. 152–9.

— (1975), 'Knowledge of language', in Gunderson, K. (ed.), *Language, Mind, and Knowledge* (University of Minnesota Press, 1975), pp. 299–320.

— (1976), 'Problems and mysteries in the study of human language', in Chomsky, N., *Reflections on Language* (Fontana/Collins, 1976), pp. 137–227.

Chomsky, N. and Katz, J. (1974), 'What the linguist is talking about', *Journal of Philosophy*, 71 (1974), pp. 347–67.

Cooper, R. (1979), 'The interpretation of pronouns', in Heny, F. and Schnelle, H. S. (eds), *Syntax and Semantics*, 10: *Selections from the Third Groningen Round Table* (Academic Press, 1979), pp. 61–92.

Crossley, J. N. and Humberstone, I. L. (1977), 'The logic of "actually"', *Reports on Mathematical Logic*, 8 (1977), pp. 11–29.

Davidson, D. (1965), 'Theories of meaning and learnable languages', in Bar-Hillel, Y. (ed.), *Logic, Methodology and Philosophy of Science*, 2 (North Holland, 1965), pp. 383–94.

— (1967), 'Truth and meaning', *Synthèse*, 17 (1967). Reprinted in Davis, J. W. *et al.* (eds), *Philosophical Logic* (Reidel, 1969), pp. 1–20.

— (1969), 'On saying that', *Synthèse*, 19 (1968/9). Reprinted in Davidson, D. and Hintikka, J. (eds), *Words and Objections* (Reidel, 1969), pp. 158–74.

— (1970), 'Semantics for natural languages', in *Linguaggi nella Società e nella Tecnica* (Edizioni di Comunità, Milano, 1970). Reprinted in Davidson, D. and Harman, G. (eds), *The Logic of Grammar* (Dickenson, 1975), pp. 18–24.

— (1973a), 'Radical interpretation', *Dialectica*, 27 (1973), pp. 313–28.

— (1973b), 'In defense of convention T', in Leblanc, H. (ed.), *Truth, Syntax and Modality* (North-Holland, 1973), pp. 76–86.

— (1974), 'Belief and the basis of meaning', *Synthèse*, 27 (1974), pp. 309–23.

— (1976), 'Reply to Foster', in Evans, G. and McDowell, J. (eds), *Truth and Meaning* (Oxford University Press, 1976), pp. 33–41.

— (1977a), 'The method of truth in metaphysics', in French, P. A. *et al.* (eds), *Midwest Studies in Philosophy*, 2: *Studies in the Philosophy of Language* (University of Minnesota, 1977), pp. 244–54.

— (1977b), 'Reality without reference', *Dialectica,* 31 (1977), pp. 247–58. Reprinted in Platts, M. de B. (ed.), *Reference, Truth and Reality* (Routledge & Kegan Paul, 1980).

— (1979), 'Moods and Performances', in Margalit, A. (ed.), *Meaning and Use* (Reidel, 1979), pp. 9–20.

Davies, M. K. (1978), 'Weak necessity and truth theories', *Journal of Philosophical Logic*, 7 (1978), pp. 415–39.

— (1981), 'Meaning, structure and understanding', to appear in *Synthèse* (1981).

— (forthcoming), 'Meaning and structure', and to appear in *Philosophia*.

Davies, M. K. and Humberstone, I. L. (1980), 'Two notions of necessity', *Philosophical Studies*, 38 (1980), pp. 1–30.

Donnellan, K. (1966), 'Reference and definite descriptions', *Philosophical Review*, 75 (1966), pp. 284–304.

— (1968), 'Putting Humpty Dumpty together again', *Philosophical Review*, 77 (1968), pp. 203–15.

— (1972), 'Proper names and identifying descriptions', in Davidson, D. and Harman, G. (eds), *Semantics of Natural Language* (Reidel, 1972), pp. 356–79.

— (1974), 'Speaking of nothing', *Philosophical Review*, 83 (1974), pp. 3–31.

— (1977), 'The contingent *a priori* and rigid designators', in French, P. A. *et al.* (eds), *Midwest Studies in Philosophy*, 2: *Studies in the Philosophy of Language* (University of Minnesota, 1977), pp. 12–27.

— (1978), 'Speaker reference, descriptions and anaphora', in Cole, P. (ed.), *Syntax and Semantics, Volume 9: Pragmatics* (Academic Press, 1978), pp. 47–68.

Dummett, M. A. E. (1973), *Frege: Philosophy of Language* (Duckworth, 1973).

— (1975), 'What is a theory of meaning?', in Guttenplan, S. (ed.), *Mind and Language* (Oxford University Press, 1975), pp. 97–138.

— (1976), 'What is a theory of meaning? (II)', in Evans, G. and McDowell, J. (eds), *Truth and Meaning* (Oxford University Press, 1976), pp. 67–137.

— (1978), *Truth and Other Enigmas* (Duckworth, 1978).

Dunn, J. M. and Belnap, N. D. (1968), 'The substitution interpretation of the quantifiers', *Noûs*, 2 (1968), pp. 177–85.

Evans, G. (1973), 'The causal theory of names', *Proceedings of the Aristotelian Society*, supp. vol. 47 (1973). Reprinted in Schwartz, S. P. (ed.), *Naming, Necessity, and Natural Kinds* (Cornell University Press, 1977), pp. 192–215.

— (1975), 'Identity and predication', *Journal of Philosophy*, 72 (1975), pp. 343–63.

— (1976), 'Semantic structure and logical form', in Evans, G. and McDowell, J. (eds), *Truth and Meaning* (Oxford University Press, 1976), pp. 199–222.

— (1977), 'Pronouns, quantifiers, and relative clauses (I)', *Canadian Journal of Philosophy*, 7 (1977), pp. 467–536. Reprinted in Platts, M. de B. (ed.), *Reference, Truth and Reality* (Routledge & Kegan Paul, 1980).

— (1979), 'Reference and contingency', *Monist*, 62 (1979), pp. 161–89.

— (1980), 'Pronouns', *Linguistic Inquiry*, 11 (1980), pp. 337–62.

— (1981), 'Semantic theory and tacit knowledge' in Holtzman, S. H. and Leich, C. M. (eds), *Wittgenstein: To Follow a Rule* (Routledge & Kegan Paul, 1981).

— (forthcoming a), 'Understanding demonstratives', to appear in Parret, H. and Bouveresse, J. (eds), *Meaning and Understanding* (De Gruyter, forthcoming).

— (forthcoming b), 'Does tense logic rest upon a mistake?', to appear in a *Festschrift* for Donald Davidson, edited by Vermazen, B., and Hintikka, M.

Evans, G. and McDowell, J. (1976), *Truth and Meaning* (Oxford University Press, 1976).

Field, H. (1972), 'Tarski's theory of truth', *Journal of Philosophy*, 69 (1972), pp. 347–75. Reprinted in Platts, M. de B. (ed.), *Reference, Truth and Reality* (Routledge & Kegan Paul, 1980).

Fodor, J. (1968), 'The appeal to tacit knowledge in psychological explanation', *Journal of Philosophy*, 65 (1968), pp. 627–40.

Foster, J. (1976), 'Meaning and truth theory', in Evans, G. and McDowell, J. (eds), *Truth and Meaning* (Oxford University Press, 1976), pp. 1–32.

Frege, G. (1892), 'On sense and reference', in Geach, P. and Black, M. (eds), *Translations from the Philosophical Writings of Gottlob Frege* (Blackwell, 1960), pp. 56–78.

— (1893), *The Basic Laws of Arithmetic*, trans. and ed. Furth, M., (University of California Press, 1967).

— (1918), 'The thought: a logical inquiry', trans. Quinton, A. M. and Quinton, M., *Mind*, 65 (1956). Reprinted in Strawson, P. F. (ed.), *Philosophical Logic* (Oxford University Press, 1967), pp. 17–38.

Geach, P. T. (1963), 'What are referring expressions?', *Analysis*, 23 (1962/3). Reprinted in Geach, P. T., *Logic Matters* (Blackwell, 1972), pp. 95–7.

— (1964), 'Referring expressions again', *Analysis*, 24 (1963/4). Reprinted in Geach, P. T., *Logic Matters*, pp. 97–102.

— (1968), *Reference and Generality* (Cornell University Press, 1968).

— (1969), 'Quine's syntactical insights', *Synthèse*, 19 (1968/9). Reprinted in Geach, P. T., *Logic Matters*, pp. 115–27.

Graves, C. *et al.* (1973), 'Tacit knowledge', *Journal of Philosophy*, 70 (1973), pp. 318–30.

Grice, H. P. (1957), 'Meaning', *Philosophical Review*, 66 (1957). Reprinted in Strawson, P. F. (ed.), *Philosophical Logic* (Oxford University Press, 1967), pp. 39–48.

— (1968), 'Utterer's meaning, sentence-meaning and word-meaning', *Foundations of Language*, 4 (1968), pp. 1–18.

— (1969), 'Utterer's meaning and intentions', *Philosophical Review*, 78 (1969), pp. 147–77.

Hausser, R. (1979), 'How do pronouns denote?', in Heny, F. and Schnelle, H.S. (eds), *Syntax and Semantics*, 10: *Selections from the Third Groningen Round Table* (Academic Press, 1979), pp. 93–139.

Hazen, A. (1976), 'Expressive completeness in modal languages', *Journal of Philosophical Logic*, 5 (1976), pp. 25–46.

Heny, F. and Schnelle, H. S. (1979), *Syntax and Semantics*, 10: *Selections from the Third Groningen Round Table* (Academic Press, 1979).

Hughes, G. and Cresswell, M. (1972), *An Introduction to Modal Logic* (Methuen, 1972).

Humberstone, I. L. (1979), Critical Notice of Keenan, E., (ed.), 'Formal semantics of natural language', *Australasian Journal of Philosophy*, 57 (1979), pp. 171–82.

Kamp, J. A. W. (1971), 'Formal properties of "now"', *Theoria*, 37 (1971), pp. 227–73.

Kaplan, D. (1977), 'Demonstratives: draft no. 2', (unpublished).

— (1978), 'Dthat', in Cole, P. (ed.), *Syntax and Semantics, 9: Pragmatics* (Academic Press, 1978), pp. 221–43.

Kripke, S. (1963), 'Semantical considerations on modal logic', *Acta Philosophica Fennica*, 16 (1963). Reprinted in Linsky, L. (ed.), *Reference and Modality* (Oxford University Press, 1971), pp. 63–72.

— (1971), 'Identity and necessity', in Munitz, M. K. (ed.), *Identity and Individuation* (New York University Press, 1971), pp. 135–64.

— (1972), 'Naming and necessity', in Davidson, D. and Harman, G. (eds), *Semantics of Natural Language* (Reidel, 1972), pp. 253–355 and 763–9.

— (1976), 'Is there a problem about substitutional quantification?', in Evans, G. and McDowell, J. (eds), *Truth and Meaning* (Oxford University Press, 1976), pp. 325–419.

— (1977), 'Speaker's reference and semantic reference', in French, P. A. *et al.* (eds), *Midwest Studies in Philosophy, 2: Studies in the Philosophy of Language* (University of Minnesota, 1977), pp. 255–76.

— (1979), 'A puzzle about belief', in Margalit, A. (ed.), *Meaning and Use* (Reidel, 1979), pp. 239–83.

Lemmon, E. J. and Scott, D. S. (1977), *An Introduction to Modal Logic*, ed. Segerberg, K., (Oxford, 1977).

Levin, M. (1977), 'Explanation and prediction in grammar (and semantics)', in French, P. A. *et al.* (eds), *Midwest Studies in Philosophy, 2: Studies in the Philosophy of Language* (University of Minnesota, 1977), pp. 128–37.

Lewis, D. (1969), *Convention* (Harvard University Press, 1969).

— (1972), 'General semantics', in Davidson, D. and Harman, G. (eds), *Semantics of Natural Language* (Reidel, 1972), pp. 169–218.

— (1973), *Counterfactuals* (Blackwell, 1973).

— (1975), 'Languages and language', in Gunderson, K. (ed.), *Language, Mind, and Knowledge* (University of Minnesota Press, 1975), pp. 3–35.

— (1980), 'Index, context, and content', in Kanger, S. and Öhman, S. (eds), *Philosophy and Grammar* (Reidel, 1980), pp. 79–100.

Loar, B. (1976), 'Two theories of meaning', in Evans, G. and McDowell, J. (eds), *Truth and Meaning* (Oxford University Press, 1976), pp. 138–61.

McDowell, J. (1976), 'Truth conditions, bivalence, and verificationism', in Evans, G. and McDowell, J. (eds), *Truth and Meaning* (Oxford University Press, 1976), pp. 42–66.

— (1977), 'On the sense and reference of a proper name', *Mind*, 86 (1977), pp. 159–85. Reprinted in Platts, M. de B. (ed.), *Reference, Truth and Reality* (Routledge & Kegan Paul, 1980).

— (1978), 'Physicalism and primitive denotation: Field on Tarski', *Erkenntnis*, 13 (1978). Reprinted in Platts, M. de B. (ed.), *Reference, Truth and Reality* (Routledge & Kegan Paul, 1980), pp. 111–30.

— (1980), 'Meaning, communication, and knowledge', in van Straaten, Z. (ed.), *Philosophical Subjects* (Oxford University Press, 1980), pp. 117–39.

— (1981), 'Truth-value gaps', to appear in Łos, J. and Pfeiffer, H. (eds), *Logic, Methodology and Philosophy of Science*, 6 (North Holland, 1981).

McGinn, C. (1981), 'Modal reality', to appear in Healey, R. (ed.), *Reduction, Time and Reality* (Cambridge University Press, 1981).

Mendelson, E. (1964), *Introduction to Mathematical Logic* (van Nostrand, 1964).

Mitchell, D. (1962), *An Introduction to Logic* (Hutchinson, 1962).

Mostowski, A. (1957), 'On a generalization of quantifiers', *Fundamenta Mathematicae*, 44 (1957), pp. 12–36.

Peacocke, C. (1975), 'Proper names, reference, and rigid designation', in Blackburn, S. (ed.), *Meaning, Reference and Necessity* (Cambridge University Press, 1975), pp. 109–32.

— (1976), 'Truth definitions and actual languages', in Evans, G. and McDowell, J. (eds), *Truth and Meaning* (Oxford University Press, 1976), pp. 162–88.

— (1978), 'Necessity and truth theories', *Journal of Philosophical Logic*, 7 (1978), pp. 473–500.

Plantinga, A. (1974), *The Nature of Necessity* (Oxford University Press, 1974).

— (1978), 'The Boethian compromise', *American Philosophical Quarterly*, 15 (1978), pp. 129–38.

Platts, M. de B. (1979), *Ways of Meaning* (Routledge & Kegan Paul, 1979).

Putnam, H. (1973), 'Meaning and reference', *Journal of Philosophy*, 70 (1973), pp. 699–711.

— (1975), 'The meaning of "meaning"', in Gunderson, K. (ed.), *Language, Mind and Knowledge* (University of Minnesota Press, 1975), pp. 131–93.

Quine, W. V. O. (1960), *Word and Object* (MIT Press, 1960).

— (1970), *Philosophy of Logic* (Prentice-Hall, 1970).

— (1972), 'Methodological reflections on current linguistic theory', in Davidson, D. and Harman, G. (eds), *Semantics of Natural Language* (Reidel, 1972), pp. 442–54.

Rescher, N. (1962), 'Plurality-quantification', *Journal of Symbolic Logic*, 27 (1962), pp. 373–4.

Russell, B. A. W. (1905), 'On denoting', *Mind*, 14 (1905). Reprinted in Marsh, R. C. (ed.), *Logic and Knowledge* (George Allen and Unwin, 1956), pp. 41–56.

— (1918), 'The philosophy of logical atomism', in Marsh, R. C. (ed.), *Logic and Knowledge*, pp. 177–281.

Sainsbury, R. M. (1977), 'Semantics by proxy', *Analysis*, 37 (1976/7), pp. 86–96.

— (1979), *Russell* (Routledge & Kegan Paul, 1979).

— (1980), 'Understanding and theories of meaning', *Proceedings of the Aristotelian Society*, 80 (1979/80), pp. 127–44.

Schiffer, S. (1972), *Meaning* (Oxford University Press, 1972).

— (1977), 'Naming and knowing', in French, P. A. *et al.* (eds), *Midwest Studies in Philosophy*, 2: *Studies in the Philosophy of Language* (University of Minnesota, 1977), pp. 28–41.

— (1978), 'The basis of reference', *Erkenntnis*, 13 (1978), pp. 171–206.

Searle, J. (1958), 'Proper names', *Mind*, 67 (1958). Reprinted in Strawson, P. F. (ed.), *Philosophical Logic* (Oxford University Press, 1967), pp. 89–96.

— (1969), *Speech Acts* (Cambridge University Press, 1969).

Segerberg, K. (1973), 'Two-dimensional modal logic', *Journal of Philosophical Logic*, 2 (1973), pp. 77–96.

Stalnaker, R. C. (1976), 'Possible worlds', *Noûs*, 10 (1976), pp. 65–75. Reprinted in Loux, M. J. (ed.), *The Possible and the Actual* (Cornell University Press, 1979).

— (1978), 'Assertion', in Cole, P. (ed.), *Syntax and Semantics*, 9: *Pragmatics* (Academic Press, 1978), pp. 315–32.

Stich, S. (1971), 'What every speaker knows', *Philosophical Review*, 80 (1971), pp. 476–96.

— (1972), 'Grammar, psychology, and indeterminacy', *Journal of Philosophy*, 69 (1972), pp. 799–818.

— (1978), 'Beliefs and subdoxastic states', *Philosophy of Science*, 45 (1978), pp. 499–518.

Strawson, P. F. (1950), 'On referring', *Mind*, 59 (1950). Reprinted in Strawson (1971), pp. 1–27.

— (1959), *Individuals* (Methuen, 1959).

— (1961), 'Singular terms and predication', *Journal of Philosophy*, 58 (1961). Reprinted in Strawson (1971), pp. 53–74.

— (1964a), 'Intention and convention in speech acts', *Philosophical Review*, 73 (1964). Reprinted in Strawson (1971), pp. 149–69.

— (1964b), 'Identifying reference and truth-values', *Theoria*, 30 (1964). Reprinted in Strawson (1971), pp. 75–95.

— (1969), 'Grammar and philosophy', *Proceedings of the Aristotelian Society*, 70 (1969/70). Reprinted in Strawson (1971), pp. 130–48.

— (1970a), *Meaning and Truth* (Oxford University Press, 1970). Reprinted in Strawson (1971), pp. 170–89.

— (1970b), 'The asymmetry of subjects and predicates', in Strawson (1971), pp. 98–115.

— (1971), *Logico-Linguistic Papers* (Methuen, 1971).

— (1974a), *Subject and Predicate in Logic and Grammar* (Methuen, 1974).

— (1974b), 'Positions for quantifiers', in Munitz, M. K. and Unger, P. (eds), *Semantics and Philosophy* (New York University Press, 1974), pp. 63–79.

— (1980), 'Reply to McDowell', in van Straaten, Z. (ed.), *Philosophical*

Subjects (Oxford University Press, 1980), pp. 282–7.

Tarski, A. (1956), 'The concept of truth in formalized languages', in Tarski, A., *Logic, Semantics, Metamathematics* (Oxford University Press, 1956), pp. 152–278. Excerpt reprinted in Davidson, D. and Harman, G. (eds), *The Logic of Grammar* (Dickenson, 1975), pp. 25–49.

Taylor, B. (1976), 'States of affairs', in Evans, G. and McDowell, J. (eds), *Truth and Meaning* (Oxford University Press, 1976), pp. 263–84.

—— (forthcoming), 'Articulated predication and truth-theory', to appear in a *Festschrift* for Donald Davidson edited by Vermazen, B. and Hintikka, M.

van Benthem, J. F. A. K. (1977), 'Tense logic and standard logic', *Logique et Analyse*, 80 (1977), pp. 395–437.

van Fraassen, B. C. (1977), 'The only necessity is verbal necessity', *Journal of Philosophy*, 74 (1977), pp. 71–85.

Vendler, Z. (1967), *Linguistics in Philosophy* (Cornell University Press, 1967).

Vlach, F. (1973), ' "Now" and "then": a formal study in the logic of tense anaphora' (UCLA doctoral thesis, 1973).

Wallace, J. (1965), 'Sortal predicates and quantification', *Journal of Philosophy*, 62 (1965), pp. 8–13.

—— (1971), 'Convention T and substitutional quantification', *Noûs*, 5 (1971), pp. 199–211.

—— (1972), 'On the frame of reference', in Davidson, D. and Harman, G. (eds), *Semantics of Natural Language* (Reidel, 1972), pp. 219–52.

—— (1975a), 'Nonstandard theories of truth', in Davidson, D. and Harman, G. (eds), *The Logic of Grammar* (Dickenson, 1975), pp. 50–60.

—— (1975b), 'Response to Camp', *Noûs*, 9 (1975), pp. 187–92.

—— (1977), 'Only in the context of a sentence do words have any meaning', in French, P. A. *et al.* (eds), *Midwest Studies in Philosophy*, 2: *Studies in the Philosophy of Language* (University of Minnesota, 1977), pp. 144–64.

—— (1978), 'Logical form, meaning, translation', in Guenthner, F. and Guenthner-Reutter, M. (eds), *Meaning and Translation* (Duckworth, 1978), pp. 45–58.

Wasow, T. (1979), 'Problems with pronouns in transformational grammar', in Heny, F. and Schnelle, H. S. (eds), *Syntax and Semantics*, 10: *Selections from the Third Groningen Round Table* (Academic Press, 1979), pp. 199–222.

Wiggins, D. (1976), 'The *de re* "must": a note on the logical form of essentialist claims', in Evans, G. and McDowell, J. (eds), *Truth and Meaning* (Oxford University Press, 1976), pp. 285–312.

—— (1980a), 'What would be a substantial theory of truth?', in van Straaten, Z. (ed.), *Philosophical Subjects* (Oxford University Press, 1980), pp. 189–221.

— (1980b), '"Most" and "all": some comments on a familiar programme and on the logical form of quantified sentences', in Platts, M. de B (ed.), *Reference, Truth and Reality* (Routledge & Kegan Paul, 1980), pp. 318–46.

Wright, C. (1976), 'Truth conditions and criteria', *Proceedings of the Aristotelian Society*, supp. vol. 50 (1976), pp. 217–45.

INDEX